THE HOUR OF LAND

Sarah Crichton Books   Farrar, Straus and Giroux   New York

THE HOUR OF LAND

A Personal Topography
of America's National Parks

-<- ->-

TERRY TEMPEST WILLIAMS

Sarah Crichton Books
Farrar, Straus and Giroux
18 West 18th Street, New York 10011

The chapters "Gates of the Arctic National Park, Alaska" and "Gulf Islands National Seashore, Florida and Mississippi" originally appeared, in slightly different form, in *Orion Magazine*, September/October 2014 and November/December 2010, respectively.

Owing to limitations of space, all acknowledgments for permissions to reprint previously published material can be found on page 397.

Library of Congress Cataloging-in-Publication Data
Names: Williams, Terry Tempest.
Title: The hour of land : a personal topography of America's national parks / Terry Tempest Williams.
Description: New York : Sarah Crichton Books/Farrar, Straus and Giroux, 2016.
Identifiers: LCCN 2015042477 | ISBN 9780374280093 (hardback) | ISBN 9780374712266 (e-book)
Subjects: LCSH: National parks and reserves—United States. | National parks and reserves—United States—Pictorial works. | National parks and reserves—Social aspects—United States. | Landscapes—Social aspects—United States. | Williams, Terry Tempest—Travel—United States. | Natural history—United States. | Human ecology—United States—Philosophy. | United States—Environmental conditions. | BISAC: NATURE / Essays. | TRAVEL / Parks & Campgrounds. | TRAVEL / United States / General.
Classification: LCC E160 .W54 2016 | DDC 333.780973—dc23
LC record available at http://lccn.loc.gov/2015042477

Designed by Abby Kagan

www.fsgbooks.com
www.twitter.com/fsgbooks • www.facebook.com/fsgbooks

1   3   5   7   9   10   8   6   4   2

Frontispiece: *Clearing Storm and Cathedral Group*, photograph © 2001 Edward A. Riddell

For
Steven Barclay

My heart found its home long ago in the beauty, mystery, order and disorder of the flowering earth.

—LADY BIRD JOHNSON

A NOTE TO THE READER

L ANGUAGE AND LANDSCAPE are my inspiration. The poet Jorie Graham has been my muse in *The Hour of Land*. Her poem "WE," published in the *London Review of Books* on January 8, 2015, has led me line by line through the unknown territory of these twelve national parks. Her prescience on the page and insightful intelligence offered me a poetic crossing.

Edward Hirsch defines "a poetic crossing" as that "which follows the arc from physical motion to spiritual action . . . into another type of consciousness, a more heightened reality. It is a move beyond the temporal, a visionary passage."

When walking in the desert, I look for cairns to guide me, the careful placement of stones stacked one by one as a small monument to direction. Jorie Graham's words have been my directive. She has graciously given permission to use these thirteen lines as a passage into these parks. For this, I am grateful. Each of her lines is represented in italics at the beginning of each essay.

As a poet and a friend, Jorie remains a fierce and uncommon grace.

Frish Brandt has guided the curation of the photographs inside *The Hour of Land*. Her wisdom and artistic edge as president of the Fraenkel Gallery have not only expanded my view of national parks, but shaped it. I honor her joyous contribution and the generosity of all the photographers who agreed to be part of this project. Their images create an emotional landscape alongside the physical one explored through each park in this book. By touching the essence of a place, another kind of poetic crossing is made.

Collaboration is the only way forward.

MAPPING THE TERRITORY

AMERICA'S NATIONAL PARKS

By definition

I N BIG BEND NATIONAL PARK, the Rio Grande is so low because of drought, locals are calling it the Rio Sand. The river that separates the United States and Mexico is shallow enough in some places that a person can walk across the river in ten steps, maybe less. American children skip stones across its surface—one, two . . . the third skip lands abruptly on the other side. The same stones are picked up by Mexican children who skip them back across to the other bank in Boquillas Canyon. The game continues back and forth until parents intervene. On one side of the Rio Grande, tourists stand. On the other side, men and boys are herding goats. Breach the border and you will be arrested, American or Mexican, it doesn't matter. Border police could be anywhere. Black phoebes fly across the river, occasionally touching water like the stones skipped across international lines. In the twenty-first century, borders are fluid, not fixed, especially in our national parks.

Earlier in the day, I met a veteran from Desert Storm, the first Gulf War. His name was Bill Summers. Bill was a tall man with hair cut short; lean and muscular, rugged-looking in his camouflage fatigues—the kind of handsome that can't be brought down by a few missing teeth. I had noticed him picking up trash along the Ross-Maxwell Scenic Drive; his backpack, with his sleeping bag and bedroll, was propped against the hillside by the side of the road.

We ran into each other at the Panther Junction Visitor Center on the interpretive trail. "Purple-tinged prickly pear—now there's a mouthful," he said.

"Yes, it is," I said, "especially, if you try to say it fast."

We began talking about cactus, how well adapted they are to drought conditions and arid country.

"I've been a volunteer in Hawai'i Volcanoes National Park," he said. "The plants around the craters are also skilled at surviving harsh conditions." A brown shirt with the Hawaiian park's insignia was neatly tucked into his fatigues.

"How long did you volunteer there?"

"Three years."

"And you're here now?"

"Hoping to be. Just turned in my application today, ma'am."

"Does it look like they'll hire you?"

"It's lookin' that way."

"Why Big Bend?"

"The desert suits me, ma'am. Not a lot of people around here."

We moved to the next plant—cholla.

"The Devil's Stick," I said.

"That could do some serious harm to a man's leg," Bill replied.

"How long have you been volunteering in the national parks?"

"Since I returned home from Iraq in 1991. Served some time in the Grand Canyon; I've been all over. Our national parks are the most important thing we've got going in this country," Bill said. "As the human population increases, the wild places not only become more valuable but more threatened. It's another way for me to protect our homeland, ma'am."

Bill Summers reminded me of my friend Doug Peacock, a vet from the Vietnam War. Doug and I met on a trail in Glacier National Park in 1982 and shared a similar conversation. Doug served two tours as a medic in the Army Special Forces, a Green Beret. A decade later, he would describe in his memoir, *Grizzly Years: In Search of the American Wilderness*, how a topographical map of Yellowstone National Park kept him half-sane in an insane war. Every night, he'd pull out the map and run his fingers over familiar country, transporting himself out of the jungle and into the mountains. He left Vietnam on the first day of the Tet Offensive, January 30, 1968.

Peacock returned home with wounds no one could see, and he disappeared into Yellowstone. Then he took a job as a volunteer on a fire lookout in Glacier National Park, where he not only watched for smoke, he watched for grizzly bears, and when he found them, he passed whole days in their presence. He didn't fear them, he was in awe of them. As he came to know individual bears, his heart slowly began to open to the beauty of the world. The grizzlies returned him to a life he could believe in. As payback, Doug Peacock would become one of the grizzly bears' fiercest advocates.

"Where are you from?" Bill asked.

"Utah."

"Now, there's a place to live."

"We live near Arches and Canyonlands."

Bill nodded. "Gorgeous parks. Been there."

"So, Bill, when you're a volunteer in a park, what do you do exactly?"

"Anything that's needed, ma'am, everything from backcountry rangering to trail maintenance to assisting people in trouble. You name it, I've done it, and believe me, with the Park Service hurting for funds, there's a lot to be done."

The conversation shifted to Big Bend.

"Have you been to the border of Boquillas near Rio Grande Village?" I asked.

"Not yet."

I told him about the kids skipping stones across the border.

"I read today that Congress is trying to introduce legislation to build a wall along the entire U.S.-Mexican border," he said.

"Can you imagine a wall in Big Bend?"

"Personally, I don't think much of fences, ma'am, and that goes for walls, too."

He bent down and rubbed his fingers across the small waxy leaves of the next plant. "Have you smelled creosote?" he asked. "Mighty fine scent."

"Last night, after the rain, the air was fresh with it."

"People don't come to places like these to see a damn wall." Bill shifted his weight and stuck his hands in his pockets. "I think there needs to be more emphasis on taking care of what's here, not what's over there."

Our conversation grew more personal. He asked whether I had ever worked for the Park Service. I told him that I, too, had been a volunteer in the parks—Grand Teton National Park, in 1974. I was a year out of high school. I took early-morning bird walks down by Blacktail Ponds along the Snake River, but I kept seeing birds that had never before been reported in Grand Teton, so the park officials grew suspicious of me.

"I only lasted a season," I said.

Summers laughed.

"In fact, one of the birds in question was an acorn woodpecker. I saw one today in the Chisos Basin and it was like seeing an old friend."

Bill told me he grew up on a farm in central Florida. "Course any farm boy's itchin' to leave, so I joined the military, enlisted in the army and took advantage of what they could give me. Then Iraq blew up and I went over. Came home pretty messed up. Paddled around the swamps in South Carolina to clear my head. There was a lot going on with me, wild places can unwind a mind. You calm down a bit. I found my way to the national parks. It was a free place to live without being bothered. And then, I learned about volunteering. The Park Service gives you a place to live and enough money for food and incidentals. That was more than enough for me."

"I have a friend who served in Vietnam and worked in Glacier National Park—grizzly bears saved his life . . ."

"That wouldn't be Doug Peacock, would it, ma'am?"

"You know him?" I asked.

"Doug Peacock's my hero. George Washington Hayduke." Peacock served as the model for the character of Hayduke in Edward Abbey's novel *The Monkey Wrench Gang*. Bill turned around. "I love that book. Love Ed Abbey. They've been a real source of inspiration for me."

Bill Summers's eyes steadied for the first time. "You see, ma'am, I guess it's a small world out here in the big open for us veterans. Tell Mr. Peacock hello for me next time you see him." He paused. "And tell him, thank you."

America's national parks were a vision seen through the horrors of war.

On June 30, 1864, not long after the Civil War's most deadly battle, at Gettysburg, President Abraham Lincoln signed the Yosemite Land Grant into law, protecting for the first time—for all time—land secured for the future. Yosemite Valley and the ancient, giant sequoias of the Mariposa Grove located there were written into law as America's inaugural nature preserve ceded to the state of California, later to be expanded and established as a national park in 1890. Though this war-weary president would never see the glory of El Capitan or the beauty of its reflection in the Merced River, he had experienced them through the images of photographers—Carleton Watkins, Timothy O'Sullivan, and Eadweard Muybridge. These magnificent lands were alive in Lincoln's imagination and he believed they might offer a unifying peace for a divided nation.

The irony was this: Fourteen years prior to the signing of the Yosemite

Land Grant, another war had been fought here—the Mariposa Indian War, from 1850 to 1851.

It is a chapter buried in America's history. In the midst of the California Gold Rush, the Mariposa Battalion, a volunteer militia company under the banner of California, had gone to battle against the Ahwahneechee Indians who lived in the Yosemite Valley. The Ahwahneechees resisted the invasion but were eventually defeated. In an act the military leadership deemed respectful, they named the lake where the war was fought after Chief Tenaya, leader of the Ahwahnee, but to the chief, this well-intentioned gesture served as a final humiliation. In the name of Manifest Destiny, Tenaya and his people were removed from their home ground and assigned to a reservation near Fresno, California. This reservation was short-lived as Congress did not ratify any of the eighteen treaties made with California Indians between 1851 and 1852. As a result, Miwoks, Monos, and Yokuts remained living in their traditional homelands with no claim to the land, always on guard against white settlers.

This is a book about relationships inside America's national parks, and as is always the case with relations, the bonds formed, severed, and renewed within these federal lands are complicated. They are also fundamental to who we are as a country. Whether historical or ecological, political or personal, the connective tissue that holds together or tears apart our public lands begins with "We, the People."

Our national parks receive more than 300 million visitations a year. What are we searching for and what do we find? As we Americans and visitors from abroad explore the 400-plus sites within the national park system that includes national parks, monuments, battlefields, historic sites, seashores, and recreation areas located in all fifty states, perhaps it is not so much what we learn that matters in these moments of awe and wonder, but what we feel in relationship to a world beyond ourselves, even beyond our own species.

I was raised in the state of Utah, where five national parks and seven national monuments are commonplace. We took them for granted: Zion, Bryce, Arches, Canyonlands, and Capitol Reef were in our backyard, the land where our families gathered and we roamed free. We hiked the Zion Narrows and escaped a flash flood.

On that same trip, my brother and I camped against a red rock wall and in the morning when we awoke, a boulder had fallen between us. We cross-country skied in Bryce Canyon, convinced the pink and yellow pinnacles of stone were lit from the inside out, especially at night. In Capitol Reef, we picked peaches from orchards planted by Mormon pioneers. We knew that Arches and Canyonlands were an acquired taste, a bare-boned landscape more akin to Mars than to Earth. Natural Bridges had the darkest, star-struck skies, the place where I almost died falling off a cliff, with 136 stitches running down my forehead like a red river and a lifelong scar to prove it. We learned early on we live by wild mercy.

But it was standing inside Timpanogos Cave (a national monument) as an eight-year-old child that marked me. We hiked up the steep mountain trail that rises a thousand feet from the valley floor in a short mile and a half. We were hiking with our church group from Salt Lake City, just an hour north. We reached the entrance of the cave and were ushered in by a park ranger. Immediately, the cool air locked inside the mountain enveloped us and we wore it as loose clothing. Immense stalactites and stalagmites hung down from the ceiling and rose up from the floor, declaring themselves teeth. We were inside the gaping mouth of an animal and we were careful not to disturb the beast. We passed through Father Time's Jewel Box and the Valley of Sleep, traversing the cave on a narrow constructed walkway above the floor so as not to disturb its fragility. But it was the Great Heart of Timpanogos Cave that captured my attention. When everyone else left the charismatic form, I stayed. I needed more time to be closer to it, to watch its red-orange aura pulsating in the cavernous space of shadows. I wanted to touch the heart, run the palms of my hands on its side, believing that if I did, I could better understand my own heart, which was invisible to me. I was only inches away, wondering whether it would be cold or hot to the touch. It looked like ice, but it registered as fire.

Suddenly, I heard the heavy door slam and darkness clamp down. The group left without me. I was forgotten—alone—locked inside the cave. I waved my hand in front of my face. Nothing. I was held in a darkness so deep that my eyes seemed shut even though they were open. All I could hear was the sound of water dripping and the beating heart of the mountain.

I don't know how long I stood inside Timpanogos Cave before our church leader realized I was missing, but it was long enough to have experienced how fear moves out of panic toward wonder. Inside the cave, I knew I would be found. What I didn't know was what would find me—the spirit of Timpanogos.

To this day, my spiritual life is found inside the heart of the wild. I do not fear it, I court it. When I am away, I anticipate my return, needing to touch stone, rock, water, the trunks of trees, the sway of grasses, the barbs of a feather, the fur left behind by a shedding bison.

Wallace Stegner, a mentor of mine, curated a collection of essays and photographs called *This Is Dinosaur*, published in 1955 by Alfred A. Knopf. The book made an impassioned plea for why Dinosaur National Monument in Utah should not be the site of the Echo Park hydroelectric dam that would flood the lands rich with archaeological history adjacent to the Green and Yampa Rivers.

In the first chapter, called "The Marks of Human Passage," Stegner wrote:

It is a better world with some buffalo left in it, a richer world with some gorgeous canyons unmarred by sign boards, hot-dog stands, super highways, or high-tension lines, undrowned by power or irrigation reservoirs. If we preserved as parks only those places that have no economic possibilities, we would have no parks. And in the decades to come, it will not be only the buffalo and the trumpeter swan who need sanctuaries. Our own species is going to need them too. It needs them now.

The dam was never built. Today, six decades later, Dinosaur National Monument remains an oasis of calm, home to the Fremont people, who once inhabited these desert lands, and the Ute people, who still live here in lands adjacent to the oil and gas boom currently under way in the Uintah Basin, now the site of America's first tar sands mine.

As we mark the centennial of the National Park Service, my question is this: What is the relevance of our national parks in the twenty-first century—and how might these public commons bring us back home to a united state of humility?

The creation of America's national parks has been the creation of myths. I grew up with the myth that when Yellowstone National Park was established in 1872 it was void of people. No one told me that our first national park was the seasonal and cyclic home of Blackfeet, Bannock, Shoshone, and Crow Nations. I was told instead that the steaming basins with geysers and fumaroles, hot springs and boiling waters were avoided by Indians—it was superstitious ground; Indians kept their distance. Like any good story with the muscle of privilege behind it, it seemed believable. And I never asked the question, "Who benefits from the telling of this particular story?"

The truth is, the federal government did not want visitors to Yellowstone to encounter Indians. Full stop. And so they either banned tribes from the new preserve or relegated them to the margins, where they could continue to hunt game—unseen. This was the era of "Indian removal" and westward expansion. Reservations were being established at the same time as national parks.

But it wasn't just our national parks that were displacing tribes: American progress was on the move in every state and every territory, rolling over whoever and whatever got in the way. Nor was it just Indians who complicated a mythical landscape. Elk and deer were lovely to look at, an enhancement of a pastoral vision. But wolves and grizzly bears were another matter—there was no place in this pretty picture for predators—and in Yellowstone they were hunted, trapped, and killed.

A fuller and more honest narrative has emerged over time, mostly from tribal historians who want to right a historical wrong. Knowledge matters. Justice matters. Hindsight shows us our blind spots and biases; we can recognize ourselves as human beings caught in the cultural mores of a specific time. This is not to excuse the brutal and tenebrific acts of the past, but to consider them in the light of what we know now.

By definition, our national parks in all their particularity and peculiarity show us as much about ourselves as the landscapes they honor and protect. They can be seen as holograms of an America born of shadow and light; dimensional; full of contradictions and complexities. Our dreams, our generosities, our cruelties and crimes are absorbed into these parks like water.

The poet Rumi says, "Water, stories, the body / all the things we do are mediums / that hide and show what's hidden." So much has been lost.

Restoration is what is required today. Can we engage in the restoration of a different kind of storytelling, not the stuff of myths, self-serving and corrupted, but stories that foster integrity within a fragmented nation? Can we change America's narrative of independence to one of interdependence—an interdependence beautifully rendered in the natural histories found in our public lands? These are the parables of change and transition that might offer us maps to help us navigate our future in the era of a warming planet. We have never been here before.

It has been said there are two stories in the world: an individual goes on a journey or a stranger comes to town. I am telling both of these stories and adding a third, a story of homecoming within my explorations of twelve national parks and monuments. Some I visited for the first time, like Big Bend

National Park in Texas. Others I had visited before—Theodore Roosevelt National Park in North Dakota, which I returned to with my father. And then there are those parks like Grand Teton National Park and Canyonlands, in Wyoming and Utah, that I consider home ground. In the case of the Gettysburg National Military Park in rural Pennsylvania, I returned repeatedly, in all seasons, trying to make sense of a war that in so many ways has never ended.

In my wanderings among these dozen national parks, my intention was to create portraits of unexpected beauty and complexity. I thought it would be a straightforward and exuberant project, focusing on the protection of public lands, as I have done through most of my life. But, in truth, it has been among the most rigorous assignments I have ever given myself because I was writing out of my limitations. I am not a historian or a scientist or an employee of a federal land agency privy to public land policy and law. My authority is simply that of a storyteller who lives in the American West in love ' with this country called home.

I have been inspired by the photographs and people included in this book. I have learned that there is no such thing as one portrait or one story, only the knowledge of our own experience shared. I no longer see America's national parks as "our best idea," but our evolving idea; I see our national parks as our ongoing struggle as a diverse people to create circles of reverence in a time of collective cynicism where we are wary of being moved by anything but our own clever perspective.

"The purpose of life is to see," the writer Jack Turner said to me on a late summer walk at the base of the Tetons. I understand this to be a matter of paying attention. The nature of our national parks is bound to the nature of our own humility, our capacity to stay open and curious in a world that instead beckons closure through fear. For me, humility begins as a deep recognition of all I do not know. This understanding doesn't stop me, it inspires me to ask more questions, to look more closely, feel more fully the character of the place where I am. And so with this particular book, I have sought to listen to both the inner and the outer landscapes that spoke to me, to not hide behind metaphor or lyricism as I have in the past, but to simply share the stories that emerged in each park encountered.

At a time when it feels like we are a nation divided, I am interested in how a sense of place can evolve toward an ethic of place, especially within our national parks.

Oren Lyon, Faithkeeper of the Turtle Clan of the Seneca Nations of the Iroquois Confederacy, recently said, "It can no longer be about the color of our skin, but the color of our blood."

Our national parks are blood. They are more than scenery, they are portals and thresholds of wonder, an open door that swings back and forth from our past to our future. "This something we call America lives not so much in political institutions as in its rocks and skies and seas," wrote the photographer Paul Strand.

This is the Hour of Land, when our mistakes and shortcomings must be placed in the perspective of time. The Hour of Land is where we remember what we have forgotten: We are not the only species who lives and dreams on the planet. There is something enduring that circulates in the heart of nature that deserves our respect and attention.

Whenever I go to a national park, I meet the miraculous.

On June 2, 2015, my husband, Brooke, and I celebrated our fortieth wedding anniversary. We chose to spend it in Yellowstone. We rose before dawn in the Lamar Valley not far from where wolves were reintroduced twenty years earlier. A silhouette of coyotes feasting on a bison carcass, surrounded by bald eagles and ravens, appeared in our binoculars. As the light grew stronger the coyotes became nervous and left. The eagles flew. The ravens vanished. A large gray wolf entered.

Morning light illuminated the bison body, now more bones than flesh. We watched the wolf disappear into a red cavern of ribs. He emerged stained.

In the several hours we watched, the wolf's stomach expanded with each mouthful of bison ripped from the scaffolding of bones until he stopped eating, looked over his shoulder, sniffed, and walked back into the woods.

At dusk, we returned to the Lamar Valley. We wondered whether the wolves might be back on the carcass. Instead, two coyotes were picking on bones covered by a buffalo robe. The coyotes disappeared into the shadows with the last light of day.

An indigo sky deepened. A mile away, a herd of a hundred bison or more grazed unconcerned. Seven left and walked single file toward the remains of the mother bison. They circled her twice, sniffed her, nudged her body, and tightened their circle as they lowered their heads. They stayed with her until twilight. Then the bison left as they came, walking single file back toward the herd—save one lone bull who stayed behind.

GRAND TETON NATIONAL PARK,

WYOMING

-<- ->-

Keep promise

O N MY FATHER'S EIGHTIETH BIRTHDAY we saw a bear, a grizzly, standing upright. We had just hiked to Grand View Point in Grand Teton National Park, where Emma Matilda Lake and Two Ocean Lake appear below, and if you turn around, the glory of the Teton Range looms behind you.

We were a party of four generations (the youngest just one year old), and we were resting at the base of the trail when the grizzly appeared. Instead of being afraid, we stood as the bear did, trying to get a better look at the elusive beast. The bear bolted into the woods. Gone. My niece smiled and looked to her grandfather. "Happy Birthday, John."

Like so many families, our family has been coming to the Tetons for generations.

Grand Teton National Park was a cherished landscape for my great-grandfather, John Henry Tempest Sr. He passed his affection for this place on to my grandfather, John Henry Tempest Jr., who passed it on to his sons, John Henry Tempest III and Richard Blackett Tempest, who passed it on to us and another two generations past mine. Our entire Tempest clan can be found here most summers, climbing peaks, hiking trails, and cherishing the wildflowers and wildlife, knowing each species by name.

Our national parks are memory palaces where our personal histories reside.

My father was known as "Teton Tempest" to his college friends because every Friday after work he would drive four hours north, never stopping to eat, intent on reaching Jackson Hole, Wyoming, and camp. At dawn he'd slip on his Ray-Ban aviators, take one green look at the Tetons, and he was gone. No canyon was off-limits. He hiked each one, week by week, in his Levi Strauss and work boots, without a shirt, never a shirt, unless a storm came up, and then he'd put his shirt back on and keep walking. He was young and strong, suntanned and fearless. On Monday morning he was back in the trenches, laying pipe.

Not long ago my father and I were hiking to Taggart Lake, a short, lovely walk to the base of the Tetons. As we walked up the trail, we heard a horn blow repeatedly. Around the bend, a man in a Harvard sweatshirt, half-crazed with fear, was holding a bear horn out in front of him, pressing the button every fifteen seconds or so. A large canister of bear spray hung low from his belt, and numerous bear bells dangled from his backpack. He looked like a one-man marching band. The expression on his face when he met us head-on was one of sheer terror.

"Good God, man," my father said. "You look like you belong in the circus, not in the Tetons. I've been hiking this trail for seventy years and never seen a bear on it yet. Cut the horn."

I forget what the hiker said in response, but I do recall my father's parting comment: "If I were you, I wouldn't advertise where you went to school."

This was the kind of impatience and candor I was raised with, in spite of the grace of my mother and grandmothers.

We were told as children that *teton* meant "breast" in French, and that early French explorers, confronted with these mountains for the first time, named them Les Trois Tetons. I was embarrassed by this story, but it was another tale to mull over, alongside the story of Yellowstone as a place Indians feared.

These peaks didn't look like breasts to me; they looked jagged in shape not soft and round. But early impressions make their mark, and language has power. I didn't know what to make of what I'd been told, so I invented my own story. The Grand Teton would become my mother mountain. No one had to tell me which peak was the Grand; it was clearly the one that loomed largest, the one that was massive, the one that looked like it held a skillet of snow that was always reflected in the calm waters of Oxbow Bend. I would worship her with my own gestures as I saw my father worship these mountains with his. Each time we visited the park, I quietly bowed to the Grand Teton.

One morning, I must have been ten years old, our family rose early at the top of Signal Mountain to look for elk. A pair of sandhill cranes were flying across the valley. I pointed to them, saying, "Look, the sandhills are crossing in front of the Grand."

My father turned to me. "That's not the Grand Teton," he said. "That's Mount Moran—you know that."

I didn't know that. Suddenly I was being told that the immense square-shaped mountain who wielded her broad influence over the valley and seemed to watch over us was something else. And not only was she not the Grand, she was being diminished as I was being scolded to look south, not north.

My father stood behind me, moving my shoulders with his hands until I was looking squarely at what he was now calling "the Cathedral Group," with the Grand Teton, Mount Owen, and Teewinot creating some holy trinity. They were no longer breasts but the Godhead. Mount Moran was left behind. Inconsequential.

I kept looking back at my mountain. My father kept pointing to his. "The

Grand Teton is close to fourteen thousand feet—the tallest peak in the range," he said.

From this angle, there was no doubt that it was the sharpest peak cutting through clouds, but from this distance I thought it looked cold and aloof. It was a knifepoint, not a mountain. I did not want to be turned in the right direction.

I did not want to be told where to look for power. I no longer believed in the names of things. I knew where the power was held for me.

I turned around. We were the only ones left on the summit.

Grand Teton National Park was established in 1929 to honor the rugged Teton peaks, with their singular mountain range and alpine lakes. In truth, it was an expansion of Yellowstone worthy of its own identity.

In the early days of the park, most of what was protected was "rock and ice." The entire Snake River valley, with its sagebrush steppes—home to pronghorn antelope, elk, moose, bison, and bears—was vulnerable to development. Horace Albright, the superintendent of Yellowstone National Park at the time (and later to become the second director of the National Park Service following Stephen Mather), carried the dream of a larger park. He knew it would require an exceptional donor of great wealth who could understand the vision and necessity of incorporating the valley from which the Tetons rose—John D. Rockefeller Jr. was his man.

Albright invited Mr. Rockefeller (the son of John D. Rockefeller Sr., who made his fortune from Standard Oil) to visit the Tetons. Rockefeller accepted and came West. And the two gentlemen drove down the dirt highway along the east side of Jackson Hole. Albright stopped the car at the overlook above Hedrick Pond, where the men could take in the whole valley, with the Grand Tetons as a backdrop. The Snake River meandered through cottonwoods, timbered islands, and a sea of sage, with herds of bison grazing in the foreground. John D. Rockefeller Jr. knew instantly that Grand Teton National Park had to be more than a mountain range; it had to include the entire valley, or it would soon become just another honky-tonk town in the West.

"I want to buy this land," Rockefeller told Albright, and together they developed a scheme of secrecy. The lands would be bought over time, surreptitiously, with the intent of eventually donating them to the federal government. Which is exactly what John D. Rockefeller Jr. did over the next decade, under the guise of the Snake River Land Company. Piece by piece, ranch by ranch, Jackson Hole was being purchased—in collusion with the National Park Service—for the sole purpose of expansion. As the historian Robert W. Righter says in his fine book *Crucible for Conservation: The Struggle for Grand Teton National Park*, the connection between the Snake River Land Company and the National Park Service "was, of course, totally within the letter, but perhaps not the spirit, of the law. Their actions were legal, but not always just or equitable." Complex deals were being made with individual landowners and executed by savvy attorneys, and homesteads that had not been "proved up" by settlers were purchased anonymously. Locals were growing increasingly suspicious of who was behind these skillfully maneuvered land purchases, and rumors of the New York philanthropist backing the sales were increasing in intensity.

On April 6, 1930, Rockefeller and Albright came clean. It was time to tell the truth through a carefully crafted press release that reached western newspapers. John D. Rockefeller Jr., with the full involvement and support of Horace M. Albright and the National Park Service, had amassed large holdings within Jackson Hole in order to expand Grand Teton National Park.

The word was out and spread like wildfire, as it does in small towns. The Wyoming congressional delegation started making noises in Washington. Jackson Hole was a cow town, and they were not happy to find the federal government corralling their lands—especially lands bought up by a fancy easterner. Hearings were held nationally and locally to debate whether an expanded Grand Teton National Park was desired, needed, or warranted. Albright and Rockefeller's plan was tossed back and forth in the halls of Congress like a Ping-Pong ball.

President Franklin D. Roosevelt—acutely aware of the outcry that would ensue if he accepted Rockefeller's gift of the land—stalled. Rockefeller was offering more than thirty thousand acres of some of the most exquisite country in all of America—and the U.S. government refused them.

This fight went on for more than a decade, until finally, on November 27, 1942, a frustrated John D. Rockefeller Jr. wrote a letter to Secretary of the Interior Harold Ickes, giving the government an ultimatum. In a nutshell: Take this land now, or I will sell it off to developers. The threat worked.

FDR, the ever-astute politician, decided to use his authority as president under the Antiquities Act (signed into law by his cousin Theodore Roosevelt in 1906) to establish the Jackson Hole National Monument, which would include Rockefeller's lands. Prior to this, the Antiquities Act had been reserved primarily for the protection of archaeological sites, not parklands. Never before had this much private land been deeded over to the federal government under the stewardship of the National Park Service.

But on March 15, 1943, by executive order, a proclamation was made declaring Jackson Hole National Monument (a mosaic of public and private lands totaling 221,620 acres), located at the base of Grand Teton National Park, now under National Park Service control. The anticipated political firestorm erupted in Congress.

Meanwhile, in Wyoming, an act of civil disobedience was occurring, with all the theatrics of a spaghetti Western. A local rancher and county commissioner named Cliff Hansen led a stampede with other "heavily armed" ranchers to protest the new monument. With yips and hollers and hats raised high, the cowboy rebels unleashed 550 yearling cows onto the newly established federal lands. It's the stuff of legend. Wyoming's boys were fighting for their lives in Europe while their land was being pulled out from under them at home! It was more than an outrage, it was treason, the fiery Hansen declared.

The story appeared as a sensation in *Time*, with one of the ranchers stating, "It may be a monument to Ickes, but it's a tombstone to me."

In the midst of World War II, the politics surrounding the new monument became increasingly ugly. Inflammatory language—calling those in favor of the monument "Nazis"—only escalated the political wrath and rhetoric. A bill to abolish the Grand Teton National Monument was passed by both the House and the Senate. As was expected, FDR vetoed it, with the concession that he would "support legislation that would guarantee the ranchers grazing rights and offer tax concessions to Teton County."

Seven years later, after seemingly endless legal battles and various bills lost and won in Congress—one of the most epic fights in conservation history— the Jackson Hole National Monument would finally be absorbed into Grand Teton National Park. John D. Rockefeller Jr. would write to his old friend Horace Albright in 1950, "The project which you then initiated, and the significance of which I was quick to appreciate, has taken much longer to work out than either of us dreamed."

Cliff Hansen would later become Wyoming's governor and a United States senator. And before he died, he would admit that he had been on the wrong side of history.

"I want you all to know that I'm glad I lost, because I now know I was wrong," Hansen said as a man in his eighties. "Grand Teton National Park is one of the greatest natural heritages of Wyoming and the nation, and one of our great assets."

If, as historians say, Grand Teton National Park was established in a series of three episodes—from the mountain park in 1927 to the national monument in 1943 to the full expansion of Grand Teton National Park in

1950—I would argue that there is a fourth episode that has everything to do with an unspoken vow made between John D. Rockefeller Jr. and his son and fulfilled some seventy years later.

> *A feather floats on Phelps Lake—*
> *a cradle of light*
> *rocking with the breeze.*

Two great stories of philanthropy exist in Grand Teton National Park. One of them is the story of John D. Rockefeller Jr. quietly buying up ranches in Jackson Hole in the 1930s for the purpose of expanding the park. The other story belongs to his eldest son, Laurance S. Rockefeller.

In 1949 it was Laurance who delivered the final Snake River Land Company land deeds into the hands of the National Park Service. The following year, the new monument was absorbed into the whole of Grand Teton National Park. The Teton Range and the Snake River, which meandered through glacial moraines and sagebrush flats, were united in common cause— the continuation of a largely intact ecosystem.

However, at Laurance's urging, during all those decades of fighting for a conservation solution resulting in the expansion of the park, John D. Rockefeller Jr. held on to the JY Ranch, which became a summer retreat for the Rockefeller family. The ranch was chock-full of history—it had been the first dude ranch in Jackson Hole, homesteaded by Louis H. Joy in 1906, and was later owned by Henry Stewart, a Pittsburgh businessman who sold it to the Snake River Land Company for $90,000 in 1932. It became a place where many U.S. presidents came not only to visit but to stay, a gathering place for diplomats, artists, and literati. Owing to its historical value alone, the Park Service by law could not dismantle it, nor did it want to.

Laurance S. Rockefeller decided, late in his life, to complete his father's original vision. The JY Ranch would be returned to the American people. He would relocate the ranch itself to a site outside of Grand Teton National Park, and in the process he would restore the land the ranch was situated on to its natural state.

If John D. Rockefeller Jr.'s vision was to establish an expanded Grand Teton National Park in the twentieth century, Laurance S. Rockefeller's vision was to reestablish the experience of tranquillity for the park visitor of the twenty-first century. "What will be needed most in the future will be one more wild lake, not one more historic cabin," he said.

He acted on his own judgment. His children learned of their father's plan through a letter delivered to them by Federal Express, and it came as a terrible shock. There had been no conversation, nothing to negotiate; there was only a decision to accept. Their ranch in the Tetons, enjoyed through the generations, was about to be dismantled without a trace.

"This completes the vision of my father," Laurance would say to his family.

On May 26, 2001, he deeded the JY Ranch to Grand Teton National Park. The 1,106 acres that surround the eastern half of Phelps Lake at the base of Death Canyon now belong to all of us. This gift marked a continuation of John D. Rockefeller Jr.'s philanthropic legacy to national parks. The ranch, purchased in 1932 for $90,000, roughly $45 an acre, is valued today at more than $160 million. But as Laurance Rockefeller said, "Father's greatest gift to the national park was not his generous donation of land, but rather his vision that people can live in harmony with nature."

Was it a promise Laurance made to his father that prompted him not only to give the land of the JY Ranch back to the National Park Service but also to rewild it? We can only speculate, but the younger Rockefeller never forgot the fervor of his father's passion for parks as a centerpiece of a democratic society. Laurance witnessed the spirited conversations between his father and Horace Albright on why a larger Grand Teton National Park was necessary, and he understood the politics involved with *any* park. John D. Rockefeller Jr. was instrumental in creating Acadia National Park in Maine, with its network of carriage roads; Grand Canyon National Park in Arizona; Great Smoky Mountains National Park, along the Tennessee–North Carolina border; Shenandoah National Park in Virginia; and Crater Lake National Park in Oregon, in addition to Yosemite and Yellowstone. Laurance would personally champion Redwoods National Park, which was established in 1968 in California.

What is needed to establish a national park? Money obviously helps, as the Rockefellers, the first family of national parks, knew. But they also knew that it takes tenacity, a shared vision by citizens, and generational patience.

In 1965 President Lyndon B. Johnson put Laurance S. Rockefeller in charge of the White House Conference on Natural Beauty. Rockefeller said, "How we treat our land, how we build upon it, how we act toward our air and water, in the long run, will tell what kind of people we really are."

Between 1969 and 1983 Laurance transferred close to 2,300 acres from the family trust to Grand Teton National Park, but no one had expected the dismantling of the JY Ranch and the rewilding project.

The legacy of Laurance Rockefeller not only builds upon his father's legacy, but transcends it in important ways. By acting on behalf of the future and, at the same time, articulating a spiritual imperative that says all life has dignity and deserves protection, and we must now minimize our impact in the name of restoration, Rockefeller the younger shows us not only what is possible but what is necessary.

"In the midst of the complexities of modern life, with all its pressures, the spirit of man needs to refresh itself by communion with unspoiled nature," Laurance Rockefeller said. "In such surroundings—occasional as our visits may be—we can achieve that kind of physical and spiritual renewal that comes alone from the wonder of the natural world."

Wind speaks through pines.
Light animates granite.
An Eagle soars—its shadow crosses over us
All life is intertwined.

At ninety-one, Laurance oversaw the transformation of the JY Ranch and the restoration of thousands of acres surrounding Phelps Lake in the heart of the Tetons. He hired his longtime friend Clay James as project manager for what would be named the Laurance S. Rockefeller Preserve. The two men had worked together in the 1950s on the building of the Jackson Lake Lodge. Douglas Horne and his design firm, D. R. Horne, of San Francisco, was chosen to carry forth the mission. And John and Nancy Carney of Carney Architects, a local firm in Jackson, would design the seven-thousand-square-foot lodge, more akin to a Japanese farmhouse than a visitor center. This singular structure would set a tone of simplicity and reverence for visitors as they began the two-mile walk to Phelps Lake.

"Mr. Rockefeller expressed his hope that the preserve would become a place of physical and spiritual renewal, that it would be a model for achieving balance between preservation and public use, demonstrating how citizens can work in partnership with their government," Doug Horne said.

Every tree cut, every stone removed and returned, every curve created in the eight-mile trail network through sagebrush meadows, forests, wetlands, and creeks, were part of a deliberate and deeply thoughtful plan to create "a different kind of experience" for the visitor in Grand Teton National Park.

Equally deliberate were the steps taken in the relocation of the JY Ranch. Thirty cabins were lifted from their foundations and repositioned, but only after meticulous documentation by cultural anthropologists. Every detail of every cabin—down to how many inches an ashtray sat from the edge of an end table—was recorded. Each Navajo rug, each painting, and shelved book was described. The extensive Indian basket collection housed in the cabins was curated with copious notes as to provenance and placement.

The nucleus of the ranch, including the main lodge, dining room, family cabins, and recreation center, was moved to a site on the north end of the Snake River Ranch, outside the park boundary, which had been sold to the Rockefeller family by the Resor family. This is where the Rockefeller clan now convenes.

Larry Rockefeller, the son of Laurance, told me not long ago that in his grandmother's diary he found a reference to John D. Jr.'s fondness for Phelps Lake at the mouth of Death Canyon (the site of the JY Ranch), while his wife, Abby Aldrich Rockefeller, preferred the long view, looking north toward the entirety of the Teton Range.

"Almost a hundred years later," Larry said, "we as a family are now experiencing the wisdom of my grandmother's perspective. I am coming to appreciate 'the long view.'"

> *We see the Great Peaks*
> *Mirrored in water—*
>
> *Stillness.*
> *Wholeness.*
> *Renewal.*
>
> *Reflection leads to restoration.*

I met Laurance Rockefeller at the Murie Ranch in Moose, Wyoming, in 1974. He and Mardy Murie were sitting on her cabin porch, and I remember listening to the two of them discussing Alaska. It's strange the details you recall. Mr. Rockefeller was a soft-spoken man with an unexpected wit. His green sport coat matched the scenery, and he looked rather like a bird, it seemed to me, with his sharp, narrow nose. There was to be a ribbon-cutting ceremony at the Teton Science School, newly housed at the old Elbo Ranch in Grand Teton National Park, and as a young naturalist working at the Science School, I had been asked to drive Mardy (who served on their board of directors) and Mr. Rockefeller to the festivities.

The Rockefellers and the Muries have both left a legacy of leadership in Grand Teton National Park. Olaus and Adolph Murie were respected biologists who worked for the U.S. Biological Service (now the U.S. Fish and Wildlife Service) in close partnership with their wives, Mardy Thomas Murie and Louise Gillette Murie, who were half sisters. The Muries' work and advocacy led to the protection of the Arctic National Wildlife Range, which was set aside by President Dwight D. Eisenhower in 1960 and designated as the Arctic National Wildlife Refuge in 1980 by President Jimmy Carter. The Muries' groundbreaking biological research on coyotes in Yellowstone and wolves in Mount McKinley National Park (now Denali National Park and Preserve), which focused on predator-prey relationships in the 1930s and 1940s, changed our understanding of basic ecology.

According to the historian Robin Winks, in the 1950s, when Laurance S. Rockefeller partnered with the New York Zoological Society to create what was essentially a zoo in Grand Teton National Park, "Olaus Murie bitterly opposed penning up wild animals and fought the wildlife preserve at Oxbow Bend, resigning from the Jackson Hole Preserve, where he and Mr. Rockefeller served on the board of directors."

From their ranch inside Grand Teton National Park, the Muries remained fierce but gracious defenders of wilderness. When Olaus Murie was president of the Wilderness Society, the Muries' cabin in Moose became its western headquarters and a gathering place for a Who's Who in American conservation, including such towering figures as Aldo Leopold, Bob Marshall, Howard Zahniser, and Celia Hunter. The Wilderness Act of 1964 was drafted there.

Mardy Murie was not only my mentor but a close friend and confidante from the time I was a college student working at the Teton Science School in the 1970s until her death in 2003. It was Mardy who opened the door for me to serve on the Wilderness Society governing council, Mardy who inspired my husband, Brooke, and me and countless others to fight for wild places without compromise. And it was Mardy who gave me her long silk underwear with pearl buttons when Brooke and I went to Alaska for our honeymoon.

Mardy told us more than once that when Olaus was asked what he thought should happen to the Murie Ranch after they died, he said, "Burn it down and let it go back to the wild." I wonder whether the Muries and Mr. Rockefeller ever had that conversation about the JY Ranch.

On September 1, 1975, I heard Laurance Rockefeller speak at the twenty-fifth anniversary of the expansion of Grand Teton National Park. "Let us all, here and now," he said, "pledge ourselves anew to maintain these majestic surroundings so that millions more through the years to come may also enjoy the peace and splendor that is here."

Nature quiets the mind
by engaging with an intelligence
larger than our own.

Laurance Spelman Rockefeller died in his sleep on July 11, 2004. He was ninety-four years old, and his dream of restoration was in motion, with the rewilding of the eastern shore of Phelps Lake well under way. In 2003, the last time he was at the JY Ranch, he told a friend, "I hope one day my family will forgive me."

Mindful of different ways of being,
Our awareness as a species shifts—
We recognize the soul of the land as our own.

In 2005 I received a telephone call from Clay James, asking if I would write a prose poem for the Laurance S. Rockefeller Preserve. I was stunned. I had just finished reading Robin Winks's biography of Rockefeller the day before.

"It would be an honor," I said.

The next day, I met with Clay at the construction site of the visitor center, where I was introduced to Doug Horne. They rolled out their plans for this ambitious project. I saw the fingerprints of Mr. Rockefeller on the blueprints of the construction site. How does one create a visitor center that doesn't simply educate but evokes a different way of being in the world? Clay and Doug showed me maps of meandering trails, a mural made of a mosaic of images, and plans for a small sound theater in the round, where children could listen to elk bugling, coyotes howling, and the falling of snow. Most of all, I could sense the power of a group of people who were committed to feeling the land, not just using it.

What they wanted from me, they said, was poetry, not prose, something simple, something felt, something true to the land. These words would guide the visitors through the exhibits and prepare them for the meditative walk to the lake.

For two and a half years I worked on what would become a poem of twenty-seven lines. I read everything I could get my hands on about or by Mr. Rockefeller. I visited his homes in New York and Vermont. I read his speeches and listened to interviews he had given. His voice became familiar. And I fell in love with his words.

His nephew, Steven Rockefeller, a man I greatly admire for his work on the Earth Charter, shared stories about his uncle, speaking of the tenderness of their relationship and the complexities of the man. He told me that Laurance, a lifelong Christian, had become in his later years a student of meditation. In fact, Steven had introduced him to Buddhism, something the two of them shared privately. He urged me to find the original footprint of the

"retreat cabin." He told me that if I could find its location, I would understand more fully what the lake and the land at the base of Death Canyon had
meant to his uncle.

> *The path of wisdom invites us*
> *to walk with a humble heart*
>
> *recognizing the dance*
> *between diversity and unity,*
> *action and restraint.*

I stood for the first time on the east shore of Phelps Lake, looking west.
The mouth of Death Canyon was open; Albright Peak was commanding.
I had never seen either of these landmarks from this perspective. Throughout
my life I had seen the green-roofed cabins of the JY Ranch from the vantage
point of the ridge on our way to Death Canyon, but it had been "the Rockefellers' place"—private and off-limits. Now the land before me was an open
space, white with snow, with hardly a trace of evidence that this was once a
colony of prestige and power. What remained was a deep and penetrating
stillness.

Clay had given me a map of where the cabins had been. I located "Steven's
Cabin" on the map. Laurance had built this cabin for Steven as a wedding
present. Steven and his wife, Anne-Marie, had spent their honeymoon there.
In later years Laurance and Mary would take that same cabin for themselves
when they stayed at the JY. The retreat cabin Steven had referenced in our
earlier conversation, the cabin used for meditation only, had to be nearby.

"A deep condition of mindfulness leads us to insights that can influence
our own lives and interactions with others and with nature," Laurance S.
Rockefeller wrote.

The two cabins were located on the other side of the small bay—separated from the main lodge. You approached them by a footbridge that was now dismantled. With the map in hand, I walked the long way around the lake until I found what I thought to be the footprint of the retreat cabin. There was little vegetation sticking up from the snow; the land seemed uncommonly level. I followed the view line to the water and sat down on a log and stared at Phelps Lake for a long time.

Phelps Lake was a perfect loneliness held. The water was dark green, almost black. Two white boulders in the center of the lake appeared as eyes, Buddha's eyes, reflecting a radiance. I sat in silence as a shroud of clouds enveloped the mountains, and when it began to snow, I started writing.

The words came quickly, more as an evocation than as a poem. I trusted them. I believed I had found the place where Mr. Rockefeller spent much of his time in solitude, in peace.

But I was still missing something, something essential.

A month later I made a pilgrimage to 1 Rockefeller Plaza in New York City.

I took the elevator to the top floor, where I was met by Mr. Rockefeller's secretary. Each of the Rockefeller brothers had a corner office: David, Nelson, and Laurance. David's office registered as an art museum, with paintings by Renoir and Monet. Nelson's office, maintained even after his death, was filled with political paraphernalia, plaques, and photographs on the walls. At the entrance of Laurance Rockefeller's office was a gorgeous painting by Gauguin. I commented to his secretary how much I admired it.

"Yes," she said. "Mr. Rockefeller took great delight in what a fine reproduction it was." She smiled. "He loved seeing people's reaction, especially, after David's magnificent art collection."

"I heard he was a trickster," I said.

"Indeed," she said as she opened the door to his office and stepped to the side. "As you can see, there's not much left."

What was left on his shelves and on top of his desk were Buddhas and scales, dozens of them. I didn't say a word. I just scanned the room slowly, noting the differences and peculiarities of each scale and figurine. His secretary left me alone and returned with a piece of paper, which she handed to me.

"I think you will appreciate this," she said.

I love the concept of unity and diversity . . . most decisions are based on a tiny difference. People say this was right and that wrong—the difference was a feather . . . I keep scales wherever I am to remind me of that . . . They're a symbol of my awareness of the distortion most people have of what's better and what isn't. LSR

"Thank you," I said. "This is what I have been looking for, this is what was missing." I had the last three lines for "Meditation on Phelps Lake" for the Laurance S. Rockefeller Preserve.

The Scales of Nature
will always seek equilibrium
A feather can tip the balance.

The Laurance S. Rockefeller Preserve was dedicated on June 21, 2008. Mr. Rockefeller's daughter, Lucy Rockefeller Waletzky, said, "My father recognized 'mind-body-spirit' as one word."

My own father was among the first visitors in Grand Teton National Park to see the eastern shore of Phelps Lake when it was finally opened to the public. As a man who has walked most of the trails in the Tetons, he walked the newly marked trail in awe, never imagining that this path would one day be open to him, too.

The Laurance S. Rockefeller Preserve has become his favorite place in the Tetons. We have walked it together well over a dozen times, and each

time, we have gleaned something new: a patch of columbines, a doe and her fawns, an unexpected headstone among the pines. The number of people who can walk there at the same time is limited by parking places, and as a result, the forest path to Phelps Lake remains a place of personal meditation—quiet, still, and solitary.

This was Laurance Rockefeller's intention.

The Rockefellers shared their wealth. Our public lands—whether a national park or monument, wildlife refuge, forest, or prairie—make each one of us land-rich. It is our inheritance as citizens of a country called America.

In the summer of 2014 Laurance's youngest brother, David, the last living child of John D. Rockefeller Jr., returned to the restored shores of Phelps Lake. Gone were the horse stables, the cabins, and the lodge. Wild gardens of columbines and paintbrush extended down to the lakeshore. Sitting in a wheelchair, one year shy of one hundred, David Rockefeller looked out across Phelps Lake toward Death Canyon with tears streaming down his cheeks.

Pine Cone and Eucalyptus Leaves, *San Francisco, California, 1932; photograph by Ansel Adams*

———

My father and his beloved, Jan Sloan, returned to Phelps Lake at the end of last summer and walked the familiar trail holding hands. I walked with them. The lodgepole pines were pungent. It had been an unusually wet summer. Even so, the yellowing grasses of fall were present and the huckleberries ripe. We walked in silence, speaking very little. Gone were the days when my father with his fifty-pound pack would sprint up Death Canyon and hike up to the Wall, where he would join the Teton Crest Trail that traverses the back side of the range. The Grand Teton no longer seemed to hold his attention as it did on that morning when he corrected me for loving the wrong mountain. What moves my father now as a man in his eighties is beauty, intimate and near.

"Look at this Indian paintbrush," he said. "Have you ever seen this color of magenta?"

At one bend in the trail, the smell of elk was strong, like urine-soaked sweetgrass, and we followed their tracks along the ridge. A stunning boulder left behind by glaciers loomed large on a slope speckled with yellow and orange lichen. Chanterelle mushrooms looked like the gold fringe of a fallen log. It was a good stopping place for lunch. The light was low, and a view opened up through the shade of lodgepoles. We sat down, ate our sandwiches, and talked. We spoke of death, not in a morbid way, but in a pragmatic one.

"It will come," Dad said. "But for now, heaven is here."

The Tetons are my Mother Park. This is the birthplace of my wonder, my first encounter of drinking deeply from Hidden Falls with my mother and grandmother, our faces wet with mist. Jenny Lake, Leigh Lake, and Emma Matilda Lake were the waters named for women. Granite Canyon, Garnet Canyon, and Cascade Canyon were the trails I walked with my brothers.

I followed my father up the flanks of these mountains, and I will follow him again after he is gone.

Not a year of my life has passed without the Tetons' jagged presence, not one.

I was not born here, but my consciousness toward a land ethic was: here in the Tetons; in Yellowstone; in Island Park, Idaho; and in the Centennial Valley of Montana—the Northern Rockies, where again and again I have witnessed wildness, what it is and why it deserves our fidelity. From space, the Grand Prismatic Spring becomes Earth's watchful eye.

To watch spring arrive on the wings of a pair of red-tailed hawks as they circle each other in amorous display is not a small thing, but a source of amazement at how they find their way back to the same nest each year.

To see the yellow fritillaries burst forth after the deep snows of winter and know that the bears are soon to follow is to be attentive to wild nature's seasonal fugue of infinite composition and succession. The great gray owl sitting on a snag near Sawmill Ponds is not simply a bird but a heightened intelligence with golden eyes behind a mask of feathers.

Not long ago I stopped at the lip of Yellowstone's Upper Falls, two hours north by car from Jackson Lake. A child had fallen to her death just the week before; she was running too close to the edge and slipped. We all grieved over her passing. I became mesmerized by the cascading waters and felt a rush of fear thinking about where we find ourselves at this moment in time—on the brink of beauty and terror—where bears appear and disappear in an instant, where bison who pay no attention to boundaries and cross them unknowingly suffer the consequences of government bureaucracy and are slaughtered on sight, and where pronghorn who continue to migrate each fall must now encounter drill rigs and subdivisions instead of open seas of sage. It is also where the triumph of one decade—the reintroduction of wolves—becomes the challenge of another decade as a murderous mythology held by many will not die nor allow them to live.

This is a chosen landscape of bugling elk, dancing cranes, and a tribe of grizzlies who spring from a glory bear named 399 who continues to amble through willows with her cubs each year, often in full view of visitors. She is an ongoing generosity who deserves more protection, not less.

Wolves howl in the bright light of the moon. Bison remain wild, not tamed. And on dark days, when everywhere we turn war is waging and violence around the world seems to be rising, a dozen trumpeter swans fly in formation over snow-covered peaks.

Just last night I watched a moose and calf so close I could count their long eyelashes through my binoculars. And coyotes are always near.

I am of this place. Family is a place, and my family is located here, those who are living and those who have passed. I am settled in the scent of sage. Mount Moran's reflection at Oxbow Bend is more than a mirror of memories; it is the joy found in river otters, a reminder that there are places in the world we can return to for peace unchanged.

After we had been gifted by the sight of the grizzly on my father's birthday, John Tempest picked up his great-grandson Wyatt and held him. "Did you see that big bear, little man?" Later that day, Wyatt would take his first awkward steps—toward the extended hands of his great-grandfather on his eightieth birthday. He would not know it then, but one day he'd be told that the day he learned to walk was the day he saw a grizzly standing upright in the presence of family, four generations that will be followed by four more and four more beyond that.

This is what we can promise the future: a legacy of care. That we will be good stewards and not take too much or give back too little, that we will recognize wild nature for what it is, in all its magnificent and complex history—an unfathomable wealth that should be consciously saved, not ruthlessly spent. Privilege is what we inherit by our status as Homo sapiens living on this planet. This is the privilege of imagination. What we choose to do with our privilege as a species is up to each of us.

Humility is born in wildness. We are not protecting grizzlies from extinction; they are protecting us from the extinction of experience as we engage with a world beyond ourselves. The very presence of a grizzly returns us to an ecology of awe. We tremble at what appears to be a dream yet stands before us on two legs and roars.

THEODORE ROOSEVELT NATIONAL

PARK, NORTH DAKOTA

≺≺ ≻≻

All this is what the wind knows

I T IS A GENTLE, PEACEFUL PLACE," my father said as we stood at Scoria Point at sunset.

The sun was slowly dropping between a stone camel's back with two humps. A pink sky was turning violet; the red flaming ball cast a crimson light on my father's face. It suited him. His life has been the reflection of passion for one thing only: work. And his work has been laying pipe throughout the American West, particularly the Intermountain West that includes Utah, Idaho, Wyoming, Nevada, and at times Colorado and Arizona.

"I have never been in North Dakota," he said. "We missed the boom here in the Bakken."

By Bakken, my father means the Bakken shale oil field that on this day, July 2, 2014, is yielding over 1 million barrels a day, making it the biggest rush of oil and gas in America's history. The migration of men and a few women over the past few years has become legion. Man camps where the transient workforce settles boast thousands spread out on the razed sage flats like jackrabbits, creating a dust devil of their own making. Most workers are living in their trucks, the lucky ones living in what can only be described as shared storage units, six to eight men living in one space, some units without windows. It is a staggered existence, with men coming and going as they rotate in and out of the work cycle; twelve days on and twelve days off.

My brother Dan was one of these men who came to work in the Bakken in 2014 to make money. He worked during the winter on the frack line, washing off the chemicals used to break up the strata below so the oil can seep up to the surface more easily. The brutality of the weather only approximated the brutality of the work. Sixty degrees below zero in howling winds is man against nature; but week after week morphing into months of solitary darkness and freezing nights alone cramped in the cab of a truck is crazy making. Like so many of the workers profiled in Jesse Moss's revelatory documentary about the Bakken oil field, *The Overnighters*, one of the roughnecks hoping to turn his life around by the big boom said, "I arrived broken and left shattered." What began as a dream becomes a matter of survival, and for some, as in the case of my brother, just barely.

My youngest brother, Hank, works in the family business in Utah, sometimes Wyoming, often Arizona, laying the pipe that carries natural gas to subdivisions and homes, answering a family's needs for heat: a gas stove, the luxury of a hot bath and a gas-flame fireplace. He is among the quiet and brave men who make our lives easy when theirs are not. These are the stories most of us don't hear.

"I'm proud of what we've done," my father says. "Not many men can say they've walked most of the major gas lines that fueled the American West's development like I have."

We are visiting Theodore Roosevelt National Park, a place on my father's bucket list. It is the Fourth of July weekend and we are alone, no other cars or visitors in sight, a reminder that not all America's national parks are overcrowded.

———

Teddy Roosevelt speaks of "the doctrine of the strenuous life," and my father sees himself as a practitioner of TR's philosophy. He admires mightily America's twenty-sixth president of the United States. Theodore Roosevelt is, after all, a man's man. In our family, the worst thing you can call someone is a "weakling." Turns out this was one of Roosevelt's favorite words. For all I know, maybe Dad stole it from the man himself, who said, "Speak softly and carry a big stick; you will go far." Tempest masculinity, a core family value, was also extended to women and children. Above all, you had to be tough, no complaining; in fact, the fewer words you spoke overall, the better: your stoicism was your power.

Yet, in the midst of the brawn was an understated and unexpected tenderness, a sharp sense of humor largely directed at oneself. My father, ruled by his emotions, is known among his men, at times, as a son of a bitch who is feared, yet always a man they respect, even love. How did he do it? He cares. My father was and remains a champion of the workingman. He attended every funeral of every man who ever worked for him. The deer hunt was a company holiday. A new rifle was given to the man who shot the trophy buck. Daily footage—meaning the amount of pipe laid in a day—became a company competition, where all the foremen and crewmen tried to best one another. Records were kept in the minds of the men, not on paper. Nothing was lost on my father. His boots walked the eroding lip of trenches every day; he knew what got dug and what got filled and by whom.

Over lunch, my father recently said, "If I was a young man again, I would work for the labor unions on behalf of the rights of workers."

I was surprised. "Union" was a dirty word around our house. But my father has watched the dignity of workers decline and he has watched how big companies exploit their workforce in the name of profit.

"They are human beings," Dad would say. "It's not always about the bottom line."

"Be practical as well as generous in your ideals. Keep your eyes on the stars, but remember to keep your feet on the ground," Teddy Roosevelt said. That sums up John Tempest perfectly.

Even as we drove into Theodore Roosevelt National Park, my father's focus was on the construction company laying the gravel on the roads. There was slope stabilization being done to halt erosion. He wanted to know who was doing it—and why. In the midst of watching white-tailed deer forage on the margins of the forest or spotting an elk on the ridge or even stopping to watch the antics of prairie dogs (at my insistence), his eye was on the infrastructure: roads, pipelines, telephone lines, and the expanding oil patch within view.

Banded hills, waving grass, green, green-yellow, rust, sweet clover, cottonwoods, red-tailed hawks, bison, crickets, sage. There is a tapestry to this country that is unique to the badlands of North Dakota. They are not bald and bare like the eroding hills of South Dakota. To my surprise, they are forested with junipers and in some cases pines. Everywhere we turn are harriers and field sparrows, meadowlarks and crows. A lazuli bunting is singing on a snag. Doves with their wings tucked tight fly like bullets down canyon. Magpies hop around us, banking we will leave something behind—shiny or edible, it hardly matters.

A rose tint casts its spell as my father and I continue to watch the blazing sun.

"It's gone," Dad says. And almost instantaneously, the sky becomes a periwinkle blue that grows deeper in its intensity. The silhouettes of deer highlight the ridges; we are not alone. The temperature drops and we return to our car. By the time we drive through the park, past the prairie dog towns, past the Little Missouri meandering through Peaceful Valley, past the lone bison still stationary, a fortress, it is dark and the lights of Medora are sparkling like a lure in deep water.

We are staying at the Rough Riders Hotel, chock-full of TR memorabilia, from sepia-toned photographs to bronze busts to signed letters to an impressive library of books authored by Theodore Roosevelt, as well as endless narratives and biographies written about him. Our national parks make fetishes of their founders and run the risk of turning history into kitsch. I am certain that if I looked into enough shops in this gateway town of Medora, I could find a pair of round-rimmed glasses, a mustache and a hat, a fringed shirt and leather chaps, and high-strung boots and appear on any one of the park trails as Theodore Roosevelt himself.

Each day at three in the afternoon, Theodore Roosevelt speaks to a full audience in the old theater. We are given a flyer of the performance when we check into the hotel. Call it entertainment or history—to the community, it is commerce.

Outside the hotel, there is a very long line to the ice cream shop.

Once in my room, I open the window so I can breathe. The moon is rising over a blue bluff.

The Superintendent

Theodore Roosevelt would have liked Valerie Naylor, the superintendent of his park.

She is formidable upon first appearance in full uniform and it is hard not to be intimidated. But her side smile gives her away. Already she is teasing my father, calling him John and offering him condolences for having me as a daughter. He is smitten. He offers to drive, she says she will, and there is no further discussion. Valerie's young cousin Cody also joins us. He is visiting from California, a high school student who has a dream of working in the oil fields north of here.

We will spend the day with Valerie in her park, the park that has been her home for the past eleven years. She received her master's degree in biology from the University of North Dakota and did her research here from 1981 to 1984, focusing on the woody draws and how small mammals like deer mice utilize them. She did comparative studies between areas grazed and ungrazed by cattle.

"I became a naturalist for Theodore Roosevelt National Park during the summers," Valerie said. "I realized I wanted to go into the National Park Service to share my love of this place with the people who visited it. This is my home park. It's where I started and where I will end."

As we drove into the park, the woody draws became evident, small oases of trees among the grasslands.

"What kinds of vegetation are we looking at?" I asked.

"It's a mixed-grass prairie with green ash, and junipers, and, of course, cottonwoods."

I see birds everywhere and hold myself back from asking whether we can stop. I guess blue-gray gnatcatchers and rufous-sided towhees. And meadowlarks are everywhere we look, especially scattered through the prairie dog towns.

"Lots of prairie dogs, Terry," Valerie says, knowing my affection for these communal rodents most people in the American West call varmints. My father has shot hundreds, maybe thousands, in his day.

"Do you love them, too, John?"

"Never mind," my father says. "Let's just keep moving."

Theodore Roosevelt National Park has large prairie dog towns that support a community of grasslands species: coyotes, foxes, burrowing owls, rattlesnakes, pronghorn, cottontails, and killdeer among them. At almost all hours of the day, red-tailed hawks and harriers can be seen floating above them with the corresponding alert calls coming from the prairie dogs.

If I had it my way, I would just sit myself among them and watch their endlessly fascinating behavior. These are black-tailed prairie dogs, not the Utah prairie dogs I studied at Bryce Canyon National Park. The black-tailed prairie dogs are much larger and more abundant than Utah prairie dogs. Historical accounts of black-tailed prairie dogs inhabiting the American grasslands at the time of Lewis and Clark report hundreds of millions of these communal animals with their towns stretching for miles across the prairie. Imagine the chatter of chirps, cries, and whistles carried by the wind that we now know from the scientists who study them to be heightened conversations with specific vocabularies and grammar on par with the language of dolphins. Prairie dog towns followed the bison herds, aerating the soil after their stampeding hooves. As the prairie dogs dig new burrows within their towns, providing endless tunnels and openings where spiders and snakes may take up residency, they loosen the tamped soils and in the process create a community for more than 243 other species of plants and animals, including predators that prey on prairie dogs such as badgers; hence, they are seen as a "keystone species," an indicator of a healthy ecosystem.

"May we just stop for just a minute or two to hear their voices?" I say to my father. I can't help myself, I am in love with these maligned creatures called "pop-guts" by my family, who have shot them for target practice.

"Here we go," Dad says.

Valerie pulls over and I step on the dry, golden grasses and lift my binoculars.

"There you are," I say. For as far as my binoculars can span the horizon, prairie dogs, in all age groups: males, females, juveniles, and babies feeding, nursing, wrestling, kissing, chirping, popping up and then abruptly disappearing into their burrows, only to pop up again in an adjacent burrow.

I focus on one clay-covered prairie dog with a black tip on its tail. He stands up on his hind legs and wails, then drops down and scurries across the grasses. Stands up again with more hearty chirps and is joined by several others. They appear as the size of small children, so much larger and stockier than our Utah prairie dogs.

"Terry exaggerates," my father says through the window that he has rolled down. Dad stays in the backseat of the truck as Valerie and I talk prairie dog. Cody also stays in the truck.

"None of us trust her."

"Our prairie dogs are pretty big, John."

I have an ally. Valerie and I met a decade ago when I visited Teddy Roosevelt Park as a guest of Dickinson State University, thirty miles east. At the time, Dickinson was a small town; now it has mushroomed with the energy boom from a population of fifteen thousand to fifty thousand.

The last time I was here, Valerie and I watched a pair of courting great horned owls in the campground by the river. We hooted back and forth in the cottonwoods at dusk until we were staring into their yellow-citrine eyes inches away. I made a vow to come back with my father, bringing back gifts of maps and guidebooks to entice a visit.

A wall of bison stand in the background, maybe a hundred or more, bulls, cows, and red calves, all swishing their tails in the midmorning heat. The wholeness of this scene asks us to imagine a large part of the American landscape stretching from Texas up to the Dakotas, looking just like this view before us.

"Let's get going!" Dad says.

Back in the truck, I turn around and say, "We're here."

Valerie is taking us up to the North Unit, which means we have to drive through the South Unit and then on Highway 85, the main route between the two units of the park.

"This is a dangerous road," Valerie says. "It's the thoroughfare from

Dickinson up to Watford to Williston, known as the gateway to the Bakken oil fields. Look at any North Dakota paper and read the obituaries, many are killed by car accidents. These big fracking trucks and oil carriers just barrel along, no pun intended," she says.

"It's energy development twenty-four seven up here. The Bakken has changed everything. Most of my job now is figuring out which oil and gas leases are going to affect the park and then meeting with the energy companies to convince them to drill somewhere else." She pauses. "Honestly, there's not enough hours in the day."

She goes on to say, "North Dakota's population was six hundred and fifty thousand before the boom, now it's over seven hundred and fifty thousand and rising. The towns of Watford City and Williston, once modest communities, are booming, with rents skyrocketing, and it's almost impossible to find a place to live. Tens of thousands of workers have descended on these towns. The locals hardly recognize the place. All hands are on deck from the governor to the state legislature, with businesses and communities now in the service of oil and gas development."

"I really want to see what's going on up there," my father says. "I know the energy boom in Wyoming and was part of it, but I've never been up here before."

"It's half an hour away," Valerie says. "We can head up there later, if you want to check it out. I know you're in the business, John. I think you'll find it fairly shocking. It's out of control and it's affecting everything."

I am listening in the backseat. Bands of pastel clays construct these badlands eroded by wind and water: white clay, gray clay, taupe. Valerie explains how North Dakota's badlands differ from South Dakota's badlands in one significant way: vegetation. And this has been the great surprise of Theodore Roosevelt National Park: it's green. The juniper forests that dot the erosional landscape appear soft and lush, a bit misleading because it's clear how wild the country really is—hard walking, little water, and a lot of wind. Whole patches of yellow sweet clover dot the landscape beneath a blue sky with herds of white cumulus clouds resembling white buffalo.

Valerie is quiet, focusing on the road. Dad and I are looking out the windows at the moving scenery. The green of the juniper becomes a mosaic with the bright yellow patches of what we learn are fields of canola oil, known as rapeseed oil. Lots of pumps not only mark the boundaries of the fields but animate them, looking like massive black crows lifting and lowering their hammer heads.

"This used to be such a leisurely drive. You could read a book as you drove, rarely even seeing another car between the two units. Now both hands better be on the wheel."

"Where were you before you became superintendent here?" Dad asks.

"Scotts Bluff. From 1999 to 2003, I was superintendent there. And before that I was at Big Bend as chief of interpretation from 1994 to 1999."

"And what changes have you seen since you started here?"

"Well, the Bakken has changed everything. My work as superintendent used to be focused on the elk herds, the bison, shoring up the crumbling bentonite hills—this park is constantly in motion." She pauses. "But now my primary job is to mitigate the drilling on the boundaries of the park, and that is more than a full-time job."

She hands a map of the park back to Dad. He unfolds it on his lap. "What's this National Grasslands area that borders the park?"

"It's a multiple-use area that still protects the ecosystem, but now it's largely being leased by the oil companies. It's being cut to pieces by energy development and it's having an impact on the park with new roads and oil pads sprouting up like corn. We'll drive out there tomorrow so you can see what's happening.

"It's like the California Gold Rush—there's no real process, no organization. It's a free-for-all, random and chaotic, and everyone wants to make a quick million and get out. And with the oil comes all the social ills associated with it: violence, prostitution, drugs—you name it, we've got it."

"Are you seeing any of this entering the park?" I ask.

"Not really, but every once in a while something strange happens, like not too long ago, a bison was shot on the side of the hill by the road. It wasn't somebody poaching a bison for food. Probably some roughnecks came into the park on the weekend, got drunk, and shot it for the hell of it.

"I don't know," Valerie says, "it's not the same. You just don't feel safe in the way you used to. I never thought twice about safety. Now I do."

"I understand what you're saying," Dad says. "During the Wyoming boom, I always kept a pistol under my seat. Always. We'd be working in Rock Springs or Rawlins and you'd be out walking the country to see where the pipe would go so you could make your bid, and guys sleeping in the sage-brush would leap up and say, 'Please hire me!' Hell, you didn't know who you'd run into.

"I mean in the seventies, in Evanston, Wyoming, you'd go into a bar off I-80, and there was a 'coat room' where it was understood that you'd leave your guns and knives and brass knuckles behind so everybody could dance or drink. It was crazy. But I have to say the oil companies did a lot of good in the town. They built recreational centers, swimming pools, and libraries. I mean, the towns benefited.

"What I can't reconcile here in North Dakota," my father says, "is this country up here is too pretty to be an oil field. Most of the oil fields I've been to have been the dredges like Baggs, Wyoming, or Big Piney—windswept land that's all but empty. But here it's so green, with these gentle rolling hills."

"I hear ya, John," Valerie says, "but like I said, I am on border control every day of every week, trying to stop the rigs from going up in our view shed. I've completely given up on our governor and the legislature. They're very tight with the energy companies. So, I've got some folks who alert me when there is a proposal for a new oil development, and then, I go directly to the CEOs of the company and ask if they will meet with me. I've had my best luck working directly with the oil companies because our state regs are so poor. I've learned over time, this is the most effective strategy."

She focuses on the road and many miles of silence pass. "But I'll tell you, honestly, it's relentless and depressing and I'm tired."

The North Unit

"We've had to close the visitor center on account of it sinking," Valerie says. "The back end of the building is eight inches higher than the front and the roof is about to collapse."

We get out of the truck and walk around the twenty-two-year-old structure.

"You can see how unstable the soil is here," Valerie points out to Cody. "It keeps slumping. The climate is really changing." She turns to my father. "Average rainfall used to be fourteen inches a year. For the last five out of six years, we've been averaging twenty inches of rain. Our badlands now stay green until September. This is unheard of. With all the rain, the clay turns into a slippery slide on the slopes and it's affecting the roads. That's all the construction you are seeing in the park, John. We're just trying to stay on top of it, but literally, the ground is moving beneath our feet."

Valerie tells us they average about six hundred thousand visitors a year to the park. She checks today's numbers: "A hundred folks so far, not bad for ten fifty-five a.m." She chats it up with the employee at the entrance kiosk, whose name is Andrew.

"What have you seen this morning?" she asks.

"Three bison thirty minutes ago," he says. "And on Mile Marker Twelve, a bighorn sheep."

"Good to know," she says. "Thanks, Andrew, thanks for the heads-up."

We continue on the fourteen-mile road that will take us in and out of the North Unit, with no idea what awaits us. This is new territory for both my father and me, roughly twenty-five thousand acres, half the size of the South Unit but more remote.

"These badlands are getting to me," my father says. "It's just so nice not to see hordes of tourists. It's all so quiet and I like how you don't have any trinket stores or restaurants inside your park."

"Me, too," Valerie says.

"Can we stop?" I ask.

"Sure, what do you see?"

"This spot of pink."

"That's ridiculous, let's keep going," my father says.

"Not a problem, John, we have all day," Valerie says.

We pull over to the side of the road, get out of the vehicle, and look.

"Wow, it's gorgeous, do you see where I'm looking, it's straight ahead to the right of the willows just down from the cliff."

"Oh, I see what you're looking at. Good eyes. It's a prairie echinacea. Pretty common around here. Beautiful. Beautiful color."

"A flower?" Dad says. I hand him the binoculars. "Hmmm."

A kingbird flies across our view. And then Valerie gets very excited. "Look, a pair of redheaded woodpeckers, up here, right here in the cotton-woods."

"Where?"

Valerie points to the middle of the cottonwood tree next to the car. I catch it in my binocs, thrilled.

"I've never seen one before. This is so great, how amazing, look at the deep red shimmering head in the light."

"There's a pair."

Dad has his binoculars focused on the woodpeckers. "Wow, I've never seen one either."

They fly across the road to another grove of cottonwoods down by the river.

We get back in Valerie's truck. "I remember the last time you were here, Terry, we saw those great horned owls in the campground."

"That was a magical night—we just kept following them—hooting back and forth together."

"Strange things happen when Terry's around," my father says. "She tells a good story, we all know that, but I've seen it. People think she's making this stuff up, but I've actually been there on some of those bizarre occasions, it's crazy, she's actually telling it straight."

"Thanks, Dad," I say, surprised by his sudden support.

"Okay, you two, if you look down the road and to your left, you'll see a remnant herd of longhorns."

"Why are they here?" Dad asks.

"It's a living history project, an homage to Teddy Roosevelt and that era. We interpret that period as having relevance to ranching, a part of the culture here in North Dakota and Montana. Historically, the longhorns were brought up from Texas, along the western cattle trails. We graze them up here. 'Interpret that period': We do a lot of strange things in the Park Service, John," Valerie says. We turn down a service road. Lark sparrows with their bridled faces fly up from the road like sparks.

"There's another redheaded woodpecker!" I say. "Look, a flock of them."

We stop and watch them, undulating from post to post. The black and white body with the bright red head is a fashion statement.

We get back in the vehicle, drive a mile or two down the road until we stop again.

"These corrals are used for the bison, we cull them for the tribes to augment their own herds. They take them for the meat, use the hide, all of it," Valerie says. "However, they are not allowed to kill them or dispose of them for a year after they receive them."

The complexities that saturate each national park are staggering and in so many ways contingent upon our understanding at the time. Yellowstone is a case study of changing and paradoxical management plans. During the early part of the twentieth century, wolves were viewed as a threat to the pastoral qualities valued at the time. Now predators are understood to be an essential component of a healthy ecosystem and were reintroduced at the end of the twentieth century.

Bison are grazing inside Yellowstone National Park, but once they step outside the park boundary they are shot by state or federal agents for fear of their carrying brucellosis, known as undulant fever, which could affect elk. Elk hunting is big money in Montana. Kill a bison to save an elk. It's that simple and it's that political—never mind there is not one documented case of a bison having given brucellosis to an elk.

Most of the issues confronting our national parks today are political. Should Devils Tower National Monument be respected as a sacred site to Kiowa people or managed as a recreational site for climbers? Compromises are made and so are mistakes. The Everglades are overrun with pythons. Some want them killed to restore a natural ecological balance, others see the killing as a cruelty. One year, a particular park is trying to control an exotic species, the next year they stop the program because their funding has been cut by Congress. Our national park management plans tend to blow with the political winds from one administration to another.

National parks can be schizophrenic. Protect grizzly bears, but if a mother bear tries to defend her cubs from a person infringing on their territory, she risks being removed or killed for being a "problem bear."

The National Park Service Organic Act, signed into law on August 25, 1916, states their mission as "To conserve the scenery and the natural and historic objects and wild life therein, and to provide for the enjoyment of the same in such manner and by such means as will leave them unimpaired for the enjoyment of future generations." On one hand, the national park service is charged with the protection of the land and everything on the land including wildlife and historical objects; while on the other hand, they have a mandate to manage the parks for the enjoyment of people. Put these two hands together and you often get a fight.

This conflict between protection and use within the National Park Service's mission may not have been apparent in the early days of national parks, when visitation numbers were low and wildlife numbers were high. But today, we see a "mission rivalry."

Robert Keiter, professor of law at the S. J. Quinney Law School at the University of Utah and author of *To Conserve Unimpaired: The Evolution of the National Park Idea*, argues that "Although the Act speaks in terms of both preservation and public use, the statutory nonimpairment standard indicates that resource preservation responsibilities should take precedence over public use in the event of conflict."

The bear should be respected.

This is why the job of the park superintendent is so crucial, for a stability of vision and being able to navigate through the inherent paradoxes of the park service mandate. In the best cases an overall ethic of care can be institutionalized, which is why Valerie Naylor is so impressive.

Being a national park superintendent is very much like being a mayor, or in some cases a governor. A sense of humor helps. I recall a conversation with a former superintendent of the Grand Canyon, Steve Martin, who told me that when he was asked why so much money was needed to reintroduce California condors, he would wryly say, "They help us locate dead bodies within days instead of weeks." That quickly silenced some of the critics, as statistics show that Grand Canyon National Park has the highest number of suicides of any national park in the country.

A national park superintendent has to be part politician, part businessperson, part naturalist, and always the diplomat. In Valerie Naylor's case, you can add fierce advocate.

———

We are looking for bighorn.

Scanning the country, I see more eastern kingbirds and several yellow warblers. Huge sandstone concretions dot the hillside beneath the bentonite hills. The work of Henry Moore is derivative.

We turn down another road and enter a spectacular cottonwood grove. To my great delight, more redheaded woodpeckers.

"This is spooky, Terry. We just don't see redheaded woodpeckers like this. They live farther east. You must have brought them."

We watch them again, their striking white secondary feathers and white rump patches contrasted with their black backs and primary feathers, with the shock of red.

As the day heats up, we are standing in an oasis of dappled light and shade. We drink some water and bring out our lunches. It is so wonderful to be able to share this with my father. He likes Valerie Naylor a lot; I can tell. With my father, you can always tell what he's thinking because he tells you.

"I think you are running this park really well, not at all like most government bureaucrats."

Valerie laughs. "Thanks, John."

In fact, Dad is right. He knows leadership when he sees it. Having run his own pipeline construction business for more than fifty years, he understands what it takes to get things done. He always told me, "Leadership is not about being liked, it's about being respected. And consistent." In 2013, Valerie Naylor received the prestigious Stephen T. Mather conservation award given by the National Parks Conservation Association "for her steadfast dedication to protecting Theodore Roosevelt National Park from the impacts of energy development, along with her successful elk management plan, and ongoing work to safeguard and elevate the importance of Theodore Roosevelt's Elkhorn Ranch."

As Valerie disappears into the visitor center to check on some things, Dad and I eat our peanut butter and jelly sandwiches under the trees.

River Bend Overlook

Why do I feel patriotic here in the Badlands? Each time I look out and see the bends in the river of the Little Missouri, these grasslands, these ships of clouds floating over the prairie, I am possessed by a sense of discovery, a vision of what the American landscape holds—this openness, these unending views, the silences, the empyreal sky. This—dare I use the word?—wholesomeness—completes me.

To be an American once meant unending possibility, and the land reflected that possibility. Always the next bend—the next ridge—the mountain range descending into the depth of canyons carved by water and wind and time.

Now, we say we have too little time, not enough time for road trips. We used to visit our national parks most often by car. Families took time and experienced the gradual approach to the park being visited. Anticipation was part of the journey as was the wildness of a family spending time together for hours and days, traversing the states. Today we arrive by plane. We miss the trek across the vast expanse of this nation. I sometimes wonder whether these special landscapes now appear as "pop-up parks," a spot of entertainment and commerce instead of an unfolding geography.

"If you want to meditate, this would be the place," I hear a woman say to her husband.

They're both in T-shirts, shorts, and sandals, with cameras in hand.

"Why don't you walk down there and stand there for me?"

"On the edge?"

"Yeah."

"How far? Is the wind with me?" the woman says to her husband.

"Good enough."

She smoothes her hair and the wind undoes it. She smoothes it again and smiles.

She looks toward the Little Missouri River from the overlook platform and he takes her picture. I wonder how many family photos have been taken here and now lie in albums across America.

My father and Valerie are talking about Mount Rushmore, a state away in South Dakota.

He tells her, "My father always wanted to see it, but he never did. So, I went with my granddaughter and her husband a couple of years ago. We had a great time. I found it really moving."

What I want to say but don't is that we took the place most sacred to the Lakota, their *axis mundi*, and carved our presidents' faces all over it. Where is the justice in that?

We look out over the vast expanse of a winding river cutting through clay and let the stillness speak. The water is muddy, brown; the sky light blue. The trill of lark sparrows surrounds us.

"Yeah," says my father, his hands in his pockets, thumbs out. "I can see why you like this place." He stands on the point, closest to where the widest curve of the Little Missouri turns again. He has always loved the long view.

The West Boundary

Valerie spreads a map on the hood of the car.

"Here's the Little Missouri National Grassland," she says. "It's over a million acres that spans four counties, the largest grasslands in the nation administered by the National Forest Service and Theodore Roosevelt National Park sits in the middle of it." Valerie explains how the various colored squares on the map indicate different jurisdictions: Indian lands are orange, private lands are white, state-owned lands are blue, the yellow squares highlight public lands administered by the Bureau of Land Management where much of the grazing of cows by local ranchers takes place, and Forest Service lands are green.

She turns to my father. "As you can see this is a vast mosaic of multiple land uses. What you need to know, John, is that ninety percent of the Little Missouri Grasslands have already been leased by the oil and gas companies."

She refers to the map again. "You can see that the North Unit of the park is the most vulnerable."

"And show me where the Bakken field is?"

"Right here is where they're 'rockin' the Bakken,' as they say out here. It's the biggest oil boom in the country right now. As you know, in the past it's been all about pool oil, but now, fracking technology has opened up everything."

"It's also freed us from the Arabs," Dad says.

"That's true, John, but the price out here has been high. Yes, we've got a million barrels a day coming out of the Bakken—but they are also burning off excess gas, costing roughly a million dollars a month and enough to fuel every home in North Dakota. You can see those flares at night."

That catches my father's attention. "Are there distribution lines?"

"Not really. It's chaos: there are few pipelines in place."

"If there were, there'd be a lot less waste," Dad says.

"Right."

"It's typical of high-yield oil fields and the boom mentality. It gets sloppy, there are no rules—"

"And a lot of people get hurt," says Valerie.

"Yes, they do."

She looks down at her map and orients it to the northwest corner of the park boundary. "So here's where we are now—see that fence, there's an oil lease just beyond it. You can see what that would do to our view shed. That's what I try to do—to keep these wells at bay."

Theodore Roosevelt National Park is an island within a sea of oil development.

Oil companies can bid for leases to drill on public lands at public auctions held by the Bureau of Land Management. Leases are purchased at ridiculously low prices, far below market value; in some cases, an acre of land can be leased for two dollars an acre. Energy extracted from our public lands produces 24 percent of global warming emissions. A national movement to keep fossil fuels in the ground is gaining momentum as climate activists are choosing to protest these oil and gas lease sales.

When Valerie speaks of view sheds she is talking about one of the most powerful features that make this park so special, a sense of the historical expanse of the Dakota territories. It was this view that I first saw more than a decade ago that brought me back. Now much of that view is oil rigs and pumps piercing the sky disrupting the horizon. Some may call this nostalgia. I see it as a breathing space central to the health and wealth of our nation. Oxygen. Valerie sees it as part of her job to protect the integrity of her park.

I ask Valerie how she has time to keep on top of all these leases popping up like prairie dogs. "I don't," she says. "It takes up most of my time, but we also have a 'geographic information specialist' who watches the leases. He's good. Gives me a heads-up. This month looks like there are three near the North Unit."

"That's the price of energy independence," Dad says to Valerie. "You environmentalists—and I will say you're better than most—but you can't have it both ways. Terry's against the war in Iraq—and against oil and gas development here at home."

"It's not that we have to stop drilling for oil and natural gas, John, we just have to think about how to do it right."

My father nods. "I agree," he says. "The haphazard nature of it all hurts everyone."

As we've talked, we've been watching bison and cows going nose to nose. The bison are nudging up to the cattle just outside the park on the other side of the fence.

"Well, I've never seen that before," Valerie says as she shoots a couple of pictures with her camera.

We climb back in Valerie's vehicle. "So here's a story for you. A young BLM archaeologist saw that a well was scheduled right on the park boundary. He called me. Sure enough, True Oil, a company out of Wyoming, had the permit and was ready to act on it. I met with the Wyoming outfit, plus the rancher whose land it was on, and the BLM person in charge. It was really important to do this. The rancher said, 'Where you are proposing to put your well is right in the middle of our calving pasture. Can't you do it by the road or in some other place?' The land manager working for the oil company said, 'I'm sorry, we can't do that.' But the company geologist, after looking at the site, ended up agreeing with the rancher and me to have it relocated.

"The land manager goes back to Wyoming and attends the oil and gas commission hearings. And I end up testifying on behalf of the oil company—a surprise to many people, and not without controversy, as you can imagine. We got the company to agree to move the drilling site two miles away from the park boundary. It was a win-win situation for all of us."

"That's impressive," Dad says.

"No, it's just what we have to do, but that takes time and, as you well know, it's all about relationships. I've learned it's actually easier and more effective to deal directly with the heads of the oil and gas companies than dealing with our governor or legislature."

Driving the last miles to the end of the park road, we are quiet. It was a lot to take in—this beautiful, still country, and the assault on its boundaries. Who decides where a national park vista ends and where an oil field begins? A map is politics made visual.

I thought about lines—the lines we draw, the lines we write; the lines we cross, the lines we cross out. An actor's lines, deadlines, hemlines, borderlines—lines drawn in the sand; lines we never forget, the lines we leave behind. A circle is a line touching.

"This is our last stop," Valerie announces.

We get out and are slapped by the wind. Dad walks to the edge of the Oxbow Overlook. "So, we are facing east?"

"That's right. You have a good sense of direction, John."

"Well, I've spent my life reading maps and walking the lines where pipe was going to be laid. I like knowing where I am."

The light is intense, and the wind is whipping so furiously, it's hard to hear. Birdsong rises from the meadows below in a staccato rhythm. The striated hills, so colorful, have gone flat in the noonday sun. Dad holds on to his hat. I am looking down at my feet. The path is paved with scoria, pieces of scorched red earth.

"Before all these companies became so arrogant, the oil companies would fly me all over Wyoming to tell them how much it would cost to run the pipe over this ridge or beneath that river. They wanted to know the cheapest and most efficient way to move the natural gas from one place to another based on the terrain we were seeing."

My father turns to Valerie. "It's funny, when I look out on this country, I still mentally figure out how to lay the pipe, how we would cross the Little Missouri, how we'd take the pipe down this hill, run the trench over there, which is what Terry objects to about our work, but I'm proud of the scars I've left in the West."

The Bakken

The town of Watford City is fifteen miles from Theodore Roosevelt National Park. We are driving north on Highway 85. The landscape looks no different from the North Unit—the same vegetated badlands meet us on either side of the road. There are fields of alfalfa and soy, but the same red-tailed hawks soar above with kestrels perched on telephone wires.

"Watford is a young town, only a hundred years old," Valerie says as she drives. "In 2005, the town spent a lot of money investing in their community.

They built a visitor center, a museum, and a theater. Some new restaurants and local businesses sprouted up. They realized they were a gateway community to the park. It became a real charming town and then the oil boom hit, and, you'll see, the town looks like it's in shock."

"I'll bet there's a lot of wrecks on this road," Dad says.

"You got it," Valerie says, and she ticks off the deaths of people she's known . . . volunteers, friends. "It's a sad place right now, believe me. The landfill for Watford was planned for fifty years. They have now determined it may be filled in two. Watford is one big bald patch for rigs, trucks, fast-food joints, and storage facilities, not to mention housing, which is a real problem."

The trailer parks are starting to appear outside our windows.

"Housing outside of Watford now is reduced to living inside storage units and containers."

Since we've left the North Unit of Theodore Roosevelt National Park, I've counted thirty-five pickup trucks on the road and seventeen fracking trucks carrying sand and chemicals. There is a septic cleaning truck in front of us. Prairie View trailer park is up ahead and I compulsively count 275 units lined up neatly on a razed patch of prairie.

Neon signs along the highway into Watford tell the story of what the "oil boom" means to business: "Express Laundry," "Oil Fuel Supplies," "Rental Storage," "U-Haul," "Trailer Park Two," "Lutheran Social Services," "Firestone," "ALCO," "Liquor," "Red Wing," "Bobcat," "Chiropractic Office," "Emerge-A-Care," "Free Showers."

Everywhere we look: scraped land, trucks in traffic, dust. We pull up to a red traffic light. "Watford didn't even have traffic lights before the boom," Valerie says.

A steady stream of trucks are turning left in front of us. Suddenly, a mallard with eight ducklings waddling behind her begins to cross the intersection with trucks speeding through the traffic light. Valerie and I bolt out of our vehicle.

"Stop!" Valerie screams, planting herself in the center of the highway, hands out. I'm trying to corral the mother and her ducklings and lead them back to where they came from—a trashed clump of cattails a few yards away from a bunch of tires tossed by the side of the road. A glint of water shines in the midst of the dump, and the ducks disappear into the postage stamp wetland.

"That wasn't too smart," Dad says, looking at us.

Valerie studies my father. "You okay, John?"

After lunch, we head out on a dirt road. Dad wants to see the man camps.

"I've heard so much about these, I want to see them for myself," he says.

"North Dakota's a cold, harsh place, but other things made up for it—big open country, everybody knew everybody else, nobody ever locked their houses or cars. Now it's just a cold, harsh place," says Valerie.

Horned larks fly out of the ruts of the dirt road. Up ahead, like a mirage, row after row after row of storage containers appears against the horizon. As we get closer the shine dulls.

Each storage container appears to be divided in half, each with its own door and windows. Some have dents in them, most likely kicked in by a drunk or rammed by a truck, accidentally or deliberately. Almost all the trucks parked out in front have cracked windshields.

"Bakken Acres—Best Value Housing—Prairie View."

"We're talking at least six men to a unit, with different men coming and going depending on their shifts," says Valerie.

Behind the rows of storage containers, we can see three rigs, pumps moving up and down like mechanical blackbirds pecking for seeds. Behind them, flares from another oil patch rise like quick-match strikes.

"Mind if I get out?" Dad asks.

"No, sir."

Dad walks down the rows of beat-in units, stepping around beer cans and bottles, most of them broken. Some of the container units have lawn chairs out front; one has a flower box, planted with red and white petunias. There are a lot of NFL stickers on the units, a few American flags.

I've lost my father, so I follow footprints; I know his boots. Even at eighty, he can outwalk me.

After a half hour or so, we gather back at the car and drive farther down the road.

"You know, for years, I've felt guilty that we couldn't put our men up in motel rooms one summer when we were working out near Rock Springs, Wyoming. I went to the army supply store and bought a dozen army cots and sleeping bags, cooking pans, plates, utensils, you know—and we put them in a circle—and camped by the river. And, you know, we ended up telling stories and eating together, sleeping under the stars, and it built up a real camaraderie among the men and by God, if we didn't bore under that river in record time." Dad pauses. "There's none of that here. You can feel it. Hell, I bet these men have never met one of the owners of these companies. The men are like ants, expendable, kill one, there's a hundred more coming to replace them."

Cody turns to my father and tells him this is where he wants to work after high school. "It's about the money, John."

"I understand that, but I wouldn't advise it," Dad says. "Go to college, get some training for a steady job with marketable skills, like a welder. But if you do decide to work here, find a company where you can talk to the owner, the man in charge, show up with your work gloves in your back pocket and your lunch box in hand, so it gives the message you're ready to work."

Cody was listening.

Down the road there are more man camps, this time rows of shiny white trailers, dozens of them. A sign reads "Watford Ridge."

"These are renting for about twenty-five hundred a month," Valerie says.

"One of my friends runs a park like this, full all of the time, and the minute one's empty, it's filled again."

Beyond Watford Ridge are a bunch of two-bit toolsheds made out of plywood: "Adele's RV Oasis—Studio Apartments."

"You'd have to see this to believe it," Dad says. "There's no dignity here."

We pass a refinery on the same road heading toward the dusty horizon, a gathering plant before that, and before that a gas processing plant.

"Hell, it looks like the men have to drive two hours to even get out to the rigs," my father says. "Think about that, they're working twelve days on and twelve days off. What are you going to do on your off days but sit in those piss-poor storage units and drink yourself to death or get on the highway so tired you drive into a ditch or another car and kill someone."

He turns around. "See, Terry, they're using a twelve-inch gas pipe taking it from the gathering plant to the refinery. The pipe is hardly buried, they just run it cheap, to get where it needs to be."

"And when do you pick up the gas?" I ask.

"We run the gas lines from the refinery into the communities into the subdivisions into people's homes so they have heat."

I realize how little I understand about this process of my family's work, which has literally placed them in the trenches of the development of the American West. I think of my brothers again: Dan, who spent part of a winter here working and living in his truck, half-crazed with the cold isolation of sleeping in his cab. And Hank, who, with his fellow crewmen, faithfully goes about the work of upholding the infrastructure we all take for granted, and not without physical cost—white forehead and sun-leathered cheeks in summer; frostbite in winter, with a litany of scars, bad backs, and torn muscles to show for it. Just last year, Hank contracted desert fever in Tucson, which grew into pneumonia and resulted in a rare abscess that cost him half his lung.

"This boom is forecasted for five generations," Valerie says. "So, this is the envelope that Theodore Roosevelt fits inside. We are an island in a sea of industrial development. Seen enough?"

A gray fox spots us; stops, runs, disappears. We turn around and drive back toward Highway 85. Once we're on the road, the glare of the sun highlights a bison in silhouette, standing alone on a bluff.

My father is silent. He looks straight ahead, his eyes focused on the road.

Independence Day

It's the Fourth of July in Medora, North Dakota, and the staff of the Theodore Roosevelt National Park will be in the parade. They plan on decorating the Park Service truck as a float, with people dressed as prairie dogs poking up and down in the back.

"May I volunteer to be one of them?" I ask Valerie. "I've got the prairie dog moves down, I promise you." My father rolls his eyes.

"Not necessary, I've got our naturalists on board," Valerie says.

"I'd love to—honestly."

"No."

Valerie Naylor is not a person you argue with, so my father and I line up on the sidewalk with all the tourists to watch. Teddy Roosevelt makes a convincing appearance—"A bully hot day, isn't it? But we're having a bully good time!" Several horses pass. A wagon full of actors, dancers, and musicians from the Medora musical passes by; the musical runs every night to a full house throughout the summer. Town officials in cowboy hats and boots are waving, while a motorcycle gang speeds past in black leathers. Several square-dancing clubs twirl along; the local police run their sirens—and toward the end, the national park float appears, with Superintendent Valerie Naylor in the passenger seat of the cab. She's waving to the crowd, in full uniform: gray shirt, green pants, badge, belt, and straight-brimmed hat. In the back of the truck, her staff of prairie dogs are popping up and down, throwing candy. The crowd loves them. My father looks at his watch and tells me the parade lasted approximately thirty-five minutes.

That night, Dad and I go see the Medora musical, at my request. It is a tribute to America through song and dance in a three-story outdoor amphitheater that holds 2,853 people, complete with an escalator. It's billed as "the rootin'-tootinest, boot-scootinest show in all the West," featuring "the Queen of the West" and the Burning Hills Singers, with live horses onstage. Seated with humanity in front, back, and on either side, it's hard to concentrate in the midst of so much toe-tapping cheerfulness. Especially when Mr. Bubble, the pink bath product personified, drives in a circle onstage, singing the brand's slogan, "Makes Getting Clean Almost as Much Fun as Getting Dirty!"

The link between Medora and Mr. Bubble is this: Mr. Bubble was the lucrative brainchild of Mr. Harold Schafer and the Gold Seal Company, which was founded in North Dakota in 1942. Mr. Harold Schafer loved the North Dakota badlands. He also felt a kinship with Teddy Roosevelt. After Schafer made his millions, he bought up the town of Medora, which was then a shabby little cow town, and he transformed it into what it is today, a mock-up western town embroidered with kitsch.

From the restored Rough Riders Hotel, to the theater where visitors can meet Theodore Roosevelt—a reenactor performing as America's twenty-sixth president—and hear his bully pulpit, to the North Dakota Cowboy Hall of Fame, Medora itself can be seen as its own destination.

Mr. Schafer (who passed away in 2001) and his wife, Sheila, are worshipped in this town for their generosity to all things Medora, the gateway to Theodore Roosevelt National Park.

As the evening wore on, my father and I wore out. After each live scene depicting historical moments of the "Wild West" (most of them starring Teddy Roosevelt), "the Queen of the West" belted an enthusiastic refrain of "God Bless America." Each rendition edged us closer and closer to an exodus. The grand finale included an invitation by the Burning Hills Singers for all war veterans to stand and be recognized, as an enormous billowing American flag was digitally superimposed over the actual prairie that appeared behind the open-air stage. Dad said to me louder than he knew, "This is so silly, I am embarrassed to stand. Take me back to the man camps—at least it's quiet."

It took us an hour to get out of the amphitheater. "I wonder how many of these three thousand people have visited the park?" Dad asked as we walked back to the car.

According to my informal poll (my methodology included asking people in line for the restroom during intermission), not many. Of the twenty-five people I randomly asked, three had been to the park—when they were kids.

We stayed up to watch the fireworks set for ten o'clock. We stood in the parking lot of the Rough Riders Hotel with a clear view east toward the butte where the display was being launched. While the crowd gathered, I tried to persuade my father that the flaming orb I was seeing floating over town was actually a UFO. Dad kept shaking his head until with enough beer, he, too, became convinced.

And then, without warning, the fireworks erupted with such force that it felt more like a war than a holiday descending upon the badlands. The endless explosions, echoing off the butte, one after another, rained down on us like a patriot's hallucination, creating the fantasy of fire flags waving above Medora, then morphing into descending profiles of Lincoln and TR himself.

The fire-popping processions of pyrotechnic glee just kept coming faster and faster, one after another, as fuses were lit, looking like snakes being charmed until they bit the sky, detonating more fireworks, each one more dazzling than the last. My father and I, now deaf and mute, watched the sky tremble in an ecstasy of explosions that finally ended in a propulsion of rockets that unleashed rockslides and cheers, until the grand finale merged spates of cannon fire with red, white, and blue chrysanthemums erupting above us as the band played "The Star-Spangled Banner."

And then it was over.

Elkhorn Ranch

"This is the birthplace of conservation," Valerie Naylor says, as we stand at the gate of the Elkhorn Ranch, the place Theodore Roosevelt credits for igniting his passion for preservation. "It's the solitude that makes this ranch so special. And it's the solitude that is now threatened." She pauses. "We are trying to protect this experience."

We can see one well on the ridge and I can hear it, too, the whining and whirring of the black metal pump moving up and down rhythmically.

"An oil well was staked out right here," Valerie says, pointing to the land adjacent to the Park Service sign.

"Right here?" Dad asks.

"Yeah, right here, last year."

She tells us the story of finding out about the well and calling the Forest Service supervisor to say, "It can't go there!" And he said, "According to our plan, it can."

It could go there, he said, and it would. Valerie listened to all his reasons, and then she simply said, "You do this and it's going to be on the front page of every paper in North Dakota, not to mention the United States."

She called XTO, a subsidiary of ExxonMobil, who had the lease. After a long conversation with an executive there about the placement of the well, she invited the man to come visit the site. He'd never been there. It was a blank spot on the map. He made the trip.

He saw the close proximity to the historic ranch of Theodore Roosevelt. Valerie shared its history and then she encouraged him to walk the mile-and-a-half path down to the foundation stones that remain of the Elkhorn Ranch, which he did. An hour or so later, the ExxonMobil executive returned.

"How many visitors come here in a year?" he asked, wiping his forehead with the back of his hand.

"One," Valerie replied.

"Excuse me?"

"I said, 'One.'"

"No, I mean how many people visit Elkhorn Ranch annually?"

"One."

They stared at each other.

"Our twenty-sixth president of the United States was altered by his singular experience of solitude. This is the experience we are trying to preserve for each visitor, the experience you just had, sir. Each person who comes here is deeply affected. So, my answer remains the same: one."

By the end of the afternoon, in Valerie's words, "We got very creative."

XTO agreed to a compromise. They agreed to drill straight down ten thousand feet from another unit where they held the lease, behind the ridge beyond the Elkhorn Ranch, and then, from that unit, drill laterally into this unit so that there would be no visual impact, but they could still capture the oil. "It is a story with a moderately happy ending. But . . ." says Valerie. "So we stopped this particular well, but look around, all these lands are leased." She turns around 360 degrees. "Each lease that comes up we have to deal with on a case-by-case basis. What if we miss one? I tell you, the stress on my conscience . . ."

She can't finish her sentence.

It's a well-known story in Theodore Roosevelt's life: Valentine's Day 1884, his wife and his mother died on the same day. That day he scratched an *X* in his journal and wrote, "The light has gone out of my life." His wife had succumbed to complications following childbirth. Their daughter, Alice, was three days old. So distraught was TR that he handed Alice to his sister and a few months later headed west on a train, intent on living the rest of his life as a rancher in Dakota Territory. He was desperate to leave his former life behind, including politics. His daughter was safe with his sister. He could disappear.

His train stopped at Medora, the outpost in the Dakota Territory where a year earlier he had come to shoot one of the last bison left in North America. Before he'd left, he had plunked down $14,000 for an interest in a cattle ranch called the Maltese Cross.

But the ranch now proved too crowded and too complicated for his grieving soul, so he saddled his horse and rode north, along the Little Missouri River. He was a lost man seeking solitude, which he found in a remote, pleasant valley about thirty-four miles away, and there he paid a squatter $400 to vacate. He would settle there in the protection of a cottonwood grove alongside the river and build himself a ranch house. And he would call this place home for the next three years and name it the Elkhorn Ranch.

He arrived an "eastern dandy," dressing in leather garb complete with fringe, and a silver monogrammed belt buckle and spurs from Tiffany (it was hard to take him seriously). But during these years at the Elkhorn, he transformed himself into a bona fide cowboy, competent and respected.

He learned the life of a cowboy, not by reading about it but by living it.

"Whenever you are asked if you can do a job, tell 'em, 'Certainly, I can!' Then get busy and find out how to do it!" he said, and he took his own advice. He learned how to rope and brand a cow. He worked the same hours as the men he hired and could ride as fast and furiously on his horse as anybody. When he hired Bill Sewall and Wilmot Dow, two Maine woodsmen, to build his ranch house as "a long, low house of logs," in the winter of 1884–85, he felled half the trees himself.

Roosevelt faced his house toward the river and designed it with a high pitched roof, wooden floors, and imported glass. It was constructed out of cottonwood. He had the men build a large porch where he placed his rocking chair, and would later write: "In the hot noontide hours of midsummer, the broad ranch veranda, always in the shade . . . I can sit for hours at a time, leaning back in a rocking chair."

His possessions at the Elkhorn Ranch were modest by New York standards: a good chair, a desk and writing table, a few chairs for guests, a couple of bedrooms. He covered his bed with a buffalo hide. The land was his extravagance. He saw himself as a steward to thousands of acres.

Teddy Roosevelt loved the ranch. He would write and read for days at a time, talking to no one, listening only to the whispering leaves and the river's currents.

"When the days have dwindled to their shortest, and the nights seem never ending then all the great northern plains are changed into an abode of iron desolation," he wrote.

The mourning doves made him feel less lonely in the world. "There can be no more mournful sound of unending grief than the sound of a mourning dove."

Here at Elkhorn Ranch, Theodore Roosevelt was comforted in stillness and emboldened by the badlands. Penning thousands of pages in his journal, he may have written himself back to a renewed state of mind.

The winter of 1886–87 was brutal and took its toll on Roosevelt's livestock, reducing it by 60 percent. The sight of shriveled carcasses strewn across his land from starvation devastated him. He left Elkhorn and the badlands shortly thereafter and returned to politics, ready to reengage with the world he had left. He would later say that it was his years in North Dakota that gave him the character he needed to become president of the United States.

"I am a westerner at heart."

"It's true that TR was a nature lover before he built the Elkhorn Ranch," Valerie says, "but it was not until he settled in the badlands, and discovered the vulnerability of this fragile ecology to profit-seekers from the outside, that he began to ponder the policies that culminated in his unsurpassed achievement as our first conservation president."

She and my father were standing beneath the cottonwood trees next to the stones from the foundation.

I arrived with my shoes off, wanting to walk the path barefoot.

"Rattlesnakes!" Valerie says, disapproving. "They're here, you know."

"Only lazuli buntings," I say.

"And here's some more of your redheaded woodpeckers."

Sure enough, another pair flew through the cottonwoods.

"These were all trees that Roosevelt knew," Valerie says.

I look up through the silver-green heart-shaped leaves. The birdsong intertwined with the melancholia of the doves must have been familiar sounds to TR. The enormous cottonwood tree I'm standing next to has deep grooves in its bark. My hand turned sideways disappears inside its mighty trunk.

"You would appreciate this fact, Terry, a silver-plated mechanical pencil was found here . . . most likely, Roosevelt's."

My father returns from walking down to the riverbank. "The river's moved since Roosevelt was here," he says.

"You don't miss much, do you, John?"

"I was just trying to imagine his view and if the house was built here and he liked to watch the river, well, it's not in view anymore, it's logical that it's moved in a hundred-plus years."

"You're right."

Dad turns and says to Valerie, "I wouldn't have picked this spot. But I guess if isolation was what he was looking for—"

Valerie nods. "I love his quote, 'The farther one gets into the wilderness, the greater is the attraction of its lonely freedom.' TR was a man of courage, but the courage to face his own grief at Elkhorn may have been among his most heroic acts."

As my father and Valerie keep walking the boundaries of the Elkhorn, I slip my boots back on and head down to the river. The heat is searing: close to a hundred degrees. Gnats like winged cyclones swirl in place. I can see why the herds of bison we saw the previous day were frantically swishing their tails.

Sitting by the river—this meandering river—at midday in the middle of the summer—I find it hard not to dissipate into the heat wave riding through the badlands, melting grasses into gold. I am Theodore Roosevelt watching the currents as grief gathers like a whirlpool and finally flows downriver.

Life and death, we are kneaded back into the accumulated soil of the prairie.

The personal shock and assault of death that drops us to our knees in time becomes a tapping, a turning, a gesture like any other—we are not special, just part of the river, this river, rushing by me now.

Our fear of death enslaves us to the illusion that we will live forever. Theodore Roosevelt knew firsthand that we do not. And so he lived large and he never forgot the source of his own healing and strength.

"There can be no greater issue than that of conservation in this country," he wrote.

He was a man of his word. During his administration, Theodore Roosevelt was responsible for protecting 150 national forests, 51 federal bird preserves, 4 federal wildlife preserves, 18 national monuments, and 5 national parks, 230 million acres in all.

Wind Canyon

This is a terrain of verbs—break, erode, collapse, slide, slough, slump, fold, burn, smolder, steam, dry, crack, blow, fly, settle, shift, swirl, shake, sing, flow, fall, rise, carry, commence, radiate, reflect, freeze, thaw, melt, accept, change, grow.

Two bull elk in velvet stand on the edge of the prairie dog town at dusk. It is our last night in the North Dakota badlands.

My father and I walk the Wind Canyon Trail at sunset accompanied by the melancholy cries of doves.

The sky looks like tarnished silver and a half moon is suspended above us. Coyotes taunt one another. Meadowlarks are warbling. The green rolling hills of Theodore Roosevelt National Park, with their patches of sweet clover, are holding light.

I watch my father focus on the horizon. He is a beautiful man.

◄- -►

—the stones, the steel, the galaxies—

SAY THE WORD "MAINE" AND I SWOON. It is everything my home in the American West is not. It is not wet. It is not green. Nor does it exist on the edge of the continent. Say the word "Acadia" and I see pink granite cliffs absorbing the shock of pounding waves, very different from the granite blocks I know that built the temple of my people in Salt Lake City. Say the words "Schoodic Point" and the taste of salt from the splash of tides reminds me of the inland sea that raised me in Utah's Great Basin.

"The edge of the sea is a strange and beautiful place," writes Rachel Carson.

It is here in "the settled wild" of Maine that I find sanctuary from the painful politics surrounding western wilderness. I don't know enough to have my heart broken in the east. What I do know is that over the past three decades I have been coming to Acadia National Park, this landscape has entered my DNA.

As the Colorado River shrinks from its historic banks due to drought, it is a comfort to sit on Acadia's Otter Cliff, a place of shimmering waters in the midst of a seeming apocalypse.

From a distance, the mountains in Acadia appear blue and rounded, not at all like the toothed peaks of the West with hanging canyons and glaciers. You can climb them in an afternoon, wearing a skirt. Their grandeur belongs not to ruggedness but to a gradual ascent toward grace. Once you're on top of the bald summit, a view of a watery planet inspires.

On my first trip to Maine I couldn't account for how familiar it felt—this place—this place where I had never been registered in my blood like heat. It didn't make sense. I didn't want to leave. I had to return.

It began with my aunt and uncle, Ruth and Richard Tempest, being called to serve on a mission for the Mormon Church in Cambridge, Massachusetts. Maine was part of their jurisdiction. While they were in church meetings on Sunday in Kennebunkport, my cousin Lynne and I would drive to the coast and explore.

Acadia National Park became a favorite haunt for our extended family. Our grandparents would stand on the edge of the continent looking east. It mattered to them, as westerners, to face Europe and remember both the sacrifices and courage of their ancestors and how they came west. Acadia became a tender point on the map for them. They said it reminded them of a time more genteel and predictable than the chaos and confusion of modern life.

For me, it became my secret respite. Here is where I come to meet my perfect solitude; where nothing is expected of me. There are times when the drama of the American West and Pacific Northwest exhausts me. We hear news that another grizzly bear has been killed in Yellowstone because they are afraid it is "a problem bear." Or another river has been fouled by an unexpected toxic spill from a spent gold mine, not far from Rocky Mountain National Park, or a coal train is going to be rerouted near North Cascades National Park in Washington.

This forested edge of the sea far, far away from the fossil fuel development in the American West shows us that what follows the story of destruction can be the story of restoration. The great fire of 1947 burned half of Mount

Desert Island. Today, the woods are dense and lush. Maine's forests have been clear-cut and burned and cut again as recorded through photographs of the great Penobscot River choked with logs, eventually floating their way down to mill towns such as Bangor throughout the late nineteenth century. Timber and steel built America. Oil and gas are now fueling it.

My momentary retreats from my home ground in Utah allow me to breathe.

I love walking up Cadillac Mountain at dawn to see the sunrise, the first glint of light that appears in the United States from equinox to equinox. I love seeing the bodies of blue islands surface like whales at low tide and disappear at high, and the lobster buoys sprinkled over the waters like confetti. I love walking the rocky coast and finding brittle stars with outstretched legs crawling on wet, slippery rocks. I love how the sea anemones open and close like flowers with the inrushing tide. And I love retreating from the edge of the water into the damp woods soft with moss and fresh with fir. In the midst of birches and maples, lichen-drenched boulders in dappled light become the stage set for Noh Theater.

Acadia National Park is a cultural ecotone where civilization and wildness meet. In landscape ecology, an ecotone is defined as "the border area where two patches meet that have a different ecological composition." Think forest meets the ocean; meadow meets the woods; a desert becomes flush with a river. These edges create lines of tension. Call it a mete of creativity where the greatest diversity of species merge.

It is also a transition zone between those who leave and those who stay. In Maine there has always been tension between "summer people" and locals, where the human ecotone down east usually has to do with wealth—the lobstermen and clammers on one hand and the Astors and Rockefellers with their summer cottages on the other. In between, you have the nature lovers, or "rusticators," as they were called in the early twentieth century.

On a gently raining day, Brooke and I hike up Champlain Mountain, and as we do we imagine the era of rusticators not far removed from my grandparents had they lived here. We walk the stairs cut from granite so thoughtfully spaced, one after another, up the steep incline. We can envision the women lifting their long skirts so as not to slip on the rain-soaked stairs, now worn with time. It all feels so civilized. There is little delineation between sea and sky, only a soft gray-blue that folds into one graceful curve of cloud. The sound of foghorns guiding boats through rough water turns guttural. The rain stops and we eat our sandwiches on the summit. As we do, a stream of light breaks through the clouds. Below, a galaxy of stars dance on the Atlantic.

For all of us, Acadia is another breathing space. Perhaps that is what parks are—breathing spaces for a society that increasingly holds its breath. Here on the edge of the continent in this marriage between wind and sea, the weaving of currents offers a tapestry of relief.

Blue mussels, clam shells—broken and whole—slipper shells and limpets, lobster tails spent, buoys abandoned; a new world is at my feet. I wear an ankle bracelet of rockweed, bright yellow. A seal bobbing in the tide is watching.

Renascence—both the word and the poem by Edna St. Vincent Millay—returns to me, the revival of something that has been dormant.

> *All I could see from where I stood*
> *Was three long mountains and a wood;*
> *I turned and looked another way,*
> *And saw three islands in a bay.*
>
> *So with my eyes I traced the line*
> *Of the horizon, thin and fine,*
> *Straight around till I was come*
> *Back to where I'd started from;*

And all I saw from where I stood
Was three long mountains and a wood.

Over these things I could not see;
These were the things that bounded me;
And I could touch them with my hand,
Almost, I thought, from where I stand.

Acadia National Park is personal for me. If Virginia Woolf speaks of a room of one's own, how about a place of one's own, not to be shared or spoken of except with the 2.5 million other visitors that come to Acadia each summer? I am not alone in my affections. In 2014, Acadia ranked as one of the top ten most popular national parks in America.

It is a privilege to visit Acadia, and it is privilege that has protected it. Established in 1916 as America's first national park east of the Mississippi (then known as Lafayette National Park), it was the first park to be created entirely out of private land and it is unique in that most of the land was donated. Every person associated with it acted out of love. Acadia's first superintendent, George B. Dorr, wealthy by inheritance, died virtually penniless, having given all he had to the cause of the park. Charles W. Eliot, president of Harvard, founded the Hancock County Trustees of Public Reservations to watch over it. And John D. Rockefeller Jr. donated more than eleven thousand acres of land to create it, and gave $3.5 million to support it. And then there were the carriage roads. This was Rockefeller's extraordinary obsession: a network of forty-five miles of roads meant only for horse-drawn carriages. Rockefeller wanted to make certain that his beloved Mount Desert Island did not succumb to the automobile era (the irony that his fortune came from his family's ownership of Standard Oil and the advent of the automobile was not lost on him). He wanted to preserve a way of life that valued civility and slowness that he saw rapidly slipping away. Nostalgia in Maine is a virtue.

Between 1913 and 1940, Rockefeller saw these roads cut into green up-holstered mountains, and curve around spruce and hemlock forests, and with each turn deliver yet another breathtaking view of the Atlantic.

The Park Service did not entirely appreciate Rockefeller's vision. They saw a system of roads at odds with protecting the wildlands of Mount Desert. Rockefeller saw it as another form of protection—protecting a way of life, and the peace that comes when time slows down and we venture into an aesthetic where nature and culture exist in harmony, not one without the other. And he saw the carriage roads as a way to open up the woods for those who may not be able to walk in the wilderness on their own. With a network of carriage roads, more people, the elderly included, could access the interior of the park. Rockefeller saw this as a democracy of experience, a way beyond privilege so that everyone could "own" these lands—a shared inheritance as American citizens.

As Horace M. Albright, director of the National Park Service from 1929 to 1933, said in Rockefeller's defense, "I believe Mr. Rockefeller had a gen-uine distaste for the garish advances of civilization . . . so he took every opportunity he felt possible to step in and save his fellow humans from the onslaught . . . of an industrial society."

A local told me that John D. Rockefeller Jr. said he spent so much money creating carriage roads throughout Acadia that he might as well have paved them with rubies. Last fall, I walked miles on one of his ruby-paved roads, red not from gemstones but from maple leaves. The path glistened from rain. Chipmunks and squirrels ran across the road with stuffed cheeks. Hermit thrushes foraged in the leaf litter, their spotted breasts becoming points of light in the elongated shadows of late afternoon. A kingfisher flew ahead, letting me know water was near. I left the road and entered the woods for a different point of view. In the canopy, a redstart snatched flies. I didn't know the underside of balsam fir looks like feathers, or of the deep, deep quiet that abides among these trees.

Back on the road, a wooden sign pointed to Aunt Betty's Pond. At the rate I was walking, stopping every few feet to look at a bird, a leaf, or an acorn, whether I would ever get to my destination was questionable. It was a six-mile meditation. There was no one else on the road. Up ahead, an orange pine needle hung twirling in the breeze—suspended from a high branch extended over the road from a single strand of spider's silk. The air was crisp, saturated with the scent of pine. All things were primary—red maples, yellow birch, and the sky, cerulean blue.

The glare from golden grasses and cattails told me Aunt Betty's Pond was close. There, I'd been told by a naturalist earlier in the day, brook trout, banded killifish, and sticklebacks live in the pond's marshy water, barely a yard deep.

Around the bend, Aunt Betty's Pond appeared like a table set with lily pads.

This is a park to grow old in, I thought.

Centuries before the rusticators and the Rockefellers laid claim to Mount Desert Island, the Wabanaki, "People of the Dawn Land," lived here. Their presence for millennia is evidenced by shell mounds found throughout the island, and they continue to live in close proximity to the park. Maine remains Indian Country.

In the 2000 census, 7,098 Mainers identified themselves in Maine as American Indian; 0.6 percent of the state's total population of just a little more than a million people. There are four federally recognized members of the Wabanaki Confederacy: the Maliseet, Micmac, Penobscot, and Passamaquoddy.

The Penobscot Indian Nation's reservation is located on the Penobscot River on Indian Island in Old Town, Maine. The name Penobscot comes from "Panawahpskek," meaning "the place of the white rocks." Their presence continues to be a force on the land. The most recent example of tribal influence and leadership is river restoration. Recent dam removals have freed the flow on the Penobscot River and restored traditional spawning grounds, as well.

In the summer of 2012, the Great Works Dam was taken down. "Today signifies the most important conservation project in our ten-thousand-year history on this great river that we share a name with, and that has provided for our very existence," said the tribal chief, Kirk Francis. The runs of salmon, shad, sturgeon, alewives, eels, and smelt are being restored.

The Passamaquoddy/Wabanaki Indians see themselves as a people aligned with trees, particularly the brown ash.

"We trace our creation story to the ash tree," Theresa Secord, director of the Maine Indian Basketmakers Alliance, said. "Gluskabe, our cultural hero, shot an arrow into the tree and from the ash came the People of the Dawn, the Wabanaki."

In a story called "Dawn Land": *The Creator knew after he had made the plants and the animal people that the Earth was missing something and so he created humans. He saw some stones and shaped them into Stone People, but the Stone People walked heavy on the Earth, destroying whatever was in their path. The Creator was not pleased and he shook the Earth until they were destroyed. He tried again; this time he made the people out of the ash tree. The people emerged soft and supple in relationship with their Mother the Earth. They say the people danced like leaves in the wind.*

Born from trees and sustained by them, the Wabanaki continue making baskets from brown ash, "basket trees," where it is difficult to see where one strand begins and another ends—like creation itself. Theirs is a woven world in the midst of a contemporary one. The burning of braided sweetgrass endures.

"Everything starts with a story. You may think you came here today to listen to me, but you're wrong. You are here because you have been called by one of your ancestors. Your task today is to find out which one and why," said the

Dr. Reverend Khadijah Matin, a dynamic African-American woman, also of Native-American descent, who focuses on ancestry. "Quite simply, you are being tapped."

It was Black History Month. The Church of Jesus Christ of Latter-Day Saints was featuring a speaker's series on genealogy at the Family History Library on Temple Square. At the time, I was teaching a class on memoir. We took a field trip to explore our roots. I looked at my students after the lecture and said, "Okay, find out who's trying to reach you and come back with a story."

"Cynthia Celestia Bunker" was the name that came to me. She is my great-great-grandmother on my maternal line: mother to Vilate Lee Romney, mother of my grandmother Lettie Romney Dixon, who was mother to my mother, Diane Dixon Tempest.

Cynthia Celestia Bunker had always been a mystery to me. Only one small photograph of her has survived, having been passed down through our family. With beautiful deep eyes, dark skin, and black hair, she is racially ambiguous and has always been framed as an outsider. In family narratives recorded in journals, she was largely absent.

I knew some details of her life from my great-grandmother Vilate Lee Romney: that her mother, Cynthia Celestia Bunker, was one of eleven siblings; that Cynthia's sister, Abigail, married George Washington Lee and died in childbirth; that Cynthia took care of her sister's four children and eventually married Mr. Lee; that they lived in Bunkerville, Nevada, where she had two children of her own, Lucina Lilywhite and Vilate; that Cynthia Celestia Bunker died in childbirth as well, leaving my great-grandmother, Vilate, motherless at age three.

That's all I knew.

Rows of computers confronted me, an invitation for a front-row seat to view one's ancestry. I sat down and typed in her name, "Cynthia Celestia Bunker" and—voilà!—a family tree appeared.

Cynthia Celestia Bunker was born on December 12, 1861, in Toquerville, Utah, to Emily Abbott and Edward Bunker Sr. Emily Abbott was born on September 19, 1827, in Dansville, New York. Edward Bunker Sr. was born on August 1, 1822, in Atkinson, Maine. Edward's parents, Silas Bunker Jr. and Hannah Berry, were also born in Maine, as were the parents of both Silas Bunker Sr. (born in 1746 and died in Blue Hill, Maine, in 1829) and his wife, Mary Foss (born in 1743 and died on Mount Desert Island in 1831). Mary's parents were also born in Maine: Benjamin Foss (1709–1785) and Silence Winch (1718–1757). And then there was Benjamin Bunker, father to Silas Bunker Sr.: born in Dover, New Hampshire, in 1710, died in 1818 on Mount Desert Island.

Mainers! Who knew? All of my ancestors preceding from Cynthia Celestia Bunker Lee's patrilineal line were Mainers, rooted in the very county I had staked my own modest claim: Hancock County. And most of them lived on Mount Desert Island, now Acadia National Park.

The connection I felt to this place in my blood and bones was real. I had been called back to the home of my ancestors. In time I learned that Cynthia's father, Edward Bunker, was the first to leave Maine. He was driven by his desire "to escape the confinement of trees." His wanderlust led him on a circuitous path to the Mormons where he heard leader Martin Harris bear his testimony about the Book of Mormon in Ohio. "It was the most thrilling night of my life," he wrote in his journal. "I became convinced of the truth of Mormonism, and was baptized in the month of April, 1845. Then I knew why it was that I had been led from my father's house and left my dear old mother whom I loved dearly."

Edward Bunker followed "the saints" to Illinois, where the prophet Joseph Smith had anchored the church. He met Emily Abbott in Nauvoo, Illinois, and was smitten. They were married on February 19, 1846, and "their wedding journey was to cross the Mississippi on ice." With the little they had they walked the Mormon trail, following Brigham Young to "the promised land" to the Great Salt Lake Valley in Utah. Soon after, Edward was called to join the Mormon Battalion to fight in the Mexican-American War; it was the only religious-based military unit in U.S. history. Emily was left behind in Garden Grove, Iowa, in a one-room adobe hut, pregnant, where she would give birth to her first of eleven children, Edward.

Edward Sr. would travel the Mormon Trail four more times; serve a mission to Scotland; and take two more wives under the Mormon doctrine of plural marriage. Emily would write in her journal, "Poverty and polygamy were a great trial to me, but I lived them both the best I could with the nature I had."

Doing some quick math with dates, I figured that Cynthia Celestia would have been conceived in March 1861. Suddenly, Edward S. Bunker Sr. took a third wife on April 20, 1861, a fourteen-year-old Scottish girl named Mary McQuarrie.

Emily gave birth to a baby girl on December 12, 1861, en route from Ogden to Dixie (now St. George), where they had been called by the Mormon prophet Brigham Young to fulfill a mission in southern Utah. It was noted in Edward Bunker's journal that Emily's daughter was born in Toquerville, Utah. "Toquer" mean "black" in Paiute.

According to the Utah census in 1860, there were fifty-nine blacks in Utah, twenty-nine of whom were slaves. The majority of African-Americans lived in Ogden, working on the railroad (not far from where the Golden Spike would later be driven to connect the Transcontinental Railroad in 1869).

In the various family journals, there is little or no mention of Emily Abbott's seventh child, Cynthia Celestia, "Lettie," for whom my grandmother Lettie Romney Dixon was named. It was from her lips that I first heard the word "mulatto" whispered between her and my mother.

The Bunker family helped colonize St. George, Utah, and eventually settled near Mesquite, Nevada, which was named Bunkerville in honor of Edward Bunker's leadership.

Edward Bunker's father, Silas Bunker Jr., and his father, Silas Bunker Sr., were Maine farmers who settled in Hancock County. They never left, nor did they ever see Edward again. Their ancestor Benjamin Bunker and his wife, Abigail Goodwin, came down east from Harpswell, Maine, known as "Merriconeag" by the Abenaki. The American Indian Wars being fought between Indians and settlers throughout the United States reached Maine in 1725, the same time Benjamin and his wife thought it would be a good idea to migrate north toward Mount Desert Island. The Bunker clan, reported to be seekers of solitude, would eventually move to Great Cranberry Island off the coast of Mount Desert Island "sometime after July 22, 1759."

After the French navigator and cartographer Samuel Champlain sailed by the large forested island in 1604, naming it "Isle des Monts Deserts," for the bare mountains rising above the trees, the ongoing land dispute between the French and the British continued to rage until the Revolutionary War won America its sovereignty as a nation. Prior to the war, however, in 1763, the Massachusetts governor, Francis Bernard, secured a royal land grant and surveyed the area north. His surveyor, John Jones, recorded that he found on Great Cranberry Island, just off the coast of Mount Desert, "Bunker's house" and "Bunker's seawall on which Benjamin Bunker dwells."

We know this from "Jones Field Notes" at the Maine Historical Society and the Bunker genealogy submitted by Edward C. Moran on August 1, 1961. The record goes on to say, "Since it is not known exactly when Benjamin Bunker arrived, but we do know the approximate time . . . the distinction of being the first settler in the whole Mt. Desert region, in addition to his clear title as first settler on Great Cranberry Isle, may well belong to Benjamin Bunker."

No doubt this "distinction" is debatable, as families everywhere are very proprietary about settlement, especially on Mount Desert and its islands. The Somes family history, for example, reports, "Abraham Somes, wife Hannah (Herrick), and their then four children (daughters Hannah, Patty, Lucy, and Prudence) were the first settlers of European descent on Mount Desert Island."

In a letter penned by Abraham Somes, he describes his arrival on Mount Desert Island: "I came down immediately after the War was over and peace ratified between Great Britain and the French and Indians—so that I could be safe in moving into the Wilderness; I came to this place which was in the autumn of the year 1761 and made a pitch on this Lot [where] I now live and in June, the year following, I moved my family and settled on the same lot and have occupied the same ever since."

If Abraham Somes was the first settler on Mount Desert Island, then perhaps it is true that Benjamin Bunker, great-great-grandfather of Cynthia Celestia Bunker, was among the first settlers of European descent on the Cranberry Isles.

Benjamin Bunker would die on Mount Desert Island in 1818, as would his daughter-in-law, Mary Foss Bunker, on June 8, 1831. Their daughter, Jennie Bunker, was born on Mount Desert on March 13, 1789, and though the date of her death is unknown, records show she lived on Mount Desert Island until the end.

Today, the mail boat that ferries folks from Northeast Harbor to Great Cranberry Island bears the name *Beal & Bunker* and is a business owned and operated by David Bunker.

Justin Bunker, skipper of the boat, is the son of David Bunker. Both live on Great Cranberry Island. Both are direct descendants of Benjamin. I introduce myself as a relative. Justin's standing at the helm of the boat with a half smile as I tell him about my obsession with Cynthia Celestia

Bunker, that we are from Utah, and that I'm interested in finding family graves.

"You'll find some, all right," he says. "We have a whole cemetery of them." Jason's dressed in a black rain jacket and well-worn jeans with holes in the knees. His face, narrow and unshaved, is shaded by a black ball cap. I can't tell whether his eyes are blue or brown. We chat the width of water between Mount Desert Island and Great Cranberry. I learn that folks who live "on the island" historically have gone mainland to Blue Hill for doctors, which explains why some of the Bunkers were born there—or buried there.

While we are talking, a woman from Little Cranberry Island heading back home with crates of food is already on the phone with Justin's father. "David, there's a woman on the boat who says she's related to you. Do you want to talk to her?" We don't hear the response, but she hangs up the phone.

"Everyone knows everything before anyone ever steps on Cranberry," she says with a laugh. "My name is Susie. For your information, Bunkers are everywhere, all over Maine, on practically every island."

It's a foggy day and Brooke and I are with Nick Sichterman and Mariah Hughs, friends from Blue Hill. There are four other people on the boat, two of them brothers trying to figure out how to ferry a kelly-green 1948 Plymouth onto Cranberry Island.

"David Bunker will barge it over for us," Jim Singerling says.

When we ask him where he lives, he says, "On the edge of beauty."

Once we're on Great Cranberry Island, it's a jolt to see freshly painted white clapboard houses in the midst of forest, fog, and sea. The edge between gentility and wildness has been erased in a seamless expression of residency. Jim Singerling asks us whether we want a ride to the Bunker Family Cemetery, or if we would like him to introduce us to David Bunker.

"Go ahead, just knock on my dad's door, the house is a little past the cemetery—he's there," says Justin, tying up the boat on the dock.

We refuse both offers and walk down the main road of the island. I am sure I want to see the cemetery. I am not sure I want to barge in on David Bunker. We walk through the small gate to the cemetery. Bunkers are everywhere, indeed, grave after sunken grave: John W. Bunker, son of Samuel and Hannah A. Bunker, died July 25, 1876; Captain Samuel Bunker, died July 19, 1899; Hannah A. Bunker, died 1902. The oldest grave we find belongs to Abigail Bunker, wife of Captain Joseph Bunker, born in 1798, died September 21, 1852.

As we leave, shutting the gate behind us, a blue pickup truck pulls alongside us. "You must be the folks from Utah looking for Bunkers. I'm Phil Whitney; I work at the Historical Society here. I'm a relative of yours through Comfort Bunker through the line of Joseph E. Spurling. I'll be working in the basement. Feel free to stop by."

We are walking down the road toward David Bunker's house as I debate whether to visit when another vehicle pulls up behind us. This time, it's Jim from the boat. He's driving a fancy all-terrain golf cart.

"Get in," he says. "It's farther than you think to David's. I'll show you the island first."

Jim drives us up and down the gravel roads in his golf cart to shingled houses boarded up until later in the summer, including locked estates with mansions where we are clearly trespassing. It's great sightseeing, but we grow increasingly nervous in these compounds of the rich. He tells us to relax and says he knows them and I don't doubt for a minute that he does. He's wearing a rain jacket with an insignia on it that to me looks like an image of Jesus with an X over him. Brooke asks Jim what it represents. Mariah apologizes for our collective ignorance. Jim is amused.

"It's St. Andrew, the patron saint of Scotland, and this is the insignia for

St. Andrews Golf Club in Scotland. It's one of the oldest country clubs in the world." He pauses. "Prince Charles is one of its members."

Jim takes us down a path that allows us to walk to the rocky shore with a fine view of Mount Desert Island. I leave the others and walk to the rocky point where waves are exploding before us. We are at the south end of Great Cranberry Island, looking out toward Acadia National Park, Cadillac Mountain piercing through the fog. These may be well-cared-for communities, but here the Atlantic Ocean is wild. The land feels tipped, the horizon is slant, and yet, I feel an unexpected equilibrium standing on the edge of the continent. Where *do* I belong? You can't belong everywhere. Or perhaps we can if we pay attention to the paths of our ancestors. Perhaps this is what it means to be American. Bloodlines originate in storylines. Some people stay in place, others move on. But if we look back far enough, we are all interconnected, interrelated, through place and race and time.

Eider ducks bob up and down in the surf. Lobster buoys have washed up on the black rocks from winter storms. And a whale vertebra gleams white even with cloud cover. It starts to rain. Walking back, a glint of light catches my eye: sea glass, sea green—its sharp edges have been tamed by waves.

Jim takes us to where the Cranberry Club is located.

"This is where ladies come from Seal Harbor and Northeast Harbor for lunch and to play cards. They come to the island in white dresses, wearing hats and gloves. Still. Quite a thing to see, quite a thing to see."

We peer in the windows of the gray-shingled cottage. A sign on the wall reads "Time Stops Here." I try to read some of the titles of the books on the shelves: *Gift from the Sea*, *Sarah Orne Jewett Short Stories*, *The Last Mrs. Astor*, *The Outermost House*, and *Crossing to Safety*. On another shelf are various field guides and children's books, *Wind in the Willows* among them.

Framed photographs are turned glass down on the dining table. Blue and white china line the shelves with stacks of teacups and saucers. Wicker furniture has been arranged in a half circle around a redbrick fireplace. There's another sign on the wall: "For Brahmins Only."

David Bunker is not a Brahmin. Jim has pulled up to his house and as we make our way to the front door, we step around Muscovy ducks, guinea hens and chickens, and various rusted metal scraps and pieces of boat equipment. Brooke and our friends have stayed in the golf cart. Jim knocks and I place myself behind him.

A large, white-bearded man opens the door. He looks tentative as he stands behind the screen.

"Hi, David, this woman's come all the way from Utah, she thinks she's related to you and would like to talk to you."

David steps out of his house and folds his arms in front of him.

"Hello, my name is Terry Tempest Williams. I'm sorry if we're bothering you. I'm from Utah, and I'm here because my great-great-grandmother, Cynthia Celestia Bunker, well, her father was from Maine, Edward Bunker, and I found out through our genealogy that Benjamin Bunker was the first settler here—"

"David Bunker was the first settler here," he says matter-of-factly. "He didn't stay long. I'm named after him. I'm not sure about Benjamin. He's not buried here."

There is a very long pause.

Jim breaks in. "I heard you had a rough winter this year, David. I just arrived a few days ago."

"Yeah, twelve-foot snowbanks with hundred-mile-an-hour winds. Bad."

"Was this the worst winter you've ever seen?" I ask.

David Bunker is quiet for a while. "No."

Well, that seemed to end our conversation. His blue eyes bored right through me.

"Thanks so much, David. I am very happy to meet you."

I extend my hand.

He pauses and then, with his broad hand, shakes mine.

We both start laughing as I read the words written on his T-shirt that his big arms folded across his chest have been hiding: "My parents said I could be anything I wanted to be so I decided to be an asshole."

"We're definitely related," I say.

There is no place to hide. We will be found. It all begins with a story. For me, the story of Acadia National Park has become the story of a family history unknown to me until I felt it in my bones and responded with my irrepressible desire to return almost every year since 1981.

I love Acadia.

On another autumn day in Acadia, friends and I took a carriage ride led by a horsewoman named Betty and pulled by two Percheron draft horses named Waylen and Willy. They must have been sixteen hands tall and well over two thousand pounds each. They took us around Day Mountain.

Betty, a retired telephone worker with a family in Winter Harbor, told us the history of the park, how the Doerrs and the Elliots wanted to keep the land wild, and enlisted John D. Rockefeller to help them achieve this goal. Again and again, we find this common story of the establishment of our national parks: a handful of people who fall in love with a place, see it threatened, want to protect it for the future, and have the passion and patience to attract the necessary funding and political clout to make it happen.

It's happening again, in northern Maine. Over the last two decades, Roxanne Quimby, the former owner of Burt's Bees, has bought up land—one hundred thousand acres of it—adjacent to Baxter State Park, in the shadow of Mount Katahdin, with the intent of creating a new national park.

She was not the first to have this dream. Her predecessors were a group of conservationists who grew tired of battling Maine's timber companies and decided to stop reacting and instead become more proactive in defense of the wild. They started an organization called RESTORE; not an anagram, just banking on the strength of the word to inspire action. Their vision was to create the Maine Woods National Park, which would protect 3.2 million acres of wilderness near Baxter State Park. Needless to say, the local mill communities reacted with outrage and opposition, convinced this would close the woods of Maine to hunting, fishing, and snowmobiling, not to mention the federal government infiltrating their towns. Further fear was ignited when RESTORE created a black-banded brochure just like the National Park Service's official maps that visitors are handed at every park entrance. The white letters "Maine Woods" written against the black background looked like a done deal. It was a stroke of genius that terrified the opposition and inspired the supporters, of which I was one. Inside the bogus park brochure was a map with RESTORE's proposal. But the plan had been slow to gain broad-based traction. Too big. Too ambitious. Too threatening to the local communities whose economies are based on logging the woods.

Along came Quimby. But her manner was blunt and less than diplomatic, and she, too, managed to inflame critics even as she galvanized others in support of protecting these wildlands in the name of a national park. Her inspiration: Edward Abbey. Again, it went nowhere.

Then, a few years ago, Quimby's son, Lucas St. Clair, entered the picture and things started to change. Born in Maine, Lucas took a very different approach from his mother. He is present in the communities. He is working the idea of a new national park called Katahdin Woods and Waters, and he is taking it to the people of Millinocket, Shin Pond, Patten, and Mount Chase, one person at a time. He has taken down the "No Trespassing" signs that his mother put up and opened forty thousand acres of the Quimby land to hunting and fishing, with snowmobiling paths open for use in the winter. He supports the high school band and has helped bring musicians and concerts from around the state to town and he knows the locals by name. He has spent so much time drinking coffee with them, talking about the park and sharing his ideas, that he may be courting an ulcer, but it's paying off. And there's one more thing: Lucas St. Clair really cares about the people. He would prefer not to have a national monument proclamation written by a president, he wants buy-in by Mainers themselves. And so far he's getting it. Two hundred businesses in Maine are now supporting the idea of a new national park. And in 2015, the *Bangor Daily News* endorsed the idea, with a state poll showing 67 percent of the people living in northern Maine in favor of a new national park in the north woods.

The national park proposal led by St. Clair offers up the Quimby land to the federal government much as John D. Rockefeller Jr. did with Acadia and Grand Teton National Parks. And St. Clair can foresee in the not-so-distant future that the proposed national park may be introduced in the U.S. Congress by members of the Maine delegation itself. But it's still a fight, and opponents die hard, especially with the collapse of the paper mills that underscores local fears of a changing economy.

But my prediction based on the history of our national parks in Utah and Wyoming is this: In years to come, following the designation of the Maine Woods National Park, the more radical vision of RESTORE will come to pass, with timber companies eventually selling off their lands to the federal government in the name of park expansion. Local communities surrounding the park will experience a boon to their economy, not just through tourism but because people will want to move closer to wild beauty, becoming the park's most loyal supporters.

The carriage stops at the cobblestone bridge constructed in 1917. Betty tells us this bridge was originally faced with moss-covered stones to merge more fully with the scenery. We step out of the carriage to partake of the rushing stream. I walk down to the water and disappear under the bridge, where I inhale the health of the day. To sit beneath the arch made of cobbles is to experience both a work of art and a sound chamber of water and wind singing inside the tunnel. It is an ecotone of the senses, a special niche within Acadia that belongs to the spotted sandpiper who flies upstream or down, uttering its joyous peeps as both a warning and a welcome. An echo of exuberance lingers. In a split second of solitude, I watch a white-tailed deer walking through the woods framed by the curvature of the bridge.

People on our carriage tour talk to each other not as strangers but as Mr. Rockefeller's guests, with a genuine interest and regard for each other in the spirit of conviviality, a callback to when good manners ruled the day. And just as Rockefeller appreciated the skill of driving a team of horses in challenging terrain, Betty does the same. We marvel at the dignity of these immense draft horses, how they negotiate the sharp turns in the road and pull the carriage up steep hills while hardly breaking a sweat. I find myself savoring the riches of the domesticated life and unexpectedly some tender place in me is touched, a place that still houses the longing of my ancestors who toiled in the desert without such luxuries, where faith and the lives of one's children were the only things worth protecting.

With each curve, each straightaway, the careful considerations made for the contours of the land reveal an ocean view or a waterfall streaming down the granite rock face. Even a white pine stands as a chosen sentinel on the journey as if to say, "Nothing is here by accident." Rockefeller wanted to create a controlled sense of awe.

There is no such thing. No matter how much we try to manage and manipulate, orchestrate, or regulate our national parks, they will remain as the edge-scapes they are, existing on the boundaries between culture and wildness—improvisational spaces immune to the scripts of anyone. Wildlife in wildlands appear without notice. Awakened is what we become in their presence. Curiosity leads us forward on an unknown path, even if it is a path of well-placed steps made out of pink granite here in Acadia. For a precious moment we touch and taste life uninterrupted. Awe sneaks up on us like love. We surrender to the ecstatic outpouring of life before us. I believe Emily Abbott called forth her own nature and gave in to the exaltation of her own wild heart and gave birth to the unimagined beauty of the daughter she named Celestia, from which the women in my family sprang.

Truth eventually reaches us like the crashing surf at Thunder Hole, the place in Acadia where unexpected waves can pull us into the sea.

Our national parks hold our stories in inexplicable ways. Acadia National Park may be small in size but the vista it offers across the Atlantic is a passionate genealogy of all that is infinite and alive above and below the surface.

Each breaking wave, each rush of the sea on the slope of sand, reminds me why these places of pilgrimage matter. They matter to me because in the long view, I do not. I am driftwood. I am rockweed. I am osprey and the mackerel in the clutch of her feet. I am a woman standing on the edge of the continent looking out.

Any visitor can look toward the horizon and experience the same view of the Atlantic Ocean that the Wabanaki have done for thousands of years, as have, more recently, Benjamin and Abigail Bunker, and the Rockefellers. Acadia National Park remains a place of privilege with herring gulls soaring over pink granite cliffs, crying against the crashing surf of the sea.

GETTYSBURG NATIONAL

MILITARY PARK, PENNSYLVANIA

⤙⤚

—*there is no prevailing*—

THE GETTYSBURG BATTLEFIELD is a storied landscape and it is written in blood.

A three-day battle July 1–3, 1863, cut into the landscape of Gettysburg and left a permanent scar in the psyche of America, now memorialized within a national park. In contrast, for 3 billion years the Colorado River cut through the sediments forming the Grand Canyon. It, too, is remembered and framed by a national park. What is time but a compressed view of history seen through the lens of story, personal or geologic? Both have their power and truths, both have their limitations. The perspective we are given depends on the person telling the story—season by season.

Autumn

We arrived at McMillan Woods. Our horses were saddled and waiting. Each saddle was secured on a red and blue blanket resembling the Confederate flag. We were told that, unfortunately, General Robert E. Lee would not be joining us.

"He is an older gentleman and when the weather gets rough, it's a little too much for him," the wrangler said.

I'm not particularly good at math, but if Lee was born on January 19, 1807, that would make him 206 years old. We learned that Frank Orlando, alias Robert E. Lee reenactor, was in truth sixty-four years old, and exhausted from all the sesquicentennial festivities. He is one of the many "living historians" who keep in character to tell the story of the individuals they personify.

This was new to us. Civil War buffs from both the north and the south take it for granted; reenactors are serious representatives of the war. It has been estimated there are as many as fifty thousand Civil War reenactors in America. The largest number convened at Gettysburg in 1998, for the 135th anniversary of the battle fought July 1–3, 1863. These battles are not without risks. Stories abound: One reenactor failed to check his revolver, a bullet was caught halfway in the chamber; he fired and shot another reenactor in the neck. Sickness is also a risk. Robert E. Lee was ill. We were leaderless but not without a guide. Andie Custer Donohue, a short, spirited blond woman with a commanding voice, would lead the way.

Custer Donohue left the corporate world of finance to do something different. "I've always liked horses and history," she said. "This combined the two."

Andie became licensed in 1998 and is on the current roster of the Association of Licensed Battlefield Guides. Of the 155 guides working today, only ten are women.

"It is a grueling process," Andie told me. "They only give the exam once every two years. There's two hundred and fifty questions on the written exam. They take the nineteen or twenty top scores. And that's only the first phase. You then take a more comprehensive written exam, followed by an oral exam where you must take a two-hour tour of the battlefield with licensed guides who will drill you with questions, some designed to distract you as tourists do. You have two shots at the tour." She paused. "Last year, only two made it."

It was in 1915 that the Department of War mandated federally licensed battlefield guides, after veterans from the Civil War petitioned Congress to require that battlefield tour guides be uniformly trained and accredited. In 1933, the licensing of guides was transferred to the National Park Service. Today, the process of licensing requires applicants to know hour by hour the dramatic unfolding of the Battle of Gettysburg. They must be on familiar terms with specific generals, colonels, and infantrymen while having an in-depth knowledge of the different states and their engagements as honored by specific monuments. Potential licensees must also be expert in the most minute details of the Civil War: military tactics, artillery, uniforms from the buttons to the boots. They must have an astute understanding of the political landscape, the business of growing cotton in the South and the abolition of slavery in the North, alongside the peculiar and particular knowledge of the cultural history of the era. They must know that in 1870, Daughters of the Confederacy had 3,320 Confederate bodies exhumed for reburial in the South. Concomittantly, they also have to know how much it costs to exhume and rebury a Union soldier. Answer: $1.59. They must be versed in the casualties of the war. Or the year when the last body was found on the battlefield. Answer: 1996.

Since 1915, six hundred official battlefield guides have been approved. Since 2012, of more than two hundred applicants, only two passed the written and oral exams to become federally licensed. Most of those presently serving as guides took the exam more than once, having to wait another two years or longer to reach their dream of wearing the nine-pointed gold star. Once inside the cadre, few leave except by death.

Jim Tate, a native son of Gettysburg, served as a guide for more than sixty years. Born in Gettysburg on July 25, 1918, Tate was only a year out of high school when he attended the seventy-fifth anniversary of the Battle of Gettysburg in July 1938. On that hot summer day, a quarter million people gathered in commemoration; eighteen hundred of them were Civil War veterans. Tate listened to President Franklin D. Roosevelt honor the dead, and he was able to shake hands with many of the survivors, dressed in their gray and blue uniforms.

He joined the National Guard in 1940 as part of the cavalry, when horses were still a vital part of the army, and fought in World War II as a sergeant in the Twenty-Eighth Division, 104th Pennsylvania Cavalry, in Italy, North Africa, and France. He returned home to Gettysburg in 1945, attended Gettysburg College, and worked for IBM. In 1951, he became a licensed Gettysburg battlefield guide, passing the exam on his first try. This became his lifelong passion. The memory of the Civil War veterans had never left him. With each tour, he evoked their spirits, their courage, their lives.

"The Civil War wasn't that long ago," he would tell each group of visitors.

"Can you see the Confederates advancing below?" he would ask visitors from the vantage point of Little Round Top. "Imagine the Union soldiers trying to hold the line behind these boulders."

Jim Tate died on January 15, 2014, in the Gettysburg Hospital. He was ninety-four years old. Fellow guides carried his casket. His burial service closed with a twenty-one-gun salute.

"We are storytellers," Andie said. "Keepers of memory. But today, I'm a horse soldier. Let's go see what General Lee was facing."

Brooke and I mounted our horses for the two-hour ride that would take us through the woods to where Pickett's Charge took place. My horse, a painted quarter horse, was named Desert Storm. Brooke rode a white horse named Chance. Andie's horse was Wyatt, as in Wyatt Earp from the West, specifically, Tombstone, Arizona, and the OK Corral. Four other visitors were on the trail with us.

Andie took the lead. "Don't worry about the horses," she said in her strong voice. "They are trained to follow."

We rode through the late-fall woods with leaves falling all around us.

"Here's what you have to know," Andie said, turning around, her right hand on the rump of her horse. "The war has been going on for two years before Gettysburg. The armies know each other. The Confederates have been winning all the battles. Lee is undefeated. He spent thirty years in the Union army fighting the Mexican War and he knows the other side well. Lee needs to get the war out of Virginia. Why not take it to the Potomac army the summer of 1863 and fight them on their own grounds? Eighty thousand soldiers were marching through the Appalachian Mountains. It's June twenty-eighth, Lee has men spread out like a big horseshoe where the outlet stores are—"

"What?" I was confused.

"I'm talking about the Confederate army marching on I-81. I take it you are not from the South.

"The Union is following Lee. They want the Confederate soldiers out of here. It's three days before they get to Gettysburg and Lincoln has no commander. He calls on George Meade, who goes from ten thousand men to thirty thousand men, from being a fifth-tier soldier to a commander."

The wind was picking up; it was getting hard to hear. Brooke looked at me in a way that can only be translated as misery. He did not want to learn about the Battle of Gettysburg or the Civil War on the back of Chance. It was clear he'd rather be walking.

"Everyone is tired of the war," Andie continued. "Meade checks out the location of Lee's army. Ten roads lead to Gettysburg, like the spokes of a wheel. Lee learns that Meade is on the move. Lee tells his scouts, 'Perfect, let them come.' The Union army is vulnerable out in the open. Lee is confident. If he defeats the Army of the Potomac, Washington, D.C., has no defenders and Lincoln has no choice but to surrender."

We continued along the horse trail. I thought about the trees we passed—the ash, the hickory, the great oaks—and imagined what they withstood during the great and bloody battle. Somewhere between a hundred and two hundred "witness trees" remain as sentinels at Gettysburg.

"The armies will clash on July first on Highway Thirty," Andie stopped to tell us. "The Confederates outnumbered the Union army on the first day. The Union army retreats into the town of Gettysburg, bringing the war into the streets. They head to Cemetery Hill." She paused. "The Confederacy wins Day One. General Robert E. Lee rides into Gettysburg as a rock star. It's like Elvis has entered the building."

As we crossed the road, we passed cannons, copper turned turquoise. "These are true veterans of the war. The battle they were fired in is marked on their muzzle. It's all documented in the National Archives."

Milkweed pods split open, sending silken seeds flying among a few monarch butterflies. Blackbirds flooded the fields. Oak leaves, brown and orange, cartwheeled across the road.

"Robert E. Lee rode exactly where we are riding. Think about that. The enemy army is a mile to the left beyond the ridge, invisible to the Confederate soldiers below." Andie pointed to a line of trees on our left, now visible as we rode down valley. "This is where the Union troops are waiting."

The war was alive in Andie's psyche and we were right there with her, except for Brooke, who reluctantly served in the army reserve during Vietnam. "I don't give a shit about the cannonballs," he said to me, "or what kind of nasty wounds they make." I took his picture; he was not pleased.

We passed by the Virginia monument, where a bronze statue of Robert E. Lee sits tall on his horse, the "Confederate gray" warhorse Traveller.

"We are going to stop where Lee stopped. He has just discovered that he is facing only forty thousand Union men. Lee has seventy thousand men and decides to stay in Gettysburg and fight. Imagine this many soldiers in the fields. You wouldn't even be able to see the grass."

Andie was in full control of her story. "It's the morning of July second. Lee decides to attack both flanks of the Union. With sixteen thousand men positioned to the right, the fight begins at four in the afternoon. Remember, the horizon holds the tension—what the men can and cannot see."

She led the way to Henry Spangler's farm. We arrived at the white farm-house and red barn and stopped.

"You are going to hear from the federal government that General Lee marched fourteen thousand men across an open field to be slaughtered during the bloodbath that has come to be known as Pickett's Charge. This is not true, as I will illustrate as we drop our horses down to where George Pickett and his soldiers were located . . ."

It was at this moment I finally understood that our guide sided with the Confederacy, that she was out to correct a wrong—that, in her point of view, it was a misrepresentation that the Union was fighting for a noble cause, which was the abolition of slavery.

"The Civil War wasn't just about slavery," she said. "It was about the South defending its states' rights against the tyranny of the federal government."

It is here I recognize an echo of the "lost cause" interpretation of the Civil War that focuses on the events of the war, not the causes that triggered it. What is emphasized is the honor and nobility of the Confederate soldiers, not that the South's institution of slavery was inhuman and unjust, even as it fueled the economy of cotton. Secession from the Union occurred because of the zealotry of northern abolitionists who forced the assault on southern constitutional rights. The South was fighting for their freedom and dignity. The South lost the war not because the North had a righteous cause, but because they had more soldiers.

I sit back in my saddle. I've also heard this rhetoric before in the American West, from the Sagebrush Rebels harping against public lands; from the leaders of the Tea Party; even from members of my own family—only it wasn't about the Civil War, it was about our black president, liberal America, the loss of states' rights and our ability to govern ourselves. I am just beginning to understand how the Civil War has shaped our ideologies and identities as Americans. And the simple, undeniable fact: all wars are political. We will fight for the myth that will support and sustain our point of view at all costs.

The rigor of these guides—their encyclopedic knowledge of every moment and each detail of Gettysburg—will not extinguish their biases.

As a westerner, I was slow to see this: this was not my war. It belonged to the North and South. It was their civil war.

This was my ignorance. This war, these soldiers, brother against brother, would decide the fate of the western territories. Would slave labor or free labor fuel American expansion? The lines of the dividing war were set.

"A house divided against itself cannot stand," said President Lincoln, quoting the Bible. The war that threatened the Union continued to seep into every American household, leaving no one standing in neutral territory. The plantation owners who depended on cotton and a slave economy were in direct conflict with Northern abolitionists who saw slavery as a moral crime. The Civil War was not only ripping the fabric of the United States in two, it was unraveling any national solidarity we had forged prior to this internal conflict. "Saving the Union" meant a battle for our nation's identity.

The Battle of Antietam fought in Sharpsburg, Maryland, on September 17, 1862, was the single bloodiest day of the Civil War, with twenty-three thousand casualties. The physical violence sparked a presidential action. President Lincoln issued the initial proclamation five days after Antietam. The September proclamation made the end of slavery a war aim, but it also gave the South another chance to lay down their arms, as it would not go into effect for several months. President Lincoln signed the formal Emancipation Proclamation on January 1, 1863, automatically freeing three million slaves by executive order. The Proclamation was met with resistance in both the South and the North. It did not end slavery. It did not compensate the slave owners or grant American citizenship to former slaves. But what it did do was make the abolition of slavery an explicit goal of the war, and reunite the Union.

Nearly nine months later the Battle of Gettysburg was fought for three days under the blazing heat of July 1–3, 1863.

Andie turned to face us as we rode. "See that white farmhouse in the field? Keep that in mind." We descended into a small gully. "What academics forget is that a field is not flat, there are dips and valleys. Pickett's men *did* have cover," she said. "The enemy can't see us and we can't see them. The white house we saw is no longer in sight."

She described the Union battle line building on Little Round Top and Cemetery Ridge, and why Pickett's Charge failed.

"Firing into smoke is a waste of ammunition. General Longstreet, who violently disagreed with Lee's strategy to send Pickett and his men forward, kept demanding that the Confederates fire their cannons, which is what they did for two hours."

She shook her head as the wind blew her blond hair back. "With the smoke from all the cannon fire, Longstreet gave General George Meade two hours of cover to move the Union army. Meade knew what was going on. He knew his Union center was weak. He knows Lee is going to attack it. And so, he fills it in."

We rode out of the ditch with Little Round Top now in view. "Imagine two hundred and fifty firing cannons. The Confederate army shooting into the smoke. When the firing stops and the smoke clears the Union army is in place. There is now no artillery support for Pickett's men, who find them-selves face-to-face with twenty thousand Union infantry.

"They are repulsed. After twenty minutes of hand-to-hand combat, bayonet to bayonet, Pickett retreats with the few Confederate soldiers left standing.

General Lee meets them. 'Don't blame it on yourselves—' he says to the broken. 'Blame it on me.'"

Lee lost twenty-three thousand men in three days. Before the Battle of Gettysburg was over there would be fifty-one thousand casualties, with ten thousand dead men draped over maimed ones groaning in the fields, five thousand dead horses among them.

Andie couldn't stop. Megaphone in hand, she chanted a litany of battle facts: "Torrential rains fell for five days and five more. Graves were washed open with too many bodies to dig graves for. Days turned into weeks as the bodies were rotting in the heat. Death could be smelled ten miles before even getting to Gettysburg. Seventeen acres had to be purchased for a cemetery to accommodate the sixty-five hundred unburied Confederate soldiers. Local farmers buried them in trench graves on their land. Ten years later, the United Daughters of the Confederacy raised enough money to have the bodies of their sons of the South exhumed and brought home. Six hundred to a thousand Confederate soldiers still lie somewhere beneath these grasses. Four months later, President Lincoln came to the formal dedication of the National Cemetery at Gettysburg on November nineteenth and gave his famous address."

When we returned to the Spangler barn, Andie had us line our horses up side by side until we all faced her in formation.

"The Civil War continued for two more years. Gettysburg was the turning point. This was the high point of the Union army's morale. Meade remained head of the Potomac army until the end. Ulysses Grant—and I might add, a brutal drunk and womanizer—travels with George Meade to celebrate with their men what Lincoln called 'the terrible arithmetic.' For every Confederate soldier killed, the Union could afford two more. There were about 20 million Northerners and only 11 million Southerners [what Andie didn't say as a true southern apologist was that nearly 4 million persons out of the 11 million were slaves]. On April 9, 1865, General Robert E. Lee surrendered and the Civil War ended."

We rode back in silence, past the farmhouses, past the memorials, on the trail in the woods winding between the witness trees.

Andie sidled up to me. "Well, I hope Obama isn't going to be in Dallas on the hundred and fiftieth anniversary."

"Excuse me?" I said.

"Well, you know, President Kennedy was invited to speak on the hundredth anniversary of the Battle of Gettysburg and he refused, went to Dallas instead." She squinted across the fields, then turned back to me. "Obama refused just like Kennedy did, and Kennedy faced his fate. Obama should think about that. I'm just sayin', there's a lot of talk 'round here. I hope he thinks twice before going to Dallas."

Winter

Today marks the fiftieth anniversary of JFK's assassination. I remember that day in Salt Lake City, cold and gray. I was eight years old, a third-grade student at Beacon Heights Elementary School. When Miss Atkins told us our president had been shot, some of us cried, some of us sat stoically in our seats. I was scared. I wanted to go home.

During lunch hour, a group of us set up hurdles on the green we shared with the junior high school. We stood in line, waiting our turn to sprint and leap over the black-and-white bars as though we were young track stars. Over and over, we ran and jumped, ran and jumped, ran and jumped, circling back to stand in line as if our energy could right a wrong, exerting what little power we had as children on that sad and fateful day.

Walking home after school, some of my friends said they didn't like

Kennedy, and that their parents didn't like him either. I knew my mother would be home watching the news.

For the next few days, I sat with my mother watching all of it, the news commentary, replays of the convertible in Dallas, the swearing in of Lyndon B. Johnson as our new president with Mrs. Kennedy by his side in her pink bloodstained suit, and the shooting of Lee Harvey Oswald by the man in the hat with the name Jack Ruby.

And when the funeral was finally aired, what I remember most was the riderless black horse, the pair of boots facing backward in the long leather stirrups.

Throughout it all, Abraham Lincoln and John Kennedy were linked by the word "assassination." It was a new word, an ugly word in my young vocabulary.

Brooke and I returned a season later to Gettysburg for the 150th anniversary parade, "A Day of Remembrance." We attended the local high school's celebration featuring the "Civil War Cantata—150," composed by Richard Fuchs, recounting the Battle of Gettysburg. It was directed by the music teacher of Gettysburg High School; 150 voices commemorated each year that had passed.

Before the cantata was sung, the master of ceremonies, in his radio voice, invited us to stand and recite the Pledge of Allegiance—led by President Abraham Lincoln. No one seemed surprised. Nor was anyone surprised when we were invited to participate in "the Lincoln Challenge," which tested the audience's knowledge of the Gettysburg Address. We were asked to recite the speech—*verbatim*.

Mr. Lincoln—young, tall, thin, and very earnest—sitting onstage in his top hat, said, "In case you don't know, the word 'verbatim' it means 'exactly.'"

A woman with red hair, in a green sweater, rose and performed it perfectly.

"Yes, those are my words verbatim."

A man in a parka stood, stumbled with the speech, and sat down.

"No, that is not what I said."

Another woman moved toward the aisle and made it almost to the end before making a small slip, at which point she was interrupted.

"No, that is not right. Please sit down."

A student in the front row stepped forth and, facing the president directly, delivered a flawless address.

There was a sigh in the audience and people clapped. No one else stood, even though Mr. Lincoln pleaded, as did the master of ceremonies. I was tempted to stand and recite the lyrics from Pussy Riot's "Punk Prayer": "Mother of God, drive Putin away," but Brooke held me back.

Mr. Lincoln rose up and declared, "Then I will accept my own challenge."

He faced the audience—but no words emerged from his mouth. Through the long pause, it became clear that his mind had suddenly gone blank.

We waited with him for the words to return. Finally the familiar words were spoken: "Four score and seven years ago our fathers brought forth on this continent, a new nation, conceived in liberty, and dedicated to the proposition that men are created equal."

All men. All men. "All men are created equal."

He continued on: "Now we are engaged in a great civil war, testing whether that nation, or any nation so conceived and so dedicated, can long endure—" Another long pause. "We are met on a great battlefield of that war. We have come to dedicate a portion of that battlefield"—Field. Field.—"as a final resting place for those who here gave their lives that that nation might live. It is altogether fitting and proper that we should do this."

It was touching and excruciating and we all endured the speech, not quite verbatim, but in the end a testament to the young Mr. Lincoln's courage to continue after the school principal handed him a copy of his own address, which he dropped, then bent over to pick up the paper while at the same time watching his top hat roll off the stage, nicely recovered by his mother.

The music teacher took command of the stage, with both hands raised and index fingers pointing at the two risers on either side of the auditorium. All eyes of the student choir were focused on the downbeat. The voices rose and fell with the melody and accommodated the moving harmonies that ended with notes as discordant as the war itself. The cantata was soulful and rich. As I listened, I couldn't help wonder what it must be like to grow up in a town where every house built before 1863 was used as a hospital and relics from the Civil War are as common as broken glass.

The last line of the cantata was "Judge no man by the color of his skin, we are American."

After the assembly, I found myself exiting the auditorium with the young Mr. Lincoln and his mother. It turned out this was his debut. "It was his nerves," his mother said. "You know, nerves are so big. He knew his lines at home—"

"What does it feel like to be Lincoln?" I asked.

"It's too early to tell, but I'm working on it," the young man said.

"How did you decide to become Mr. Lincoln?"

"My buddies I served with in Iraq always said I looked like Lincoln, so I thought well, I'm from Gettysburg—when I get home I won't shave for a month and see what happens. Besides, people told me the real Lincoln is getting pretty old."

"You'll see the real Lincoln in the parade today," his mother said. "He is old, but he's good, and sooner or later, he's going to need a replacement."

The parade for "A Day of Remembrance" was about to begin. Brooke and I waited on the corner of Stratton Street and Middle Street, one block up from York, Gettysburg's main street. The air was frigid and the sky overcast, but we were dressed for it. People lined the sidewalks, many sitting in lawn chairs with multiple blankets draped over them.

"Gettysburg is all about the stories," the woman sitting next to me said.

"Tell me one."

"My grandmother told me about a photograph of an unidentified Union soldier found dead in the field, his eyes still open, staring at a picture of his three children. The photographer who took the picture published it all over the South in hopes of locating his family. Finally, the soldier's wife came forward. His name was Amos Humisten. Mrs. Humisten started an orphanage. When she died it was taken over by a terrible woman who abused the children. This town is now plagued by the ghosts of those children."

Many ghost stories fly around this town.

"Here they come!" she said. "Right on time."

I heard the snare drums, then the piccolos. A soldier from the Union army appeared, carrying the American flag, and behind him marched lines of old men in blue wool uniforms decorated with medals.

President Abraham Lincoln appeared, waving to the crowd from a horse-drawn carriage. He did look old, but also convincing.

The Daughters of Union Veterans of the Civil War followed behind. Then came Generals Ulysses S. Grant and Robert E. Lee, riding side by side on their famed horses, one brown, the other dappled gray.

Block after block of infantry platoons marched by, some with their own brass bands. The parade continued on for hours. We later learned that ten thousand reenactors were here. It was, after all, the sesquicentennial parade. There were widows in black, with their large hoopskirts sweeping the street as they walked by in their shawls and bonnets, some pushing baby carriages. Sharpshooters dressed in their characteristic olive-green uniforms marched by, as did a wave of women, nurses carrying bandages and walking with the wounded. Each regiment of soldiers, both Confederate gray and Union blue, bore banners honoring the states they had served. Some

Confederate regiments marched barefoot and beleaguered. I was hypnotized by the soldiers' feet, all of them, focusing on the symmetry of legs marching in perfect rhythm, especially those enhanced by the tapping of metal mounted to the heels of their boots.

A lone white stallion was led by a Union soldier, a pair of boots facing backward in the stirrups hanging from the empty saddle.

The Fifty-Fourth Massachusetts Regiment appeared and the crowd leapt to its feet. The regiment of all black soldiers began to sing "The Battle Hymn of the Republic" a cappella, their voices deep and strong. I wept. These men were not reenactors, they were soldier brothers bridging time.

"Thank you for not referring to my uniform as a costume," Brigadier General Liam McKone said, after we asked him about his attire. "I'm part of the Vermont Second Brigade. I'm Irish and a lot of Irishmen are fighting to free the slaves. We know war and we will fight till the bloody end."

We shook hands in the parlor of the bed-and-breakfast where we were staying.

"But you can call me Billy Lee. May I join you for lunch?"

"Of course. How did you, um—"

"Become a reenactor?"

"Yes, thank you," I said. I didn't want to offend him by asking him to break out of character, and what a character he was—short, stocky, impeccably dressed in a Union-blue double breasted uniform, with a round, reddish face, long, white hair and a crescent-cut beard, curving ear to ear.

"Doors just kept opening up between worlds, what else can I tell you? This name, John Lonergan, kept appearing as a presence. I am convinced there is a scientific explanation for it. Twelve years ago, I am reading next to the stove, it was my sixth season in Vermont, mud season, and honest to God, this fellow just reached out and grabbed my ankle and said, 'Tell my story!'

Ten years later, I went to John Lonergan's grave in Burlington and placed the book I wrote, *Vermont's Irish Rebel: Captain John Lonergan*, below his chiseled headstone."

"And what's his story?" Brooke asked.

"We were born almost one hundred years apart, to the day. I'm seventy-five years old. Through some undefinable process, I had a mission as an Irish immigrant to tell this story of a brash young man who became part of the Thirteenth Vermont Regiment, the Civil War's first ethnic regiment, mostly Irishmen, who played a heroic role in defeating General Lee's army at Pickett's Charge. Lonergan was only twenty-four years old. After receiving a Medal of Honor for his valor at Gettysburg, he returned to Ireland as a general of the Irish Republican Army that invaded Canada twice. He was a military man till the day he died in 1902. His body was eventually brought back to rest in Burlington, where he was received as a Civil War hero at St. Joseph Cemetery."

Billy Lee laughed, placing his hands on his sizable belly. "Now that's the CliffsNotes version."

"But you said your name is McKone and that you're a brigadier general," Brooke said.

"We all take our liberties," he said. "I do living history and we take on a particular persona. But the person who got me here is Lonergan."

"And when you were doing research for your book, was it difficult reconstructing his life?"

"I found out most things where one finds all truth—in the Irish pubs! Let's have beer, for God's sake!"

Brooke ordered two Guinness Extra Stout.

"Do you know the difference between a company, a regiment, and a brigade?" he asked.

"No," I said.

"You need to know a few military facts before any of this Gettysburg history is going to make sense at all," said McKone. "A company is made up of a hundred men; a regiment is a thousand men; and a brigade is five thousand men. There were various kinds of soldiers: infantry (on foot), artillery (responsible for cannons, et cetera), cavalry (on horse), regular (versatile), volunteer, and militia. Of course, these are ideal figures. In truth, they shrank in size with each battle." He paused. "There were also the sharpshooters."

"We spoke with one of them today," Brooke said. "Dressed in green wool."

"Yes, but we Irish are the 'green boys from the mountains.'" He and Brooke clinked bottles. "Don't confuse us, lad. And know your numbers: thirty million people lived in the United States during the Civil War. There were twenty million in the North, ten million in the South, and four to five million slaves. By the time the war was over, America had lost two percent of its population. By today's numbers, that would translate to losing close to six million citizens. People don't realize what a bloody war it was and how deeply it cut into every aspect of American life, large and small."

Numbers kept falling from Mr. McKone, a teacher who clearly loved his subject just as Andie Custer Donohue did. "There were three hundred thousand people living in Vermont during the Civil War. Thirty-five thousand men were sent to fight, that's over ten percent of the population. Five thousand died, many from disease. What you need to know about my man Lonergan is that he was a young captain. He and his company of Irishmen were not battle-worn soldiers. They were just thrown into this horrendous fight in Gettysburg. All they had was a musket, a bayonet, a blanket, cup, and spoon. Many were barefoot. And they each had about forty rounds of ammunition."

He continued, "John Lonergan and his company were told to raid rebel soldiers at Codori's house on Emmitsburg Road just below Cemetery Ridge. Lonergan led the charge shouting the Gaelic battle cry, '*Faugh a ballagh!*'"

"Meaning?" Brooke asked.

"'Clear the way!'" McKone said. "And he didn't lose a man. Now, that was quite an action. But it didn't end there."

Our fish and chips arrived, and the server asked whether we had seen any ghosts since arriving in Gettysburg. "They're here . . ." she said.

"And you've seen them?" we asked.

"Oh, honey, I see them all the time, tell us something we don't know."

Brooke and I looked at each other. "Which room?" I asked.

"The Longstreet Suite is a popular one."

"Longstreet," McKone interjected. "What a tragedy, talk about being haunted by his own instincts, but having to carry out Lee's orders against his better judgment. Meade instructed the Second Vermont Brigade to fill in the right flank around Cemetery Ridge, but it was the Thirteenth Vermont Regiment that led the charge against Pickett's men. Imagine these Irish boys going against fifteen thousand Virginians shooting right at them in the midst of so much cannon fire you couldn't see what was in front of you. The fog of war was physical. It was a noisy place, I'll tell ya. But the Irish know the art of war and Lonergan kept going and led the charge toward Pickett's men. Can't you just picture these Union men in blue with ruddy complexions like mine, marching shoulder to shoulder, a comfort, but also a helluva target. Lonergan lost six men around him, but just kept going. By then, John Lonergan didn't even have a loaded musket, all the ammunition was gone, what they had left was their guts and a sharpened bayonet."

Our meal was almost finished.

"So you see, Lonergan and I aren't kin by blood but by country, both our countries, Ireland and America. The Civil War belongs to all of us. Lonergan tracked me down. Don't ever think the dead aren't playing with us. They use us for their unfinished business, even if it's something as simple as telling their story."

McKone disappeared, then returned with a copy of his book, which had, not surprisingly, a bright green cover. "I want you to have this. If nothing else, it will be a good door stopper—it's nearly six hundred pages. I'm proud of it. I kept my word to Lonergan. Goddammit, did I ever!"

Brooke and I returned to the battlefield in late afternoon. It was strangely empty given the number of reenactors and bystanders at the parade. We walked up Seminary Ridge, where our shadows were long. Little Round Top was in view. The bite of winter went deep and deeper still with the wind. The same McMillan Woods we'd ridden through a month earlier, flushed with fall's regalia, now was a scene of bare branches creating black signatures against a steel-colored sky. Beneath the silhouettes of oak, hickory, and birch, red berries glistened in snow.

The geography of war is named: the Wheatfield, the Peach Orchard, Big Round Top, Little Round Top, and Devil's Den. We walked down the ridge to the Pennsylvania State Memorial. A pink cast struck the largest of the stone monuments as a crimson sundown outlined the Appalachian Mountains to the south.

Thirty-four thousand five hundred and thirty soldiers from the state of Pennsylvania are honored here on their own home ground, their names recorded in bronze. I closed my eyes and read the names with my fingers, line after line, as if I were reading them in Braille, recalling words that were written in Gettysburg four days after the war: *Every name . . . is a lightning stroke to some heart and breaks like thunder over some home, and falls like a long black shadow upon some hearthstone.*

We climbed the spiral staircase, its walls covered in hammered copper. Greek key designs surprised me as they decorated the walls above the banister. Once in the open-air cupola, we could see the full circumference of the Gettysburg battlefield. Venus sparkled just above the horizon and the half moon illuminated the furrowed land. A silhouette of an infantryman on top of a nearby monument could be seen running against the sky with bloodred clouds behind him.

"Wars never end," Brooke said.

Spring

Dogwoods were in bloom. They looked like white butterflies settled in the darkened woods. Cardinals flashed red; the sloping lawn was laced with violets; and Louis Gakumba and I ate our lunch beneath a blue sky on Cemetery Hill on the edge of Gettysburg.

Louis is our son from Rwanda. He works for the Rwandan embassy in Washington, D.C., where they just completed the twentieth commemoration of the Rwandan genocide. Kwibuka 20 was acknowledged throughout the world as a reminder of "never again." The month of April is always reserved as a remembrance of the horrific spring that sparked the war among Hutus and Tutsis in 1994, but this anniversary was different. "Remember—Unite—Renew" were the words held by both Rwandans abroad and Rwandans at home. Louis is now part of the diaspora. I met Louis eleven years after the war. He was my interpreter for a project we worked on together with Lily Yeh and other "barefoot artists" to build a genocide memorial near his hometown of Gisenyi.

"What is a civil war?" Louis asked as we leaned against one of the monuments.

His question surprised me, even though I knew that while most Americans were led to believe the Rwandan genocide was a "civil war" between the Hutus and Tutsis, most Rwandans don't see it that way. They see it as a war of ideology to exterminate one race in favor of another. But his question was a fair and complicated one. It made me think.

America's Civil War was fought primarily by civilians rather than the military, and yes, both sides were from the same country divided by a cause, a derivation of the Latin phrase *belle civicus*. The South called it "the war of Northern aggression." The North called it "the war of Southern secession." Both phrases sanitize the horror and savagery of war itself. Both sides were unified in their suffering.

Historians say the Civil War was fought for three reasons: to keep the Union together, to end slavery, and to secure citizen's rights. The term "civil war" also refers to the fact that many citizens watched the fighting from the sidelines; in the early days, some battles were suspended in the afternoon for teatime among the generals. And until late in the war, hospitals treated the wounded from both the Confederate and Union armies.

"I know war," Louis said. "No war is civil."

"And the truth is hard to come by," I said.

It wasn't until 1998 that the National Park Service took on the truth of slavery within their interpretation of the Civil War and looked at the causes and context of the war, instead of just focusing on military strategies at the various battlefield sites, including Gettysburg.

Dwight T. Pitcaithley, a public historian who worked for the National Park Service for thirty years and ended his career as their chief historian from 1995 to 2000, influenced this shift in both policy and perception. In 2006, he wrote an influential essay, "A Cosmic Threat: The National Park Service Addresses the Causes of the American Civil War." He says, "Over the past several decades, Civil War–era historic sites and museums, with few exceptions, have generally avoided all discussion of the causes of the war and its consequences, or they actively or passively embraced the Lost Cause interpretation . . . Beginning in the 1990s, however, African American history in general and slavery in particular has gained fuller discussion in the public arena."

He goes on to say, "Congress played a major role in expanding the interpretation at historic sites . . . inserting language specifically instructing the secretary of the interior to interpret the park, in the larger context of the Civil War and American history . . . including effects of the war on all American people, especially on the American South."

This same shift in "storytelling" was evidenced in 1991 when Congress forced a change in interpretation at the Custer Battlefield National Monument. Custer was no longer glorified and the Sioux, Cheyenne, and Arapaho were no longer invisible or demonized. Both parties were now being recognized as holding courage on the same battlefield, calling for a name change to Little Bighorn Battlefield National Monument, creating a memorial to the Indians who had also died in the battle.

"The National Park Service is not a preservationist organization," Pitcaithley says. "It is an educational organization. We preserve these sites because they have stories to tell and we have something to learn from these stories."

We crossed the street to the Soldiers' National Cemetery, where the small brick-shaped headstones of unknown soldiers look like white stitches sewn into the lawn. Someone must have missed these soldiers back home.

"Did any black soldiers fight in the Battle of Gettysburg?" Louis asked.

"I don't know. Some accounts say there were no black soldiers on either side of Gettysburg. Others tell of a black civilian who took up arms on his own, joining the Union cause, fighting with the Ohio Fifth Regiment. But as always, it depends on who is telling the story."

Today, many black historians, Henry Louis Gates among them, are revisiting and revising the historical record: Gettysburg was not just a three-day battle but a reign of Southern terror throughout Pennsylvania involving the killing of freed slaves and other African-Americans, the burning of houses and whole communities after unimaginable horrors done to black people. I turned to Louis. "You know as well as anyone through your own experience with the war in Rwanda, and politics in general, that the 'segregation of memory' is perpetrated by those in power. Truth is another casualty of war."

The story of Basil Biggs looms large in the aftermath of the battle. Basil Biggs, a free black African laborer and veterinarian, moved his family from Maryland to Gettysburg, so his children could participate in the Pennsylvania Free Public School Act, allowing them to go to public instead of segregated schools. According to the 1860 census, 186 free black people lived in Gettysburg. Biggs bought a farm and soon found himself in the middle of a nightmare. As Lee's army approached, he fled Gettysburg with his family, knowing they were vulnerable to rogue slave hunters.

When Biggs returned home after the battle, his farm was in ruins, his land was a makeshift graveyard, and his ransacked home had been turned into a hospital—one of the busiest in the area. With carnage everywhere and soldiers suffering, it was not unusual to see "a pile of limbs higher than the fence." Biggs was sickened by what he saw. He took it upon himself to exhume the hastily buried soldiers and place their bodies in coffins with care, returning them to their homes or reburying them with proper respect in the Gettysburg Cemetery.

The task of properly burying soldiers expanded. F. W. Biesecker, a white Gettysburg resident, had won the government contract to exhume Union soldiers on the full battlefield and rebury them on newly purchased land that would become the Soldiers' National Cemetery. Biesecker turned around and hired Biggs as the subcontractor to do the actual dirty work. It is said that in October of 1863, Biggs and his team of black laborers exhumed and reburied over thirty-five hundred soldiers. They were paid $1.25 per body.

It is hard to imagine what went on in the minds of those men as they dug grave after grave after grave for the dead sons of the Civil War, but by the time President Abraham Lincoln stood on the hallowed ground of the Soldiers' National Cemetery, it was a place of order and respect. But Biggs and his men didn't stop there. Basil Biggs felt that the black soldiers who died in the Civil War (an estimated two hundred thousand African-American soldiers fought in the war—about 10 percent of the entire Union army, which corresponded to the African-American population in the nation as a whole at the time) also deserved a dignified resting place. So in 1866, Biggs joined with a man named Lloyd Watts and other black veterans of the war to found the Sons of Goodwill. Biggs, with the help of additional funding, purchased a small plot of ground near the National Cemetery for their black Civil War brothers who gave their lives to end slavery. This half acre of land, lovingly dedicated and maintained in the name of black veterans, came to be known as Lincoln Cemetery.

"There is always a story behind a story," Louis said.

Louis and I looked past the National Cemetery fence to where Lincoln stood and delivered the Gettysburg Address, fresh with his morning pencil edits written in the margins.

"Two minutes long," Louis said, "and we still recite those words. It's amazing what a few words managed to do against what the ravages of war had done."

My mind turned to Camus and what he wrote in his 1946 essay "Neither Victims Nor Executioners," one year after World War II ended: ". . . throughout the coming years, an endless struggle is going to be pursued between violence and friendly persuasion, . . . henceforth, the only honorable course will be to stake everything on a formidable gamble: that words are more powerful than munitions."

"We can go now," Louis said. "I just wanted to see the spot where Lincoln gave the Gettysburg Address."

I wanted him to see Gettysburg National Military Park, only minutes away, but Louis had seen enough.

"I don't need to see the place where people died."

He stretched out on a bench beneath a cypress tree and quickly fell asleep.

I recalled Louis's first visit to Washington, D.C. It was a full moon and Barack Obama had just been elected president of the United States. We took a cab from our hotel to the Lincoln Memorial. It was late and the moon was mirrored in the Reflecting Pool at the base of the Lincoln Memorial, with the Washington Monument directly east. We were walking up the stairs toward Lincoln when Louis stopped and turned around.

"I know this place," he said.

"How so?"

"I know this place because of the pictures I have seen. This is where Martin Luther King Jr. gave his speech." And then Louis Gakumba recited "I have a dream." Verbatim.

It was how he had learned English. "I found a book in Gisenyi called *The*

World's Greatest Speeches. I translated Dr. King's speech from English into French, and back to English again, and I memorized it."

I had no idea.

Louis emerged from his catnap and I convinced him to at least go into the park with me to see the historical Cyclorama, a 360-degree portrayal of the Battle of Gettysburg that has been beautifully restored from the original painted in 1883 by the French artist Paul Philippoteaux.

The painting itself rendered by Philippoteaux and his team of European artists is a marvel, aside from the ingenious engineering and construction required for its own custom building so it could be shown properly to the public. The Cyclorama painting is 42 feet high and 377 feet long, a canvas longer than a football field. Twenty thousand figures of men, women, and horses are painted on the canvas, with special attention given to particular details of each battle with its ensuing commanders, from Meade and Lee to Armistead and Sickles—they are all represented in the painting. The whole project required not only meticulous attention to historical facts and photographs but close to five tons of oil paint. Altogether, the painting weighs four tons.

This magnificently restored Cyclorama is a precious relic of the Victorian era, before motion pictures and DVDs that leave so little to our imaginations. When the Cyclorama *The Battle of Gettysburg* was first shown in Chicago in 1883, and then again in Boston the following year, veterans of Gettysburg flocked to see this painting in the round. They praised its accuracy as they provided their own narrative fresh from a memory still flush with the emotions and horrors of the Civil War. For many of the soldiers, it was the first time they got a sense of the overall picture, the entirety of the battle and the scale of what actually happened in those three long days.

The great Cyclorama was on display in Gettysburg from 1913 through 1965, carrying its own history of wear, decay, and destruction. Fortunately, through the efforts of visionary superintendents, over time the National Park Service joined the Gettysburg Foundation in undertaking a massive restoration project from 2002 through 2008. The masterpiece is now housed in a special Cyclorama building with a circular platform from which to view the painting as it was designed to be seen.

The Cyclorama captured Louis with its arcane beauty and terrible details, which in the round offer a panoramic perspective. The circular mural created the illusion of action using lights, sound, and narration. Each cannon fired became an explosion of light; our heads turned and turned again as another flash of light and another battle ensued. More cannons and more fire erupted, until hundreds of cannons lit up the landscape everywhere! We were caught in the magnitude of the chaos that surrounded us.

And then it ended—no more narration, no more lights, no more sound. We stood in the aftermath of the deadly battle. No one budged and no one spoke until we were asked to move on. After the show a volunteer took us aside and pointed to where a pale and wounded Lincoln appears with a figure resembling John Wilkes Booth. They are walking out the door of what looks to be a French farmhouse.

"Some say the artist took the liberty of foreshadowing Lincoln's death," the volunteer said.

Before leaving Gettysburg, we stopped and climbed the Longstreet Tower. The wind was blowing and the dry cornfields of last fall's harvest rattled like bones. "Every war is the same," Louis said, looking out over the battlefield.

Bones. A year before we visited Gettysburg, Louis and I laid down bones on the Washington Mall. One million bones were laid down in memory of the mass atrocities that have occurred in Rwanda, Sudan, Congo, Cambodia, and during the Holocaust. This was the vision of artist Naomi Natale: to have people make bones in remembrance of those who have died, without recognition, through the anonymity of war. These bones were being placed for all to see on one of the most public spaces in the world, the same green where Union soldiers during the Civil War were temporarily housed and fed, and where the wounded arriving from the battlefields of Virginia were cared for. It was here the poet Walt Whitman came after finding his brother George, who was injured in the Battle of Fredericksburg. His brother recovered, but Whitman remained for the next three years in Washington, caring for the soldiers, often consoling the wounded and the dying by writing letters for them to their loved ones at home. "They died all about us there just about in the same way—noble, sturdy, loyal boys . . ."

> *I am faithful, I do not give out;*
> *The fractur'd thigh, the knee, the wound in the abdomen,*
> *These and more I dress with impassive hand—(yet deep in my breast*
> *a fire, a burning flame.)*
>
> —WALT WHITMAN, "The Wound-Dresser"

All wars are the same, Louis repeated. "What we hold in to survive kills us in other ways. Another kind of war rages inside."

At the conclusion of the ceremony of "One Million Bones," the bones of clay, plaster, and papier-mâché made by people from all over the world blanketed the Mall from the Washington Monument to the Capitol. A collective call to end violence and the madness of war had been sounded.

Louis wrote afterward:

When I first heard about "The One Million Bones Project," my heart flinched. "Don't go—too painful," a part of me said. For me, this was not an artistic abstraction, this was my history. But another other part of me said, "Go—this will fulfill a promise . . . Honoring the dead."

We were asked to dress in white as a sign of respect, which I did. And then, we were invited to stand by a pile of bones and begin the arduous task of placing them on the lawn in remembrance of those who had died so violently.

This was the same ground I stood on a few months earlier in bone-breaking cold at the second inauguration of President Barack Obama. Over a million people had come to bear witness to the pages of history, a history that includes slavery and America's own Civil War where the bones of the dead are buried.

Looking across the sea of clay bones before me, I imagine Ezekiel in the "Valley of Dry Bones" when God asked him "Son of man, can these bones live?" I watch John Dau, one of the lost boys of Sudan holding a bone, the first bone to be laid down publically, ritualistically. I watch him remember a life he honored by kneeling on the grass and saying a grace before laying it to rest. I know the pain survivors live with, the courage it takes to go on when nothing is left of them, the strength required to keep digging in the hope of finding one more bone of loved ones. The bonds we share with the bones can never be broken.

I hold a femur in my hands made of clay. I stare at the bone of what could be a human begging for mercy, or of a child hurled against a rock, a million lives lost in Rwanda, Sudan, the Congo Democratic and else where—and then I place it on the ground with other bones, each one set inside the sacred space of memory.

The bones I continue to pick up and place on the ground, one after an-other, remind me of seeing my own bones exposed during the war when a neighbor sliced open the back of my hand with a machete. When I met Naomi Natale, the artist and architect of "The One Million Bones Project," I asked what had inspired her?

"I went to Rwanda," she said with tears floating in her eyes and words choking her throat. "The genocide piled mountains of bones," she whispered.

For the rest of the day, we lay down bones, a mosaic of bones made by hand. As Carl Wilkens writes, "When we make something with our hands, it changes the way we feel, which changes the way we think, which changes the way we act."

What are we to make of the Battle of Gettysburg or any war?

If no war is "civil," then is any war justified? Inevitably, both sides in any conflict carry on until their own moral self-destruction is ensured. Politics fuels wars. People end them.

The spring grasses feel saturated with questions.

Summer

"Shit, I don't know, I wonder if they knew what they were fighting for," Rick Bass says as we walk the fields of Gettysburg. "How can you ask farm kids to think things through?"

"Do the kids heading off for Afghanistan and Mosul know what they are fighting for?" Brooke asks. "What's changed?"

"Let's forget if they were right or wrong: they were brave," Rick says. "I know this sounds like a justification or apology from a southerner, but this wasn't about them wanting to keep their slaves—they were too poor. There was something else going on here."

We are walking in late-summer grasses, flushing up finches and sparrows.

"Go to war and participate in glory. The Confederate and Union armies were selling something that had little to do with slavery, they were selling patriotism."

"How is that any different from today?" Brooke says. "War is a propaganda machine."

The smell of sweet clover is strong among the freshly mowed fields. Peas grow on both sides of the trail. Rick bends down, picks three pods, splits them open with his finger, and eats them. Small sulphur butterflies and honeybees visit Queen Anne's lace.

The three of us have been friends ever since we made a pilgrimage to Ed Abbey's wake in Arches National Park on May 1, 1989. Brooke and I picked up Rick hitchhiking on his way to Moab. We were young writers who looked up to Cactus Ed for his passion and political irreverence. We shared a belief in saving wilderness. Now we are older writers who still believe in wild places, having just attended the fiftieth anniversary of the Wilderness Act in Washington, D.C.

I wanted to experience Gettysburg in the summer.

"What was the weather like during those three days in July?" Rick asks. "It must have been a swelter for the soldiers in their wool uniforms. Humid. I can imagine in that moment on July third when cannons were firing for hours, it wouldn't matter what color the sky was, it was so blackened by gunpowder And then, what happened when it cleared?"

His is the mind of a fiction writer always imagining the scenes from which the action springs.

"It was hot for the first two days and then, at the end, it rained and rained, until the blood from the bodies became a river," I say. "There are hellish accounts of trying to remove the dead and wounded from the fields, but there was too much mud. Wagons got stuck. I read one account of a wagon train carrying the Confederacy's wounded back to Virginia on July Fourth that was seventeen miles long, from front to back. Virtually every farm, house, church, and building in Gettysburg was a hospital or a morgue. And then, the blazing heat returned and you could smell the death stench of Gettysburg for miles."

We keep walking, flushing up crows and grasshoppers. Wild strawberries, chickory, a monarch butterfly. What remains of war? These grasses with their roots are holding down soil that was once mud-soaked with the blood of soldiers. Locals say the vultures who still haunt the fields of Gettysburg have retained a memory of human carrion. To walk the land at Gettysburg without crowds, without interpreters or reenactors or plaques telling us what to think and how we should feel, is to let the land tell its own story. The furrowed fields between patches of poison ivy and thistles still hold the faith and panic locked in the thousands of pairs of feet that tromped through this terrain. We tell ourselves the lines of soldiers, shoulder to shoulder, crossing into lines of enemy fire can be not only imagined but felt.

"What were they hoping for?" Rick asks Brooke.

"My friends who are veterans from Vietnam or Iraq tell me it's for the hope of defending their fellow soldiers and a belief that somehow, somewhere, they are fulfilling a mission to 'secure the peace.' But where is the peace of fifty-one thousand casualties left lying on a battlefield? That's what I want to know," Brooke says.

Gettysburg is not a place for pacifists.

The Union army won the Battle of Gettysburg because they took the high ground on Little Round Top to Seminary Ridge, creating a military stronghold in the shape of a fishhook. We are also told they held the moral ground, but what I hear my friend tell us is that the only ground that mattered for those boys fighting was the ground beneath their feet.

Rick is a southerner, born in Fort Worth, Texas. "That had to be surreal for the boys—from both the North and the South—who largely came from rural country and were used to hunting game," he says. "Suddenly they are given muskets not for shooting a deer but a man, and not even a foreigner, but a fellow countryman, even a brother . . . that had to be a mind-buster. The first shot had to be the hardest—after that, self-defense."

We flush a meadowlark. I didn't know they were here. Their yellow breasts are a song before they even open their beaks.

In 1999, the Gettysburg National Military Park created a twenty-year plan to return the battlefield to its 1863 appearance. This restoration project included the replanting of historic woodlots, orchards, and the removal of nonhistoric vegetation. The re-creation of original fence lines, lanes, and trails used by troops is under way now. Since the park was established in

1895, land has been acquired by both southern and northern interests: farms have been bought, houses torn down, even golf courses returned to fields, and historic view sheds have been restored—all in the name of protecting and preserving the battlefield at Gettysburg. In this instance, the national park has been a unifying force in bringing opposing sides together. By re-creating historical cultural landscapes through environmental manipulation, ironically, a more accurate depiction of the battle has been rendered from the restoration of the peach orchard to the view on Little Round Top.

We are slowly returning to the hour of land where our human presence can take a side step and respect the integrity of the place itself—paying attention to its own historical and ecological character beyond our needs and desires. This kind of generosity of spirit requires an uncommon humility to listen to the land first.

"Knowing where the wind's blowing, watching every branch, listening to every sound—the deceptions of the field—all this was going through their minds," Rick says.

I am smiling. Rick is in his own reverie, surveying the landscape both physically and historically, as a hunter. I realize I will never fully understand my friend until I go hunting with him in his beloved woods in the Yaak Valley. Montana is his adopted solitude.

Up ahead, I hear a familiar voice. Brooke turns and has the same reaction.

No doubt about it, the voice belongs to Andie, our guide by horseback in the fall.

It's the same Gettysburg-by-horse tour on the same path with the same horses carrying different riders.

We watch her through the screen of Stanton's woods. It's the same white picket fence, the red barn, the farmhouse, only this time the leaves on the trees are green not gold.

"Man, that woman is pissed—listen to her!" Rick says.

"I have . . ." Brooke says.

You will hear from the government today that General Lee sent his men to slaughter . . . Andie's voice carries over the fields.

"Good storytelling can manipulate anything," Rick says. "That's what the military counts on."

We find a hole in the fence bordered by goldenrod and cross over to where Pickett's Charge took place. Gettysburg always seems to circle back to this moment.

The horses are coming toward us, Andie in the lead.

"I don't want to have to engage with them," Brooke says.

"By the time they get to us we'll be in the woods," Rick replies.

Brooke is already gone.

We've walked a large circle and are now at Pitzer's Woods, reading a plaque at the memorial honoring General James Longstreet. He is on his horse facing the battlefield. The sculpture appears grossly out of proportion: Longstreet overwhelms his horse. Visitors have placed Lincoln pennies on the monument as offerings, a practice we have seen on many of the monuments and tombstones.

Brooke turns to Rick and me: "Didn't we hear this was made to stand on top of a tall monument or pedestal, not on the ground—but it never happened?"

"Sadly, nothing seemed to work out for the general here in Gettysburg," I say.

As a senior corps commander, General Robert E. Lee wanted Longstreet to go forward with the attack regardless of his own misgivings. James M. McPherson, the great Civil War historian, calls Longstreet's challenge to Lee regarding Pickett's Charge "a near-insubordination."

Longstreet's own words convey more than reluctance, they speak to his grief and regret: "My heart was heavy . . . I could see the desperate and hopeless nature of the charge and the cruel slaughter it would cause. That day at Gettysburg was the saddest of my life."

Some say Longstreet was scapegoated for the South's loss at Gettysburg, that the fault should rest on Lee's shoulders as his "grave miscalculation." Others say that his disagreement with Lee's tactics on Pickett's Charge on July 3 led him to stall engagement, and that his tardiness on the battlefield contributed to the catastrophic outcome for his men, sixty-five hundred casualties in fifty minutes, their bodies spread a mile across the field with more than fifteen hundred soldiers dead. But monuments tell their story in stone. Longstreet rides into history out of proportion, in ignominy, a large man on a short horse, while Lee rides proudly, upright and erect on the monument honoring the Army of Northern Virginia just up the road.

Creating a monument is a matter of taste and values and the means to get it made. Once you monumentalize a person, place, or thing, you run the risk of worship. And what we worship, for better or for worse, freezes the story.

There are 1,328 monuments dotting the edges of Gettysburg. The recent Friend to Friend Masonic Memorial, brought to Gettysburg in 1993, depicts the scene of Confederate Brigadier General Lewis Addison Armistead being assisted by a Union soldier, both of them members of the Masonic Order. Below are the words "a brotherhood undivided," even as they fought in a divided nation.

It is a well-known story in Civil War lore: Armistead, leading the Army of Northern Virginia forward in Pickett's Charge, with his hat on, his sword held high. Armistead kept his focus, bravely crossing the stone wall as he continued fighting his way through the Union line with a few other fellow soldiers, an advance that would become the Confederacy's high-water mark, their farthest reach into Union territory. Armistead took a bullet in his leg and his chest and fell, spirited and exhausted, at once, dying days later in a Union hospital. In that moment, a Union soldier who knew and admired Armistead stopped and knelt down to help his friend. On the field, Armistead is reported to have handed his gold watch to his Mason brother, asking him to give it to his dear friend Winfield Hancock, who was fighting for the Union army. At a farewell dinner prior to the Civil War Armistead had said to Hancock, "God strike me down dead if I ever lift a hand toward you in battle."

So the story goes. Gettysburg is a battlefield of legends.

My favorite memorial belongs to the state of Louisiana. It is a soaring androgynous figure, more female than male, who is sounding the trumpet in her left hand while she raises a flaming torch toward the sky in the other. The right angle made by her arms is authoritative and commanding as she rises above the body of a fallen soldier clutching his heart. Both figures are strong and muscular, unapologetic to death. The sculptor, Donald DeLue, titled it *Peace and Memory*.

But the place I return to after four visits to Gettysburg is a grove of trees where the Monument to Seventh New Jersey stands decorated with bands of Civil War bullets. Brooke, Rick, and I sit down for lunch in the shade of a great, gnarled oak tree, certainly a witness tree present to some of the bloodiest fighting that occurred in the Valley of Death below Little Round Top.

"There will never be another war that leaves the trees standing," Rick says.

"This was a war that had one foot in the past and the other in the present— musket balls on one hand, cannonballs on the other. Who could have foreseen the evolution of artillery from bayonets to nuclear bombs?"

Mountains of cumulus clouds gather above us and paint the sky in pastels. How does a place that knew such violence now register peace?

"The mockingbird's singing would have called out the Southern boys' childhood in summer," Rick says, lying on his back, looking up through the trees. "That would have been bittersweet for them."

Brooke is sitting in the grass with his back against the monument. The drone of cicadas creates a haunting dirge that threatens to drown out Brooke and Rick's talk about war strategies.

"So the sharpshooters must have positioned themselves behind those boulders up at Little Round Top and from there they could see the whole of the Union fishhook strategy to overtake the Confederate army," Brooke says.

"Yeah, the terrain and slope of the hillside look a lot more formidable from down here. The Union certainly had the geographic advantage," Rick answers.

"Look how small the people look up there, it's bigger than it looks from Cemetery Ridge."

In a letter to his pastor, a man from Emmitsburg, Maryland, with the initials A.J.B. watched the scene through a telescope. He wrote:

On Friday, the 3rd day of battle the hours of 2 o'clock and 5 o'clock, it is said it was the hardest contest witnessed during whole war. During that I watched it with intense interest: but I need not to say I for there were 50 or 60 persons present at Indian Lookout for which body all the members of the college, except Fathers John McClosky and Xopie constituted a part during which hours, some of the officers said afterwards they never before witnessed such heavy cannonading.

Flames of fire and volumes of smoke obstructed our view considerably. We have not gone to the battlefield yet, but persons who have been there since the battle say that it presents a most horrible spectacle. They say that some two or three days after the fight dead bodies and the bodies of wounded and dying were to be seen scattered over the field in every direction, and that the stench for miles around is most intolerable. The graves of some thousand are to be seen on the field where they fell . . .

Another written account by a soldier explains how after that battle he looked up at the brightness of the moon, but all he could see were "spirits flitting from Little Round Top to Devil's Den and back all night." He couldn't sleep. And all he could hear in the loneliness of the night were the groans of soldiers left to die.

Gettysburg is at risk of becoming a place of war worship. In our desperation to perceive valor and courage that may not be present in our own lives, we glorify a terrible slaughter of men and boys. The myth that war propagates and that our national memory perpetuates is that all soldiers are valiant and brave, and that American history is a history victorious instead of shadowed and scarred.

The awe-inspiring spectacle and pageantry displayed here at the Gettysburg Battlefield, reenacted again and again in our costumed imaginations, makes me wonder whether we are absorbing America's history in half-truths and, in many cases, lies.

Rick stands up. "What if all those men listed on these monuments as 'missing' just ran away when they saw what their chances were of staying alive versus being shot? Hell, I don't know what I'd do. I hope I would stay and fight, but I'm not sure if a general told me to march to my slaughter, if I wouldn't just . . . Shit, look at the numbers: I think it was on the Florida monument, did you read those numbers? It was a ten-to-one kill ratio, something like eleven hundred wounded and a hundred-plus killed with eight hundred and forty missing. That's bullshit. They ran away."

We leave the sanctuary of shade and Rick apologizes: "I'm sorry to be such a downer, I'm just saying they are keeping this war worship alive like any other God—the uniforms, the artillery, the stories. Gettysburg is not past tense. Lee is alive. Grant is alive. I just want to know if we as a country still are?"

"There's a marked absence of regret," Brooke says. "It's about the mechanics, the generals, the infantrymen, the dead, the wounded, and the missing. Here's what happened, this was the strategy, the artillery used, the casualties reported. The focus is on the *what* of war—rarely the *why*."

"It's all fucked up," Rick says. "Why all this rapture about war? Why not a landscape, a piece of music or literature?"

"I guess it's all pushing me to make some sense of why I am so taken with

Gettysburg, why I keep coming back," I say. "Maybe it has something to do with what the dead—many still buried here—want us to know."

There is no monument for Basil Biggs. There is no monument to the residents of the town of Gettysburg, largely women, who brought the injured and dying into their homes and took care of them. These are the ghost monuments that haunt me and they are as real as the ghosts of the dead who refuse to leave.

The winds blow, the branches sway. So little feels settled on this hallowed land.

Our car is back at the parking lot at Pitzer's Woods, where we left General Longstreet on his horse. A makeshift camp has been set up by a half dozen reenactors whom we pass to get to our vehicle.

"Howdy."

"How's it going?"

"Good, we're about to go bowling for Yankees."

"Excuse me?" I ask.

"We're artillery, ma'am. We're settin' up our hardware."

"I see. Forgive my ignorance, but I know very little about Civil War artillery, can you explain what you are doing?"

"Sure, we're support for the infantry, the men on foot. Artillery doesn't win wars. Feet on the ground do. We're interested in taking you out before you engage our troops."

The man I am engaging with is large, bearded, with sandy-colored hair, perhaps in his midforties. He's got an eagle tattoo on one bicep and a Confederate flag on the other, both tattoos showcased by a sleeveless gray T-shirt. He and his cohort carry what looks to be a small cannon out of the bed of his pickup.

"Our job, ma'am, is to emotionally dehabilitate you."

"And you're with the—"

"Confederate army," he says, interrupting Brooke. "We're part of the Second Company of Richmond Howitzers setting up support for the Army of Northern Virginia. Tomorrow we'll be dressed and firing up the cannons." He pauses. "This here is a twelve-pound Napoleon."

Rick is quiet.

"Where y'all from?"

"Utah," Brooke says.

"So, may I ask you a question?" I ask.

"Shoot," he says. The men start laughing.

"Coming from Utah, the Civil War wasn't something I ever really thought about. I think it's why I keep coming back here, to figure out a history I didn't know was mine. Can you explain to me what the Civil War is about?"

"It's complicated, ma'am. Let me put it to you this way: The North is more industrial with lots of textile factories. The South is more agricultural, growing cotton, sending it up north. The government is setting up heavy import taxes on us. So we're fightin' to get the federal government out of our lives. It's about economics and our right to govern ourselves. It's a state's rights thing, ma'am, the North against the South. We're the underdogs."

He pulls out some more guns and ammunition from the Civil War era.

"Do you get it? It's about the average soldier. Say you're invading my town. You think I'm gonna let that happen? The fight's local. I'm defending my homeland. Yeah, sure, the bigwigs were trying to direct things and they had their politics, Lee and Longstreet over there [he points to the fields], but in the end it's about defending your own territory. You weren't fightin' for a philosophy. You were fightin' for your buddy, for your family, for your honor. Now I'm fightin' here in Gettysburg, so people like you can stand next to me and ask me these kinds of questions."

Another one of the reenactors behind him is setting up a cook tent and hanging up cast-iron skillets and various tools.

"We're sleepin' here tonight. He's my cook." The men start laughing again.

"I mean I know you come here and think it's all about slavery, but look at it this way, the Feds can't just come in here and tell us what to do. The best way for you to understand the Civil War is to look at the gun issue in America right now. You ain't taking my guns away. Slaves. Guns. It's the same issue, just different items."

He turns to Brooke and Rick, pointing to his own chest. "It's the Big Man telling the little man what to do. You know what I'm talkin' 'bout. Nothin's changed."

EFFIGY MOUNDS NATIONAL

MONUMENT, IOWA

-<- ->-

death yes but as a gathering

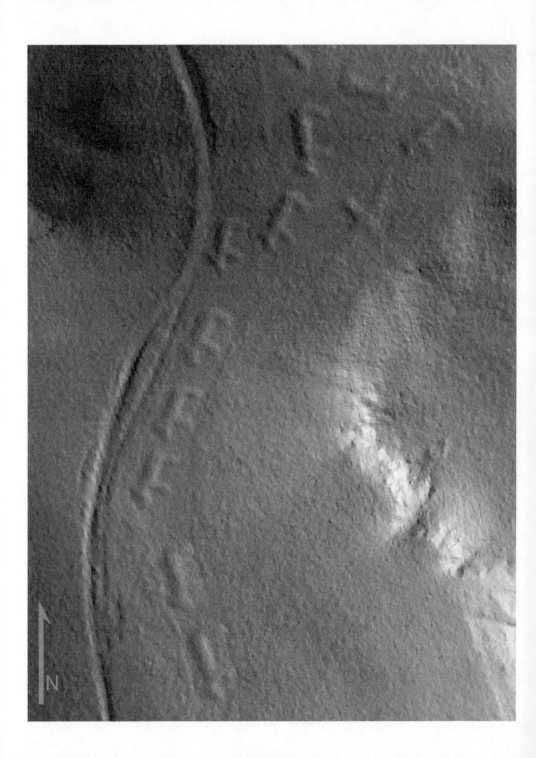

THERE IS A GREAT BIRD RESTING in the woodlands above the great river with marching bears behind her. A seasoned peace that can only belong to the prairie creates the path on the ridgetop where she can be found. Time—not blood—is the life force animating the bird and these bears. Fifteen hundred years ago these earth mounds were made by the hands of the people who lived here in the Upper Mississippi River Valley, ancestors to today's Ho-Chunk people, also known as the Winnebago. This is the "Driftless Area" where the glacial sheets of ice that stretched across the North American continent during the Pleistocene fell short of this holy site. A Ho-Chunk woman would see these figures through the gestures of ceremony: the burying of the dead; the honoring of birds and bears. As a visitor, I experience this land as a walking meditation.

Effigy Mounds National Monument is a quiet space of contemplation in the northeast corner of Iowa where the Mississippi River creates a fluid boundary with southern Wisconsin. For millennia, tens of thousands of these earth mounds dotted the midwestern territory of what we now know as the United States. Archaeologists have documented twenty-three different shapes of effigy mounds. But Manifest Destiny plowed them under in favor of fields of corn. Now very few remain in a landscape that has been transformed by industrial agriculture. Still, within Effigy Mounds National Monument there are 207 mounds, 31 of them effigies in the shapes of animals.

Most of the round mounds are believed to be burial sites housing the bones of men, women, and children who belonged to particular communities. Some burials contain bundles of bones, some charred, some dusted with red ocher. Other mounds have contained "flesh burials" where the body has remained intact. Artifacts such as Clovis points have been found nearby along with those that surprise, like a copper breastplate with twine made from basswood. Other mounds shaped from the earth are long, like a string of pearls stretched along the ridges, while others rise from the woodland floor in the shapes of birds and bears, possibly wolves, most with a view of the Mississippi River.

We approached each mound as a prayer. *Death yes as a gathering place.* Death yes honored in a seasonal pilgrimage that perhaps was the end point of a journey taken to remember one's ancestors. To visit any grave is a solemn practice. To visit these mounds is to be brought into the presence of an unseen force where the ground has literally been raised.

The Great Bear Mound facing the Great River is the largest of the bear effigies located within the national monument. Registering ninety-five feet long from rump to nose, it does not house bones but stirs belief. Imagine the equivalent of more than twenty dump-truck loads of soil being used to create this earth-sculpted bear and the people who cared enough to shape it. Breezes blow through the trees in great gusts. A vulture wavers over the clearing. The body of the Bear is a quivering of grasses. I pick up a small owl feather, remove my shoes, and begin to walk the outline of the Bear barefoot. Around and around, I walk the Bear until I feel the rhythm of ritual that transcends words. Animal effigies invoke power, a power not held by humans.

A friend of mine from the Midwest believes these raised bodies of bears are grizzlies recounted on the edge of their eastern-most range. Who translates the art of ritual? It belongs to the makers themselves. But isn't any mound, geoglyph, or pictograph a physical representation of an idea or belief? Who were these inhabitants? And where do their bloodlines flow now? What I do know is that on the other side of the ridge, the green shuddering of fields registers as a single note of corn.

Albert LeBeau, the cultural resources manager at Effigy Mounds National Monument, says "the new archaeology" expresses the Indian point of view.

"No, 'the Mounds People' didn't one day just suddenly disappear. No, there were no 'Early Woodland People' who built these mounds and left. 'The People' who made these mounds and effigies didn't self-identify—they are part of a continuum of Indian people who are still here, ancestors to the Ho-Chunk and others who have used this area for at least twenty-five hundred years. This place was most likely a seasonal stop for them, a stop of abundant game and food from fish to seeds."

He goes on to say, "The archaeological evidence supports the native understanding that these mounds were created and used for ceremonial purposes. It was a *refugio*. During a time of hardship, it was seen as a sacred area."

Albert is a large man, smart, spirited, and outspoken, with short-cropped hair and tattoos on both arms. We are sitting in his office near the visitor's center.

"Look, I chose to be an archaeologist. I cannot choose not to be Lakota." He picks up a pile of papers. "On the one hand, I belong to the bureaucracy of the National Park Service. On the other hand, I am part of my Lakota people who live in South Dakota. So you may wonder, do I want to be a historian or an archaeologist? I just want to be myself, to see the history for myself, and find the true story, not someone else's interpretation."

In the visitor's center, there are numerous interpretations of "the mound builders." They range from the earliest theories in the late seventeenth century that a race of super-Indians built these mounds and then mysteriously disappeared; to Josiah Priest and William Pidgeon's "Moundbuilder Myth" in the early nineteenth century, which promulgated that the large earthworks were built by "the Lost Tribes of Israel"; to Alfred J. Hill and Theodore H. Lewis, who in 1880 obsessively and passionately mapped more than thirteen thousand mounds, trying to record them before they were destroyed, and filling forty leather-bound notebooks in the process; to the local, self-taught archaeologist Ellison Orr, who led the Iowa Archaeological Survey from 1934 to 1936; to R. Clark Mallam, an anthropologist from Luther College who saw the earth mounds as "a public works project" tied to seasonal migrations and bringing societal cohesion to the people associated with them. The literature is contradictory and confusing, as each era perpetuated its own ideology.

Mallam, the anthropologist from Luther, recognized the "Driftless Area" comprising northern Illinois, southern Wisconsin, and eastern Iowa as the territory of the effigy mound culture. His approach was to "articulate holistically a series of economic, social, and ideological relationships."

It was Mallam who viewed effigy mounds as sacred space, "analogous to that of a shaman moving from one reality to another." It was also Mallam who with his students outlined the effigy mounds with lime so they could be seen from above and identified more clearly. This practice has been abandoned, as it is seen by the tribes as an act of desecration.

Ellis Orr, and other founding fathers of Effigy Mounds National Monument, initially sought to protect the mounds by proposing a vast Mississippi River Valley National Park. But their plan was deemed too complicated and too political, given the priority of the plow and the competing economic interests of emerging towns and cities in Iowa and Wisconsin.

And so each year they saw more mounds destroyed. The vision of one national park carried by a few became a fragmented vision promoted by many. Pragmatism trumped passion. In 1949, President Harry S. Truman used the Antiquities Act to protect the precious remaining archaeological sites and created the Effigy Mounds National Monument in the state of Iowa. It was a quiet tribute to Iowa's eight-term Republican congressman, John

Fletcher Lacey, who helped not only to write the Antiquities Act in 1906 but enact it. In 2015, the monument now holds 2,526 acres in trust along the Mississippi River, including 81.5 acres of restored prairie.

Seen from Fire Point Overlook inside the monument, the mosaic of protected lands that remain in spite of agricultural development is impressive. These lands include Pikes Peak State Park downriver, and the wooded islands and waterways in Wisconsin that make up the Upper Mississippi River National Wildlife and Fish Refuge, more than two hundred thousand acres directly across the river from Effigy Mounds National Monument.

From this vantage point, one can imagine the landscape encountered by the French explorers Father Jacques Marquette and Louis Joliet in 1673 while canoeing the Mississippi River in search of a passageway to the Pacific Ocean. But as a westerner who grew up with stories of the Great River from Mark Twain to Meridel Le Sueur, what I could not have envisioned until now was the wealth of the wilderness of the Mississippi, home to 260 species of fish (25 percent of all species in North America), walleye, bluegill, and large-mouthed bass among them, with the occasional monster pikes; more than 145 species of amphibians and reptiles; 50 species of mammals who inhabit the riverbanks and forests; and 326 species of birds, with 60 percent of our nation's migratory birds using the river as a flyway. With this kind of bio-diversity along the Mississippi River corridor, it makes sense that humans, past and present, have always sought the ecological riches of the river community, finding both mobility and stability within the Mississippi watershed.

Bob Palmer, chief ranger at Effigy Mounds, recites this history with the knowledge of a local. He was born and raised on a farm ten miles down the road. "Growing up here, we were always aware of the past," he says. "Artifacts and arrowheads were often exposed while plowing the fields." He pauses. "Effigy Mounds is a complicated place. I've been here long enough to know just how complex the relationships between the park and native people are, especially now. There is a ceiling on the world and a floor on the world and we occupy the place in between. Those of us who work for the National Park Service have a responsibility as stewards to the land and its history."

When I ask Albert LeBeau how he feels the National Park Service is managing Effigy Mounds National Monument as a sacred site of "The People," his answer is immediate:

"Horrible, absolutely horrible."

LeBeau is referring to the 2009 scandal that took place under the jurisdiction of the former superintendent Phyllis Ewing. She was responsible for seventy-eight projects valued at $3.4 million that were constructed without mandatory environmental reviews or proper tribal consultations regarding burial sites. The maintenance supervisor, Tom Sinclair, managed these projects, which included building boardwalks accessible for handicapped individuals; new trails, roads, bridges; and a maintenance shed. Although the National Park Service says no burials were damaged, one tribal elder claimed that during these construction projects near the Yellow River, the cemeteries of his ancestors were treated like "places to walk your dog."

"These projects were in clear violation of the National Historic Preservation Act as well as the Native American Graves Protection and Repatriation Act of 1990," Albert says.

A local newspaper reported, "Somewhere along the line, officials admit they lost their way. Without following required review processes, the U.S. National Park Service built three boardwalks and a maintenance shed that may have interrupted the historical integrity of the park." The "Serious Mismanagement Report" filed in 2014 states that both Ewing and Sinclair "had an inexcusable lack of understanding of the fundamental importance of the archaeological resource they were assigned to protect, along with its complexity, pervasiveness, landscape qualities and history, which enabled them to discount concerns and justify gross physical and ethical violations of a site held sacred by many."

What Bob Palmer did not tell me, as a loyal ranger of the United States Park Service, is that he is on record as a voice challenging the former superintendent.

Although a 2009 audit uncovered numerous violations, Superintendent Ewing continued her job until she was transferred in 2010 to the Regional National Park Service offices in Omaha, Nebraska, where she did "curatorial work." She was fired from the Park Service in 2014. Claiming that she had been "scapegoated," Ewing is currently suing the agency for age discrimination. She was seventy-three years old at the time of her violations.

A former national park employee at the Effigy Mounds National Monument, who asked to remain anonymous, told me, "The situation was appalling; nobody was being held accountable. Artifacts, including bones, had been found in boxes in another Park Service employee's garage. They knew exactly what they were doing and they didn't care."

Twenty tribes who recognize Effigy Mounds National Monument as a sacred site for their people signed a letter of protest, a collective call for maintaining the dignity and peace of their ancestors:

Crow Creek Sioux
Flandreau Santee Sioux
Ho-Chunk Nation
Iowa of Kansas and Nebraska
Iowa of Oklahoma
Lower Sioux Indian Community of Minnesota
Omaha Tribe of Nebraska
Otoe Missouria Tribe of Indians
Ponca Tribe of Nebraska
Prairie Island Indian Community
Sac and Fox of the Mississippi in Iowa
Sac and Fox Nation of Oklahoma

Santee Sioux Tribe of Nebraska

Shakopee Mdewakanton Sioux Community

Standing Rock Sioux Tribe

Sisseton Wahpeton Oyate

Upper Sioux Indian Community of Minnesota

Winnebago Tribe of Nebraska

Yankton Sioux Tribe

Albert LeBeau took over as cultural resources manager in 2013. "You can cut the head off the snake but it still slithers," he says. "The good news is, we are able to talk to the tribes again. We were able to show them the investigation and promise them transparency. The new superintendent, Jim Nepstad, is committed to this. We are in the process of rebuilding their trust. And my being here in this position is part of that trust."

He stops and faces me directly. "When I chose to walk this path, I chose to be a preservationist. The resource comes first. And the resource for me is the ancestors.

"I do what I do because those people don't have a voice anymore. I choose to be their voice." He pauses. "Elders are a resource, too. The National Park Service needs to remember that the old people know things—they forget that tribal people have a long knowledge based on stories passed on generation after generation. My grandfather told me long ago that the great bird and marching bears marked friendly territory for the Lakota, but that beyond that, if you cross the Mississippi, you are not welcome."

After a long and rich conversation, Albert draws Brooke and me a map of where we could walk to see the great bird and Marching Bears.

"I don't know how to explain it, except to say, there's something there—a magnetic shift and you feel it."

Brooke and I rise before dawn the next morning. The creek bed is dry. We are walking on an old roadbed that cuts through a mature forest of red oaks. Cicadas begin their rasping chorus at sunrise. Diffused light follows us up the steep incline to the top of the ridge, where it opens wide to a restored prairie dense with bee balm, sumac, and black-eyed Susans. Black swallowtails waft among the pale purple coneflowers. When we come to a stand of aspens we face an eruption of birds: rose-breasted grosbeaks, redstarts, catbirds, yellow warblers and vireos joined by chickadees, house wrens, flickers and yellow-bellied sapsuckers. It is a charged place. We are drawn to a small path that veers right from the main trail. There in the shadowed woods is a circular mound covered in ferns. Neither Brooke nor I speak, but stand silently inside a cacophony of birdsong.

Back on the main trail we follow deer tracks to another large stand of aspens where a first-year summer tanager confounds us. We are unfamiliar with its marbled plumage, red-yellow. With Albert's map in mind, we turn left down a mowed pathway wet with dew. Large ferns flirt with us, brushing against our legs as mourning cloaks and tortoiseshells float above the grasses. It is lush country. We descend into shadows overtaken by stillness. There, in a shaded clearing, are two mounds with a monarch butterfly hovering over them. Brooke and I separate.

I do not recognize the shape of this particular effigy until I draw it with my feet. Its edge is distinct, a contrast between what has been mowed and what has not. The tall grasses suggest fur. After one full rotation the vegetative body of ferns and forbs lets me know I have walked the contours of a small bear. I slowly walk the path surrounding the small bear twice. With the breezes, the body of the bear breathes.

From the eye of the moon still visible in daylight, ten bear effigies move down the spine of the mountain in single file. We walk among them. What was the impulse behind their creation? Respect? A ritualistic uprising in the relationship between humans and animals? And I wonder which came first:

Was it this particular landscape that drew the effigies into being? Or was it the animals themselves that called forth the ceremonies in the mind of the people? To be situated in place is to be engaged in a reciprocity where survival, both physical and spiritual, depends on our understanding of gestures.

I believe necessity drives us to improvisation where improbable and sustaining gestures create moments of grace that take care of us. We continue to evolve and transform who we are in relationship to where we are. We do not live in isolation from the physical world around us. Nature beckons our response. It is in the doing, the being, the becoming that meaning is made. What becomes sacred is the act itself—not what remains. Something inexplicable is set into motion. The bears are animated within the landscape.

These bears were reimagined in place through a collective belief and need. I do not know why they were sculpted into being, but their power is palpable. I may be blind to what has been buried here or held inside these effigy mounds for thousands of years, but I can read the landscape like Braille through the tips of my fingers translating the script of grasses into a narrative I can understand. The bears and birds and snakes written on the body of the Earth through the hands of the humans who dwelled here in the Upper Mississippi River Valley are a reminder that we form the future by being caretakers of our past.

As we continue down the path, the glare of the Mississippi River shines through the spaces between sugar maples and hickories as it meanders below. The temperature feels cooler, the shadows deeper. Suddenly, with a white oak as my witness, the energy of the woods shifts—in the clearing is the bird.

I stop to see the winged effigy in its entirety. Falcon enters my mind, swift and stealth. What if the wind I have been hearing is the memory of flight? This bird made of earth glimmers as light dances on the leaves and I want to touch her body, a garden, but I don't. Restraint is its own prayer. The fact that a red-headed woodpecker, now iridescent in sunshine, flies down from an oak branch to where the raptor's heart would be only makes the moment more miraculous.

For the rest of the afternoon, I walk the effigy's wings into motion. They say her wingspan is more than two hundred feet. For me, her wings span time, where the whispering of Holy Wisdom can be heard.

Great bird above the Great River, what would you have us know?

BIG BEND NATIONAL PARK, TEXAS

-‹‹- ->>-

Any wind will tell you

A NY WIND WILL TELL YOU it is the long view that counts. Big Bend National Park is the long view—stark, lonely, and soul saving. I have waited all my life to see this kind of vista.

I come to Big Bend as a naturalist only, desperate to immerse myself in natural history, not the history of humans. Gettysburg left me weary from war, Effigy Mounds left me hungry with questions, and so, for now, I want nothing more than to focus on birds. Though I have chosen to come during winter when most of the 450 species of birds recorded here have not yet migrated back to the basin, the sight of one black-crested titmouse dangling upside down in the pines steadies my heart.

"El Despoblado" is what the Spanish called this country, "the uninhabited land." It remains one of the least visited national parks in America, with roughly three hundred thousand visitors a year compared to 10 million visitors in Great Smoky Mountains National Park. And in January, visitors at Big Bend are particularly scarce, which is why I've come now. In the ten days Brooke and I explore Big Bend, it will appear empty of people.

I am leaving my own species and ten thousand years of human history behind. Forgive me. Isn't this what environmentalists like me are accused of—blatant misanthropy? It's not that I have a disdain for humankind, I just need a break. I want to be absorbed into someplace larger and more expansive than the human brain. I am seeking a different kind of circuitry, the nervous system of rivers and deserts and mountains born of fire.

At this very moment, in the winter of 2015, the U.S. Congress is considering a bill to secure the U.S.-Mexican border not with a fence but a wall, what the late, great writer Chuck Bowden called "a fucking piece of performance art." The inhumanity of such an act would be matched only by what this would do to the wildlife community, who have no understanding of man-made borders other than that it means the cessation of movement and migration. The 118-mile border that Big Bend National Park shares with Mexico would be closed not only to humans but to coyotes, jackrabbits, javelinas, ring-tailed cats, kit foxes, mountain lions, bobcats, and deer. Add lizards, tarantulas, and diamondback rattlesnakes and all other animals who would be stopped crossing a largely invisible border.

The ultimate misanthrope, Edward Abbey called Big Bend National Park an "emerald isle in a red sea." This is my desire—to simply walk and witness the Chihauhaun Desert, where thousands of species of cactus will ask nothing of me but to be left alone beneath an overarching sky.

I have brought a spectrum of small colored notebooks, one for each day, to record images and impressions.

DAY ONE—BLUE NOTEBOOK

Blue is bunting, indigo and quick. Blue is jay, its chatter like jazz. Blue is grosbeak is bluebird is blackbird turned sky. The Chisos mountains at dusk are blue. Blue is ghost-like. Twilight. Deep border blue. Once is the blue moon where panthers dance. Twice is the blue belly of lizards flashing. Blue waves are heat waves, dervishes in sand. Blue is the long song of storm clouds gathering with rain.

The desert is most alive at night. Small, dark eyes glow in the dark and then vanish. Strange cries startle. A band of collared peccaries (also known as javelinas) stand their ground as we cross the wash. Two feet tall, roughly thirty-five pounds, they look like wild boars with their characteristic tusks. In moonlight, their fur is black, silver-tipped, and spiked. The difference between fear and awe is a matter of our eyes adjusting.

A flurry of moths becomes a white-winged blizzard; stalks of sotol glow like lit tapers on either side of the road. For eighty miles, we never pass a car. We enter Big Bend National Park for the first time beneath a haloed moon surrounded by the immense silhouettes of the Chisos Mountains.

We stop the car, get out, and face the chilled silence of a crystalline night. Orion is overhead, Scorpio is rising, and very near Pegasus, the winged horse, we can see the smudge of the galaxy Andromeda.

It is 9:15 p.m. on January 25, 2015.

Big Bend becomes a deep sigh for me and with another breath, I retreat into the spaciousness between stars. Wherever you look the private is made public, what once was hidden is now exposed, even darkness—especially darkness. Spent agave look like rib cages pried open by ravenous coyotes.

Prickly pear pads, succulent and plump, decompose into a structure resembling lace.

We are standing on a blue-lit desert on the border of Mexico. I wonder who is out there holding their breath, praying not to be found. Human. Animal. I want to develop night vision.

DAY TWO—TURQUOISE NOTEBOOK

The bracelet I wear in the desert is turquoise. Turquoise is protection from rattlesnakes coiled. Rattlesnakes uncoiled move fast like a river. Downriver on the Rio Grande, a man keeps a turquoise boat hidden in willows. A turquoise boat is the color of defiance. A lazuli bunting is turquoise with wings. A mountain lion at twilight is a turquoise shadow fanning orange flaming flowers with her nervous tail. Turquoise eyes steady as stone disarm me.

Santa Elena Canyon provides our first glimpse of the Rio Grande. The water is slow moving and pink with morning light, mirroring the red-streaked cliffs rising on either side of the river. Rock wrens guide us up the narrow switchbacks. A quick altitude gain reveals ruby-crowned kinglets below, flirting in the willows. Most deserts have a memory of the sea and here is no exception. Fossils embedded in the limestone create an ancient brocade woven through the stratigraphy of stone.

I stop. I know this smell in the desert—the aftermath of a flash flood—damp sand, detritus, the layers of rotting leaves. Juncos steal seeds off the trail. I can drink the day's freshness in dew. The voice of a canyon wren registers as a scent, clear notes echoing against rock. Around the bend, the Rio Grande is flexing its muscle through ripples of currents.

These canyon walls, fourteen hundred feet high, resemble Puebloan pots—black paint on red fired clay. Gradations of black, gray, and blue come forth in late-afternoon light on burnished walls, red-orange. My skin is indistinguishable from the skin of the canyon, though stone lacks blood and flesh withers against time.

Swifts above, black crossbows in flight, are darting rim to rim. Swallows flock, skimming the river for flies.

The farther we walk down canyon, the more evidence of beaver we see. What remains of cottonwood trees, young and old, are sharpened stumps, some cut recently, others tarnished like silver. Brooke and I gather small, smooth sticks and place them as a poem along the bank. My native friends say beaver wood is medicine.

The canyon narrows. White sculpted boulders create a calm found in Zen gardens.

We can walk no farther. I sit on the sand and focus on the river. Standing waves become my meditation.

If the world ends, let me be here.

DAY THREE—GREEN NOTEBOOK

Green is not to be trusted. It is the color of water hoarded in plants. It is selfish, not kind or generous. Pinyon green is flamboyant. Juniper green is insecure. Pine green is pompous. The sharp green of yucca will slice an eye without blinking. Ocotilla is a green withheld in winter. Grass green is green glass broken waiting for bare feet. Repeat again as the river repeats, the Rio Grande is the green of opuntia, a gentler name for prickly pear, but just as disturbing. Green is the javelina's tongue after eating envy.

Big Bend is not a place of second chances. Even a blink will rob you of a sighting. Was that an owl? Did you see that flash of tail? A tumbleweed rolls in front of us. Things disappear quickly in the desert, especially the color green.

DAY FOUR—GREEN YELLOW NOTEBOOK
Lichen on cliff face igneous towers. Rock nettle. Dogweed. Evening primrose. Skeleton leaf goldeneye. Algerita rimmed with red. Green-yellow is the paint of plants that mimic butterflies gathered to drink: a two-tailed swallowtail; a lyside sulphur; a sandia hairstreak close enough to glean powder from wings. But it is the agave, silver-green that holds the pollen yellow for the bat in search of fruit. Last night, I dreamed the color I should seek is leaf-gold.

The day begins with a pair of cactus wrens and a cerulean sky. Hard to fathom "Snowmageddon" is blanketing the Northeast while the Southwest lives in drought. The Rio Grande runs so low in places that you can wade across it ankle-deep and be in Mexico. Climate-change deniers will soon disappear like the zealots who proclaimed the Earth was flat and the center of the universe.

Mayor de Blasio of New York has called for residents to "shelter in place." For a lizard to "shelter in place" means to hide under a rock when hot; for a javelina, it means be still as stone and black like lava and you will not be seen; for a jackrabbit, run zigzag. When visiting a national park, the average visitor stays fifty-seven hours before moving on: 2.4 days. A visitor to a natural park spends four to six hours a day outside; and if the park is historical, a visitor will spend only two to four hours a day outside. "Shelter in place" to humans may too often mean sitting in front of a television or computer screen, which is where the average American spends eight to ten hours a day.

Brooke and I walk to Dog Canyon. It is a six-mile saunter. Brooke takes off his clothes. I take off my shoes. We do not expect to see anyone today. The trail is not bone dry, but stone dry. We are walking inside a dry creek bed. Exposed roots, trying to stabilize the crumbling walls of the arroyo, create their own signatures of drought. The walls are now twelve feet high; and flash floods make for greater erosion. Cracked mud is the violence of heat waves made visible. The mirage we see dancing on the horizon is more than the tease of water, it is the illusion that what you want you will have.

Up ahead we see a cloud of skimmers, small orange butterflies gathered around a pothole filled with water. Blue-gray gnatcatchers are also stealing sips and fox tracks circle the tiny pool repeatedly.

I remember being told by my father when we were hiking in Utah's desert, "If you get thirsty, suck on a stone." He prided himself on not carrying water.

What is it about stones in a wash, on a beach, by a river that draws us down to pick one up and carry it home as a talisman? Do we infuse them with meaning or memory? A white stone round like the moon remains full like on the night we arrived; a stone the color of cinnamon reminds me of love; a black stone the shape of a comma will sit on my desk. The stone I pick up today is oval and pink, smooth between my fingers, warm in hand. It is a face without features. But when turned over, two eyes and an open mouth appear. Do any of us recognize ourselves for who we are? I consider my impact, hurtful and helpful to the places I call home. I cannot escape my demons. They follow me like heat waves.

The brutality of desiccated birds stiff in a dry riverbed dead from drought tells me the only essential thought in the desert is water.

My footprints walking up the wash are the ones I follow back. We are running out of water and stones to suck on will not be enough to quell our thirst. Water wars will make oil wars obsolete. Stones will be used to mark the graves of the dead. It's not so hard to imagine that scenario here in Dog Canyon, where water is scarce and bones are plenty.

In Texas, where cattle ranchers have ruled supreme, the question must be asked: how much water is being used to raise the cows we eat? The answer to this question is one of the reasons I no longer eat beef. Agricultural water in the Lone Star State accounts for 60 percent of total water usage. And the only thing in Texas more sacred than cows is oil. Add the increase of fracking for natural gas, now responsible for up to 25 percent of all water usage in the state, and Texans are realizing in this era of drought that excessive water use for beef or oil is suicide. In the last four years, the nation's leading beef state has lost 24 percent of its total cattle herds. The price of beef is down for sellers and up for consumers. The price of oil is down and dropping with a glut that serves no one.

More than thirty communities in Texas are running dry with sand in their faucets due to drought. In the town of Telingua, where Brooke and I had a drink with locals, this is what they were talking about in the Starlight Bar. The dirty secret they were telling is that water is being trucked into rural towns, and residents are drinking wastewater.

This morning at breakfast, Brooke and I asked for a glass of water. The waiter said, "Only if you are going to drink it, all of it. We're hurting out here. Water's no longer a giveaway."

"Climate change is the straw that is breaking Big Bend's back," a Park Service employee said to me. I believe her.

On the highway from El Paso a billboard reads, "Leave your cares at home. You're in Texas now." But the truth is the world is home and paradise is not around the bend. The Rio Grande is being called the Rio Sand. It is worth repeating.

I pass a young man on the trail of cracked mud.

"No shoes?"

"No, and the man behind me has no clothes."

I keep walking and then turn to look back. He turns at the same moment, scratching his head.

Brooke is a half mile behind me, turning toppled cairns into standing stones.

Rain in the west is falling in black streaks, evaporating before it ever reaches the ground. It has a name: Virga.

DAY FIVE—YELLOW NOTEBOOK

Yellow-rumped warblers; summer warblers, streaked; lesser goldfinches not lesser at all; marigolds; buttercups; cinquefoil in bloom; yellow cake cliffs uranium bright; yellow diamonds on black-tailed snakes, rattles shaking in ceremonial wakes; an amberwing dragonfly is caught by a shrike; yellow is lightning splitting grief; thunder follows the act of counting; yellow is the mountain lion hardest to find; the eye of Venus winks at dawn; the yellow rays that reach us is a fire lit.

What I know as a naturalist is that if you want to see wildlife, get up before dawn. Brooke and I rise several hours before the sun and drive toward Persimmon Gap near the Old Comanche Trail to see what animals might be present. Two stars evenly spaced like eyes peer over the Chisos Mountains; Gemini to be exact. It rained hard the night before. The pine-oiled perfume of creosote is strong.

The first line of light will not appear on the eastern horizon until 6:37 a.m. The sun will not awaken the desert until 7:55 a.m.

What happens in between?

A bull elk is caught in our headlights. He seems strangely out of place; we later learn they were introduced for "sport" in West Texas. A pair of coyotes are hunting in the wash. We see two white owls, barn owls, and many jackrabbits and cottontails darting across the road. And just as darkness is beginning to lift, four bobcat kittens cross in front of us, all legs.

For two hours, we sit on a hillside and watch light slowly come into the country. It is slow and subtle, a litany of yellow light, sun rays turning from yellow to orange to pink with clouds transposed from red to purple. We watch a black sky become indigo, then turquoise, then gold. And when the orange orb crests the horizon, birdsong erupts.

We follow the sun up Lost Mine Trail to the saddle, where a priestess made of stone raises her hands eastward. We count nine mountain ranges, one after the other, rolling toward the horizon like waves. Standing on the spine of the ridge, wide views fall on either side of us.

No map can orient us here. Where does America end and Mexico begin? This is its own country, borderless by nature, unowned, unbowed, complete. Boundaries are fears made manifest, designed to protect us. I don't want protection, I want freedom.

Wind is spirit. I feel it here. In Big Bend, we are walking on Sky Islands.

I am always astonished by where our legs can carry us. Brooke and I have been walking most of the day. I could walk forever with beauty. Our steps are not measured in miles but in the amount of time we are pulled forward by awe. This is another gift from our national parks, to be led by the vistas, to forget what nags us at home and remember what sustains us, the horizon.

Two red-tailed hawks soar over the valley.

Majesty. Not a word I often use. Today majesty is the length from where I stand to the summit of the mountain we are climbing. This mountain has majesty and holds its own authority above all others.

We have been joined by a fellow traveler from London. He rented a car to come from a business meeting in Austin to see Big Bend, a seven-hour drive. It feels good to walk, he tells us. We pass lizards on stone ledges. Ravens soar past as we continue to gain elevation.

"In London, there's nine million of us in a very tiny space. Here, there's a handful. That's it. I keep looking for people and instead, there are cactus and space. So much seemingly empty space. I am awestruck. It just puts everything in perspective." The man wipes his eyes. "I need more of this. What can I say? I'm just so grateful some people had the foresight to protect these lands for me and my children and their children for the future. I'm without words. It's very profound."

The man from London leaves us on the summit.

After a long interlude of silence, Brooke turns to me. "Are you ready to go?"

DAY SIX—ORANGE NOTEBOOK

Orange ball of sun, twisted wire of copper scorpions cross the border at Bocquilla for the price of six dollars spiked prickly pear with afternoon light orioles copperheads a coral snake caught between bands of black yellow orange monarch against blue orange are the fires burning the forests in Mexico now black with ash changes the sunsets vermillion like the flycatchers orange in the desert is the color water may become.

We have found an oasis in the desert. This shock of green belongs to a secret shared by Valerie Naylor. It was where she would go when she needed a reprieve from the heat and expanse of Big Bend back when she was a park naturalist, before becoming a superintendent in North Dakota.

"Sometimes you need the intimate places," she had told us from one of the long views in Theodore Roosevelt National Park, in Medora, North Dakota. "Sometimes in these big vistas, it's easy to lose track of yourself."

Brooke and I lean against boulders looking up at the waterfall, more of a weeping than a cascade, but emotive nonetheless. The sound of desert water reaches us as morning vespers. Longspur columbine, maidenhair ferns, and cardinal flowers frame the sound.

Band-tailed pigeons are cooing from the refuge of oaks. Green-tailed towhees are rustling in the underbrush. Quail are here, blue-gray gnat-catchers, lazuli buntings, and jays, both Mexican and scrub. All manner of warblers must flock here during spring migration to make this their home in the summer.

Saturated walls of water become hanging gardens of trumpet flowers and it is easy to imagine blue-throated hummingbirds buzzing the falls a few months from now, worthy of a return visit to see. In the time it takes to write this sentence, the wall of water turns blue, cobalt blue, defying common sense. It pays to sit and chart the changes within a morning, especially with a movable feast of light.

A pair of golden eagles circle this glint of sky. One of them is missing two primary wing feathers. I envy their range of vision. This canyon must cut deep into the geologic veins of the Chisos Mountains, adding to the mystique of these "sky islands" that rise precipitously from the valley floor, in some cases with a 4,500-foot elevation gain.

From the desert pavement of evenly spaced creosote and mats of prickly pear and ocotillo, and the broad dagger yuccas and sotol, the Chisos Mountains bring geographic relief—shade from pinyon and juniper forests and pockets of yellow pine.

For a naturalist, this is vertical natural history, where one life zone bleeds into another as it does when the desert meets the mountains. Javelinas who inhabit the lowlands are replaced by deer as the primary herbivore in the foothills. Black bears and bobcats and ring-tailed cats skirt the edges in the crepuscular hours of dawn and dusk. Peregrine falcons nest below the peaks and hunt in the valley.

We are blessed by the cool mist from the falls, and the tyranny of heat (even in January) is forgotten. Brooke and I curl inside each other and fall asleep. When I wake up, I think I am dreaming. The waterfall seems louder, fuller. Columbines are nodding in the breeze. Everything feels animated. Lines from W. S. Merwin's poem "Variation on a Theme" come to me:

> *Thank you my lifelong afternoon*
> *late in this season of no age*
> *thank you for my windows above the rivers*
> *thank you for the true love you brought me to*
> *when it was time at last for words*
> *that come out of silence and take me by surprise . . .*

Everything about Big Bend takes me by surprise.

The sound of water is behind us. We are back out in open terrain again.

I grab my hat before it blows away. The wind, always the wind—I turn around to locate its source. The canyon is tucked away but the rugged cliffs with their eroding faces are lined up like cousins. The Chisos are a force in progress, changing hourly in shadow and light. When the wind stops, the heat returns. Our pace quickens.

As we continue down canyon, the temperature rises and we take off layers. When I told Brooke I read that ground temperatures can be as hot as 180 degrees here in the Chihuahuan Desert, he said I needed stronger reading glasses. He said it was impossible. It's not. Air temperatures of 120 degrees are not uncommon in July and August, but if you were to touch the lava rocks on the playas near Castolon, you would be burned, wind or no wind. A boiling wind is imaginable.

Is wind the common presence within our national parks? I felt it in Effigy Mounds in the wing beats of ravens. I heard it in Gettysburg as ghosts; it runs on the backs of waves in Acadia like unbridled horses. And there were times in Theodore Roosevelt National Park when my father and I were unable to hear each other for the ferocity of the wind. In the Tetons, wind can be the most wicked force of all, blowing climbers off their routes in any season. But the winter winds are deadly, dropping temperatures to a bone-chill of sixty degrees below zero.

Any wind will tell you, it is impossible to escape.

Wind, water, light. These three things draw me into every national park I have visited. They are not qualities to be found but presences to be felt. Though wind can be unwelcome, it can also be a savior in summer. A whisper or a howl—what the wind knows, we can hear as an oracle or omen.

DAY SEVEN—RED NOTEBOOK

Red is the vermillion flycatcher the scarlet tanager the cardinal's tuft the robin's breast the skin burned a barrel cactus blooming the wet walls of Santa Elena the balanced rock the shock of sun the blood of snakes drunk by eagles a vulture's head fires blazing angry ants a volcano remembered a monarch seen a sky at morning a warning given a tick engorged the night eyes of coyote a man gunned down flashing lights the color of fear a ruby lost berries picked pictographs read.

Our correspondences can be read as in the red of a koan box made by my friend Lawrence Fodor, an artist who lives in New Mexico. I had seen his koan boxes in Marfa, Texas, and they intrigued me, both the saturation of color as well as what resides inside: a secret. The objects he places inside a sealed cigar box are personal: they are to remain a mystery. Only if the box is broken open can the contents be known. For Fodor, a koan box can begin as a palette thick with swirled paint and later become an art object. The palette I am interested in is the color vermillion. In Big Bend National Park, vermillion flycatchers became my obsession.

During the time I was exploring Big Bend, Lawrence and I were in conversation about a particular koan box. Emails can be a box, too, opened and shared with ideas explored.

On Thu, Feb 26, 2015, at 9:27 AM, Terry Tempest Williams wrote:

Dearest Lawrence:

Good morning. It's been so wonderful to dream about your Koan Boxes. The one that has remained with me is the vermillion box. The fire, the passion, the focus, all that burns in us as we create our work, our world together. I have always loved and feared the color red.

Koan Box Vermillion/Red/Green, 2012-13, 23kt yellow gold

This one, might it still be available?

What you have created with your boxes is something Dogen would honor, don't you think?

"The true eye of study"

Blessings,

Terry

On Thu, Feb 26, 2015, at 11:58 AM, Lawrence Fodor wrote:

Good Morning Terry,

I, too, have a curious relationship with the color red . . . while it compels me, it simultaneously repels me. But I seem always to be pursuing "the perfect red"—despite its utter elusiveness and impervious nature to fixed definitions. I think of all the colors—red, in its infinite varieties—has the most varied responses and reactions.

There is a lovely book titled, "Color—a Natural History of the Palette" by Victoria Finlay. It is a marvelous read as she describes her world travels and stories in search of the "origins" and histories of many colors. In the chapter on Red, she describes Pliny's version of the origins of vermillion as the result of an epic battle between a dragon and an elephant. In the story, the two were always fighting, and their struggles ended when the dragon coiled himself around the elephant, causing the elephant to lose his balance and fall on the dragon—crushing them both. The merging of their spilled blood created cinnabar—the basis for vermillion. It is the perfect metaphor for the chemical designation of cinnabar (a by product of mining mercury) which is equal parts mercury and sulphur. "Combined, the silver elephant and the yellow fire-breathing reptile miraculously make something that is blood red."

All through history red has been so significant, continually thrilling imaginations—how could it not? And it continues to do exactly that!

And while I am not certain that Dogen would have honored the Koan Boxes—that thought is captivating. The best boxes—always—are accomplished when I don't think about them as I paint.

Yes, the Vermillion/Red/Green Koan Box is hanging on my wall in the studio and available.

Thank you so much for the continued dialogue, the interest in acquiring a piece and our exchange of inspirations and imaginations.

With infinite appreciation,

L

On Mon, Mar 2, 2015, at 2:48 PM, Terry Tempest Williams wrote:
Dearest LF:

I have to tell you this: I went to Big Bend on Saturday for refreshment, my eyes needed a stretch from the near-sighted page.

Yesterday, I spent the morning at Santa Elena Canyon where a friend from Peru had asked me to take some water and merge it with the Rio

Grande. This I did humbly and not without consequence. When I poured the blessed water into the muddy river more green than blue, only a stone's throw from Mexico, each drop created a four-sided star that lit up water.

The bank where I was standing was steep and slippery and I had a hard time getting up, relying on the grace of grasses and roots to help me. By the time I returned to the mouth of the canyon on the beach, I was spent and laid on my back in the sand looking up at clouds and the signatures of swallows.

On my way back to the Chisos Basin, I saw a mature cottonwood grove, uncommon in the Chihauhuan desert, as you know. It required passage along a lonely dirt road. Something told me to go—which I did—and guess who was waiting inside: a vermillion flycatcher. I burst out laughing. I parked my car, walked over to him, quietly bowed and smiled. He stayed very near, doing what he does, cock his head to the side, watch for insects, fly to the ground, catch one in his beak, and fly back to his perch, repeating the gesture over and over again with great focus and intensity. I could not believe the flame of red feathers on top of his head. His brown mask and cloak defies any sense of hiding. He turns and a fire is set. The sun, the feathers, the bright shock of red, orange, vermillion—this tiny mysterious bird—a koan in its own right—Suddenly, I found myself encircled by six vermillion flycatchers, males and females, igniting the desert.

Your Koan Box Vermillion is speaking to me.

With gratitude and awe, Terry

On Mon, Mar 2, 2015, at 3:09 PM, Terry Tempest Williams wrote:
What color is an oracle?

On Wed, Mar 4, 2015, at 12:19 PM, Lawrence Fodor wrote:
Dear Terry,

I too escaped last Thursday. My partner John had a board retreat in Palm Springs for a literary foundation on whose board he sits, so I tagged along.

Instead of sitting by a pool, I rented a four wheel drive vehicle and drove to Joshua Tree National Park during the day on Friday and Saturday. I've not been since I was young . . .

While the main part of Joshua Tree is a fantastically surreal infinite diorama of diverse desert ecology—with the magnificent Joshua trees, Cholla cactus, Ocotillo and those precariously graceful massive boulder outcroppings—I spent as much time in some of the more remote and less crowded areas of the park. I entered via the south entrance where the road follows and crosses, several times, a large winding arroyo through Cottonwood Canyon . . . I stopped at several points along Cottonwood Canyon to explore the arroyo and get a closer look at the trees. I realized they were Palo Verde trees—and the red growth on them was Mistletoe berries— fully ripe and waiting to be consumed by the Phainopeplas (Feather or Black Flycatchers) that love and depend on the berries. The Black Flycatcher is not nearly as dynamic looking as a Vermillion Flycatcher, but the Mistletoe in the Palo Verde made up for the lack of "color" in the birds, who, unfortunately, didn't seem to appreciate me wanting to photograph their supper and its host. They flew off immediately as I approached. In the waning afternoon light with the sun coming and going through the high cirrocumulus clouds, timing, like in most circumstances, was critical. Luckily I was there in time and long enough to catch the fleeting sun before it set behind the high desert hills surrounding the canyon.

While reading your magical Big Bend adventure I was astonished, and yet I wasn't, that we were both on a solo track, simultaneously, of discovery in some of the most beautiful landscape in the country. The way I work, in all its intuitive configurations, is generally a trail of discovering via random wandering—either in the haunts of my studio or anywhere else I travel and explore. As artists, the beauty, and all the revelations therein, is in stumbling onto the unexpected when we are in the midst of looking/not looking for something else entirely—that sensorily aware state of not assuming anything, nor purposely looking for anything in particular but completely in touch with the moment and where we happen to be. And that is when we are afforded Vermillion Flycatchers or Palo Verde trees with red ripe mistletoe.

I loved your story of mixing the waters and the resulting stars! When I utterly give myself over to discovery, without pretense or expectations, nature always seems to validate and verify my path.

We are so fortunate to be on the planet, to be able to wander and to experience these marvelously complicated yet simple wonders.

Warmest regards,

L

On Wed, Mar 4, 2015, at 12:27 PM, Terry Tempest Williams wrote:
Isn't that true, the magic of wandering, or as Thoreau put it "sauntering." I, too, love that you were at Joshua Tree on your own trek of solace with "the Palo Verde trees with red ripe mistletoe" while I was in Big Bend. I do love the phainopeplas . . . I've never been to Joshua Tree, but want to—Thank you for taking me there through color.

Back at my desk, now in the process of translation from the eye to the page—I wonder if that is how you make art as well—by way of translation.

Always, the attempt to get it right and the realization we never can.

And then, there is always the surprise—

Six more days of heaven in West Texas—Have you stayed in the stone cottages in Chisos Basin? There is a photograph on the wall of Lady Bird Johnson looking very chic with Stewart Udall, the Secretary of the Interior, trailing behind her on the Lost Mine Trail. How am I ever going to leave? How can I beg to return?

xxx

Terry

DAY EIGHT—PINK NOTEBOOK

Sierra del Carmen is a pink-banded fortress, a prism of light; the pink voice
of doves; pursed lips of peccaries; open gills of bass; my body next to Brooke;
Boquillas Canyon at noon; limestone blushing; western coach whiptail
covered in sand; ears of mice; frogs pink from fright jumping toward water;
an eagle claw cactus draws pale blood with its spines; a paleface rosemallow
lures ants, rock wrens who eat them; trailing windmills are flowers not relics,
a bouquet of pink phlox blooms underfoot.

The Rio Grande is more than a border between the United States and Mexico,
it is home for some three dozen species of fish: longnose gar, gizzard shad,
roundnose minnow, flathead minnow, speckled chub, blue tilapia, Mexican
tetra, Mexican stoneroller, Tamaulipas shiner, Chihuahua shiner, Rio Grande
shiner, red shiner, bluntnose shiner, longnose dace, carp, river carpsucker, blue
sucker, smallmouth buffalo, gray redhorse, blue catfish, channel catfish, flathead catfish, American eel, plains killifish, mosquitofish, goldfish, warmouth,
bluegill, green sunfish, longear sunfish, redear sunfish, largemouth bass,
freshwater drum, Rio Grande perch, tidewater silverside, and the Big Bend
gambusia.

The Big Bend gambusia (*Gambusia gaigei*) is on the endangered species
list, a minnow two inches long, endemic to Big Bend National Park. Historically, it occurred in only two spring systems: Boquillas Canyon and Rio
Grande Village. Today it is found in only two small ponds in Rio Grande
Village, the largest campground and RV park in Big Bend. This tiny species
of fish now covers "the smallest geographic range of any vertebrate species in
the world."

The gambusia minnow is related to other live-bearing fish most often associated with aquariums, like the guppy, the molly, and the swordtail. They belong to an ancient family of fish known as Poeciliidae that have been on this planet for more than 100 million years.

What is the life of a minnow worth? The desert has its own currency and it is measured in water.

The Big Bend gambusia was first discovered at Boquillas Spring in 1928. The following year, the species was described by the biologist Carl L. Hubbs. Shortly thereafter, the spring dried up and the Big Bend gambusia was considered extinct.

However, in 1954, a small population of *Gambusia gaigei* was miraculously found just a mile away from Boquillas in another spring-fed pond on the edge of Rio Grande Village. But the development pressures within Big Bend National Park gave the construction of a large campground, grocery store, and gas station priority over a threatened minnow. The gambusia were also vulnerable to competing species like the mosquitofish thrown into the same pond by fishermen.

Gambusia gaigei at its lowest ebb had been reduced to three individuals: one female and two male. The tiny fish was listed as an endangered species under the Endangered Species Preservation Act of 1966. Critical measures were taken by people who cared.

Roland H. Wauer worked as the chief naturalist at Big Bend National Park during the epic story of the gambusia's survival. He and his colleague Roger Siglin collected more than 250 Big Bend gambusias from the main pond and created another pond exclusively for them, with a pump to regulate water flow and temperature. As a safeguard, they transported a hundred of the collected gambusia into a park aquarium. And once again, the pond was fouled with other fish and more minnows died. The population was again perilously close to extinction.

With the Endangered Species Act of 1973, greater protection was given to the Big Bend gambusia, but the allotted funds for habitat restoration were not adequate and the fish continued to falter.

Under careful watch by the Park Service, the aquarium gambusia were reintroduced into the pond again. This time, Wauer wrote a new message and posted it on a sign, hoping to appeal to the conscience and consciousness of visitors and fishermen.

The sign read: "FISH SO FRAGILE—This pond contains the world's population of *Gambusia gaigei*. These minnow-sized fish have lived here since Mastodons. Unique and fragile, they survive only because man wants to make it so."

In 1984, the staff of Big Bend National Park in cooperation with scientists at the University of Texas and with the Rio Grande Fishes Recovery Team, and with support from the U.S. Fish and Wildlife Service, created a comprehensive management plan for the minnow that included careful and consistent monitoring of the ponds for water quality; invasive species; and habitat protection. And for now, the *Gambusia gaigei* population at Rio Grande Village has been stabilized.

In 2012, the U.S. Fish and Wildlife Service issued a five-year review of the Big Bend gambusia, as required by the Endangered Species Act, and documented "several thousand" gambusia living in the two ponds at Rio Grande Village.

But collective vigilance is required. And the report concluded that because of the desert minnow's isolated and limited location, small numbers, and short life span of one year, combined with a barely adequate water flow and the temperature range (between ninety-two and ninety-five degrees Fahrenheit) required for a healthy population, an increased probability of extinction in the wild was likely. One flood, one malfunction of the pump system, one outbreak of disease or infiltration of an exotic species like the blue tilapia from Mexico could sink the Big Bend gambusia forever.

The five-year review also stated that although the effects of climate change are difficult to predict, "projections suggest the southwest United States may experience the greatest temperature increase of any area in the lower 48 states . . . exacerbating a region already plagued by low rainfall, high temperatures and unsustainable water use practices."

Consider the ponds that hold the shimmering lives of *Gambusia gaigei* holy.

I visited these two ephemeral ponds, where variegated meadowhawks skim the water and scarlet tanagers sing from the edges of cattails as swimming gambusia flash silver below—adjacent to the hubbub of the campground and RV park. What struck me as I witnessed these tiny fish the size of my little finger was not the miracle of their existence and how they have survived us against all odds, but how the eight hundred thousand acres of wildlands that constitute Big Bend become a moral framework for the significance of national parks.

Habitat saves species and so do people. Our national parks are a sanctuary movement for the wild. Under the watchful eye of El Pico in the Sierra del Carmen, one pond protected and another pond built by a naturalist created a revolution for a minnow.

On a rock in Boquillas Canyon, someone has left a black crocheted rosary with wooden beads. Footprints lead to the river very near where a pool of *Gambusia gaigei* once thrived.

Our fate, like the fate of all species, is determined by chance, by circumstance, and by grace.

DAY NINE—PURPLE NOTEBOOK

Purple prickly pear mountain range after range grackle sheen rock roots of trees berry cries of curve billed thrashers mockingbirds mimicking bluebonnets

in wind dinosaur plum footprints fossils and shells left inside limestone yellow
contrast with red violet blue the veins of bat wings transparent in moonlight
purple ink with stars a meteor streaking words

I have been thinking about bats, because we have not seen any here, not one. This is the price of coming to Big Bend in winter. It's too cold, the nights belong to stars. Most of the bats are in hibernation, asleep in a cave or crease in a canyon wall. Even so, I imagine seeing any one of the twenty-two species of bats recorded here, particularly the small pipistrelle with its black mask, eyes to ears, and its reddish to light brown fur and dark wings. We know them in Utah as vesper bats, who offer high-pitched prayers at dusk. Two pennies rubbed together as a copper screech will draw them close.

In caves high in the Chisos Mountains near Emory Peak lives the endangered Mexican long-nosed bat. It is found nowhere else in the park. In the heat of the summer, this bat will swoop down to a century plant that grows for a hundred years and then blooms once in its lifetime. At dusk, the Mexican long-nosed bat drinks the precious nectar.

The Colima warbler also resides only in the Chisos after migrating seven hundred miles in April from Colima, Mexico. Birders will climb the arduous South Rim trail to get a glimpse of its white eye-ring and yellow rump in the otherwise gray bird. In 1977, an Aztec thrush was sighted in Boot Canyon, a rarity reserved for the highlands of Mexico, where the elusive songbird keeps its own counsel.

Who knows what other species come and go without notice? The trail we walked up this morning to see Balanced Rock did not reveal the mountain lion's rosette tracks we saw coming down. We were followed. They say those who live among tigers wear masks on the backs of their heads when they walk, giving the big cats behind them their own sense of being watched.

Desert strategies are useful: In times of drought, pull your resources inward; when water is scarce, find moisture in seeds; to stay strong and supple, send a taproot down deep; run when required, hide when necessary; when hot go underground; do not fear darkness, it's where one comes alive.

DAY TEN—BROWN NOTEBOOK

Elk brown deer rat mice stone face of the Chisos skin of border muddy banks the Rio Grande is a meandering script hermit thrush singing inside a thicket of thorns an old wool blanket hanging on a fence post mistaken for a shepherd with goats brown white black gopher snake glossy snake bull snake hognosed a scorpion's tail when color disappears into shadows it becomes brown dull invisible.

I love the word "tinaja"—earthen jar. In canyon country it translates to potholes—where rain is held in the cupped hands of stone, home to fairy shrimp, diving beetles, and water boatmen. This is where life gathers—and, in the language of the desert, drinks deeply from the depressions.

The land is rain-blessed this morning with chartreuse lichen glistening on Casa Grande. The cactus are plump. Roadrunners upright turn horizontal with speed. Lizards vanish. Snakes coil. The desert feels anything but dormant. After rain, Big Bend self-corrects, begins anew, bluebonnets burst forth. Lavender dares to become violet.

It is a day of angled light and flat-bottomed clouds floating in a turquoise sky. We are walking in a canyon akin to Utah's sandstone fins. A whitewashed ledge foreshadows a peregrine. We watched a prairie falcon yesterday. Birdsong is an electric current lighting up the trail. And perched inside a desert persimmon bush, a black-throated sparrow sings to the small black fruits, shiny with morning dew.

The skeleton of a snake picked clean by a shrike hangs from a fence post as a necklace of bones.

Yucca with leaves like quivering swords stand next to cholla, the devil's club. In the desert, success is the understanding of limits. One false move and you die. You can't talk your way out of thirst. Bare skin burns. Face-to-face with a spitting rattlesnake, the only thing you have to negotiate is your escape. There are rules in the desert. Pay attention. Adapt or perish.

Big Bend is no place for cynics. There is too much at stake. A bedrock pragmatism refutes sentimentality through the beauty of the unexpected. What we mistake as sentimental is in fact a generosity, a willingness to stay open and acknowledge the miraculous.

Cynicism flourishes in air-conditioned rooms. Like any true place, the desert is a risk. Back into a barrel cactus and you may get hurt. But touch its yellow flowers with petals like wax and the pain from its needles lessens. Our fear of being touched removes us from a sensate world. The distant self becomes the detached self who no longer believes in anything.

Awe is the moment when ego surrenders to wonder. This is our inheritance—the beauty before us. We cry. We cry out. There is nothing sentimental about facing the desert bare. It is a terrifying beauty.

———

Beyond the arch made of balanced rocks is a landscape of sleeping dragons, mountains not yet roused by spring.

DAY ELEVEN—BLACK NOTEBOOK

Black as raven in midnight's feathers; black as desert in the absence of moon; black as lava in mountain tombs; black as the eye of chickadee in cap and chin; black as the headdress of roadrunner raised; black as the slit in Dog Canyon at noon; black as javelina's black patent hooves; black as ice in winter's break; black as bear and bats in caves; black as a widow casting her web; black sees light.

The desert is not a void. It is my unknowing.

DAY TWELVE—WHITE NOTEBOOK

White datura awakened by dreams calls forth moths drenched in pollen light
Moon and stars on water moves bright yucca stalks a canyon's mind White is
white if the eye is to believe a cottontail in motion is a life saved by speed.
Clouds cotton delusion becomes white rich with tales: Once upon a time white
wolves and camels lead soldiers back from war. In the desert, the mirage of
water as angels is replaced with sandstone the color of everything broken.

My notebook is painted with rabbit blood in one Sumi brushstroke. The morning did not begin as planned. I was prepared to walk to the Mules Ears, two volcanic plugs that have eroded into a seismic view that shakes the horizon.

Fog filled the Chisos Basin where I was staying and it was a dramatic descent into clouds. All along the road, cottontails darted in and out and I had to slow way down not to hit them. I wondered who was benefiting from the explosion of rabbits, perfect packets of protein.

Near the Upper Burrow Mesa Pour-off Trail, I saw something standing in the road. It was a red-tailed hawk with her talons clamped on a freshly killed cottontail. The rabbit's head was facing the Chisos, its ears resting back on its body, the long back legs in direct alignment with its head. It was a perfect portrait of predator and prey.

The hawk and the rabbit were close, but I wanted details. Through my binoculars the red-tail had a crest, something I had not noticed before, nor had I appreciated the sharp point of her beak and the bright yellow cere above it. The hawk's beak breaks the skull like an ice pick, beak to brain, beak to brain; red flesh is being eaten in small bites. Plucked rabbit fur is pulled apart from the muscle cartwheels across the road. Beak to brain. Tear, gulp, tear.

The raptor eats the eyes more slowly. And then, in three gulps, she swallows the ears whole. In less than five minutes, the rabbit's head has been devoured.

The shoulders are next. The hawk pulls out from the rabbit one long red strand and for a moment, predator and prey appear joined by an umbilicus.

The back legs of the rabbit are now crossed, relaxed, a headless offering.

Red-tail tightens her grip, ripping and pulling each strip of sinew and muscle with a measured ferocity, swallowing each tender whole. The hawk looks up, waits, her eyes focused on the horizon, then drags the rabbit off the road to the soft shoulder and doesn't move. Several minutes later, a truck passes. The red-tail flies down the slope with the rabbit clutched in her talons, trailing him like a bloody flag, barely clearing a yucca white with bloom. The hawk lands on an open patch of desert pavement, rearranges the rabbit, and then, beak to flesh, beak to flesh, finishes the cottontail that she has been eating, leaving behind a coil of intestines. Patches of fur now take flight as feathers. The red-tailed hawk takes three jumps before becoming airborne once again.

GATES OF THE ARCTIC

NATIONAL PARK, ALASKA

-‹‹- -››-

There is no private space

THE GATES OF THE ARCTIC ARE OPEN.

We arrived by wings.

A seaplane named Otter delivered us—

It was here, a yellow-billed loon called from the lake.

It was here, a circle of white wolves—five on the flanks of the mountain—appeared.

It was here, an emissary of crowned caribou emerged from a fold in the land.

FACING PAGE *Photograph by Sebastião Salgado / Amazonas images*

————

We arrived before the snows.

The tundra was red, gold, and green.

My presence was dark. I had just signed a restraining order against my brother, not because of him, but because of me. I was afraid for both of us. My heart had become a violence, a ticking time box that forgets nothing and holds everything red.

The tundra was red and gold with blueberries.

I picked blueberries with the bears, each of us keeping our distance. There were more than enough to share.

I was with friends and my husband, Brooke, who knew enough to let me be.

This is wilderness, to walk in silence.

This is wilderness, to calm the mind.

————

This is wilderness, my return to composure.

There was a mountain shaped like a pyramid. Each day, I sat before it. Each day, something happened. Changing light from the changing weather animated the geometry of the slope. A bear walked by. Cotton grass swayed in the breeze. Down feathers tumbled across the tundra. Morning frost melted quickly. The mountain was a glorious indifference, a repeating grace, a geologic fortress that softened in the shadows.

I walked toward the mountain. I climbed its talus slope, rocks wavering with each step. It was arduous. I kept going. My imagination reached the summit before my legs. The view was vast. I was small. I found relief.

We handed my brother's gun to the sheriff in Wyoming. What we didn't know is that in Wyoming, it is a felony to take another man's gun. We took my brother's gun. We were detained at the Teton County Jail. Felony charges were pending.

I care about my brother.

I care about wilderness.

To care is to lament.

———

My brother is a wilderness, unknowable.

Sitting with the mountain, I gain strength. A stability of soul is transmitted.

Stillness is an abiding presence in the form of a fox watching, waiting for a hare. The hare is hidden from the fox, also waiting, watching for the moment to flee. The mountain remains when both are gone.

What happens when wilderness is gone?

What will remain?

Great pains are taken for those we love: Brother. Wilderness. Fox and hare.

To take pains suggests a sustained carefulness, an effort to see that nothing is overlooked but that every small detail receives attention, as to "take pains with fine embroidery."

Before the Great Mountain this sentence comes to mind: "Weave grasses together for no reason and you will find God."

In wilderness, there is no reason, and so I weave grasses.

In our species, there is no reason, and so we go mad.

The grasses I am weaving together remove me from my mind, my terrible, violent, creative mind. The storm brewing inside me is passing. I have made a small mat of grass as a resting place for larks.

In wilderness, we are defined by the body, not the mind.

Yet, still, I, you, we

lament [l*uh*-**ment**]
1. to feel or express sorrow or regret for.
2. to mourn for or over.
3. to feel, show, or express grief.
4. a formal expression of sorrow or mourning, in verse or song; an elegy or dirge.
Synonyms for lament: bewail, bemoan, deplore.
Synonyms for wilderness: desert, waste, wild.

Gates of the Arctic is one of these.

And what is a synonym for wild?

My brother. He would love it here. If only he could see this. The horizon belongs to Rothko. Rothko, who committed suicide after completing his chapel in Houston. Fourteen canvases. Purple in one light; black in another; maroon at dawn. When I stood before one of Rothko's panels at dusk, the north painting, it became a portal—a wilderness—an ocean—the universe. And for a moment, I was unafraid of death.

Our species is committing suicide—that is a choice—and in the process, we are causing others pain.

Who cares?

Who cares about this wilderness?

This glorious indifference?

In the afternoon, I began crossing a deep, dry creek bed that if followed would lead to the river below our camp, when I noticed a thin line of water had begun trickling down from the snowfield above. I decided to wait for the rivulet and see how long it took to reach me, and when it did, I walked with the water, stopping now and again to watch the water pool behind a small gathering of stones until more drops from the melting snowpack joined them. The water pooled long enough to raise red birch leaves like boats until they, too, spilled over the tiny ledge of a flat rock in a rush of water, gaining momentum as the trail of snow tears widened and pooled again, eventually filling half the streambed, advancing pebbles along its way. And as I followed the leading edge of the rivulet that was now accepting rain, I could hear its faint, emerging voice, announcing itself to the river.

It is in our nature to survive.

My brother will survive.

Our relationship will survive.

The irony of our existence is this: We are infinitesimal in the grand scheme of evolution, a tiny organism on Earth. And yet, personally, collectively, we are changing the planet through our voracity, the velocity of our reach, our desires, our ambitions, and our appetites. We multiply, our hunger multiplies, and our insatiable craving accelerates.

Consumption is a progressive disease.

We believe in more, more possessions, more power, more war. Anywhere, everywhere our advance of aggression continues.

My aggression toward myself is the first war.

———————

Wilderness is an antidote to the war within ourselves.

In Gates of the Arctic, following caribou tracks, I am finding peace.

Would you believe me if I told you I was skipping?

We came by wings.

Our ability to travel is a privilege. But it is also a choice. Money is time. Where do we spend our time? Wilderness is not my leisure or my recreation. It is my sanity.

These valleys, these rivers—creased, folded, and pushed. What wisdom mountains house. My God—they are Gods. My God has feet of Earth. We are flickering moths in migration.

In a circumference of beauty, we join the dilemma of the Little Prince: Where do we turn our chairs? Where do we set our gaze?

The yellow-billed loon alone on the lake: Does she know her numbers are few, that she is a candidate for care under the Endangered Species Act?

The tribe of white wolves meeting on the mountain: Do they know they are an open target for helicopter hunters crossing boundaries no one can enforce?

The emissaries of caribou, crowned and rising: Can they taste the oil bubbling up through the melting permafrost?

The legacy of the Wilderness Act is a legacy of care. It is the act of loving beyond ourselves, beyond our own species, beyond our own time. To honor wildlands and wild lives that we may never see, much less understand, is to acknowledge the world does not revolve around us. The Wilderness Act is an act of respect that protects the land and ourselves from our own annihilation.

The tundra is red and ripe with blueberries. Bears with blue-stained tongues, just like mine, anticipate the winter.

It is in our nature to survive.

My brother asked me for help. What I gave him instead was rage.

I am addicted to rage.

My brother and I are both addicts. If you looked into our eyes, you would see no difference. We are not bad people. We are people who feel badly about things we have done.

Sex. Money. Oil. Drink. Aren't we all addicted to something, someone, some secret shame we harbor?

In wilderness, there is no shame.

In wilderness there is acceptance in the evolutionary processes of life. No plant or animal petitions for mercy. There are no complaints rendered or excuses made. There is only the forward movement of life and the inevitable end.

The end of wilderness scares me.

I am unsteady on my feet. Tussocks on the tundra covered in dwarf willow bring me to my knees. My eyes drop down to the level of lichen, reindeer lichen, and I note the branching of one is reminiscent of another. I look up. Nothing. Everything.

With the help of my hands, I rise and keep walking toward the knoll, visible from camp. Brooke is ahead of me. We scramble up scree. From the top, we count five drainages and three lakes, knowing from the map that there are four more beyond our view. It is this kind of scale that protects us from smugness. At our feet, a bleached caribou antler embedded in the ground appears as a graceful curve.

We fall asleep on a bed of bones—bird bones, rabbit bones, the bones of voles—and nestle inside each other as we have a thousand times in wild places. The small feathers that remain beneath the whitewashed outcropping of stone, a testament to death, suggest the perch we found for ourselves is also the perch of falcons, eagles, or owls.

My brother bands birds of prey during fall migration. As I am in the Arctic, he is on Commissary Ridge in the Salt River Range in western Wyoming, where it is not unusual to see 125 golden eagles pass through in a matter of days. He told me before our splintering that it takes three men to hold an eagle down while placing a band around its leg. He described the day he watched an eagle from afar, who was watching him, as he twirled a pigeon on a string above his head like a feathered lasso designed to catch the eagle's eye and lure him in; how the eagle, a mile and a half out, became a winged torpedo directed toward the prey, focused and deadly, and as my brother held steady, the eagle swooped down feetfirst toward him and the pigeon. I forgot the rest of the details, only that somehow, stoically, he held the great bird in its protest long enough for others to help him place a silver band around its ankle that would later glisten against a rain-hungry desert.

————

"Sorry to interrupt," our friend Kyle said, appearing on the knoll and out of breath, "but I wanted to be three instead of one." He had startled us awake. We sat up from our bed of bones. Below us was a grizzly, upright.

Brooke stood; the bear caught him in view and dropped on all fours and ran a few yards, turned, stood up again, faced us, sniffed the air, and then fell into a gallop across the terrain of dwarf birch, willows, and black spruce, never looking back. We watched the golden bear until she became a point of light moving across the great expanse. Who knows who else was watching us.

"Traditional Koyukon people live in a world that watches in a forest with eyes," writes Richard Nelson in *Make Prayers to the Raven*. "A person moving through nature—however wild, remote, even desolate the place may be— is never truly alone."

We are in a country of eyes.

We are walking in a country of eyes; a world intimately known by the Inupiat people, the Koyukon people, and the people who came before them. There is no such thing as a wilderness without humans. Our imprint on the land is a matter of time and scale and frequency.

The Gates of the Arctic Wilderness sits inside a national park bearing the same name. Covering more than 7 million acres, including much of the Brooks

Range, it is bordered to the west by the Noatak Wilderness, making this the largest contiguous wilderness area in the United States. Go east and you will find the Arctic National Wildlife Refuge. Go northwest and you will cross into the National Petroleum Reserve. Within this national park, native lands remain intact where native people exercise their subsistence rights as they have done for generations. Nothing exists in isolation, especially not wilderness.

How do we find our way back to a world interrelated and interconnected, whose priority is to thrive and evolve? What kind of belief systems are emerging now that reinforce and contribute to a world increasingly disconnected from nature? And what about the belief—my belief—in all that is wild?

I return to the wilderness to remember what I have forgotten, that the world can be wholesome and beautiful, that the harmony and integrity of ecosystems at peace is a mirror to what we have lost.

My brother and I became lost to each other. Isolation was the trigger. Isolation is always the trigger behind a gun, a drink, or a war.

Wilderness is not a place of isolation but contemplation. Refuge. Refugees. In the years to come, there will be less of one and more of the other. Communities up north in villages like Kaktovik on the edge of the Beaufort Sea are at risk of losing their livelihoods on the ice, the melting ice. The Inupiak and the polar bears now moving inland are watchful and waiting, trying to adapt.

———

Have you heard the thrumming of the Earth? It is here.

This morning, while we were drinking tea, a short-eared owl banked its underdown and quill so close to us her beauty and power startled. Death is a talon away.

Was my brother safe?

Am I?

Wilderness is a knife that cuts through pretense and exposes fear. Even in remote country, you cannot escape your mind.

The call of the wild is not what you hear but what you follow.

I want to follow the owl and dare to touch that which threatens to kill us—

"Wait, I see something—" say the Koyukon.

Wilderness is the surprise of tenderness. The relationship we think is destroyed can be restored.

———

Perhaps this is the definition of pristine: a sustained integrity; a vow of health and renewal; an ecological body of knowledge uncorrupted.

My brother, this wilderness, and I are approaching a pristine place of understanding.

In wilderness, I see my authentic reflection in the eyes of Other: an owl, a caribou, a bear.

My brother is Other, and so am I.

Can we love ourselves enough to change?

This was the question my brother and I asked ourselves on a morning walk in the Tetons before we broke apart.

This is the question I am asking myself again.

I have not seen my brother since I passed through the Gates of Wilderness.

———

I await his return. He awaits mine.

The scales of equilibrium can be found in wilderness.

A feather can tip the balance.

It is time to forgive—

my brother, myself, this wilderness.

I want another chance.

Change is coming.

The Great Mountain I have been watching, courting, studying as my mentor, is shivering. Rocks are falling. A small slide is apparent. Snow is accumulating on the pyramid peak, threatening to erase it, and there is a quality emanating from this massive presence that I recognize as reverence. Nine caribou are traversing the white-tipped tundra. They stop and stand resolute in the deepening storm. When the winds arrive, and they will, this quieting will become a blizzard capable of taking our lives.

———

I am facing the mountain, this glorious indifference.

I am watching as someone is watching me.

Wilderness is the source of what we can imagine
and what we cannot—the taproot of consciousness.

It will survive us.

GULF ISLANDS NATIONAL

SEASHORE, FLORIDA AND

MISSISSIPPI

⤙⤙ ⤚⤚

what more shall we do to others. To otherness

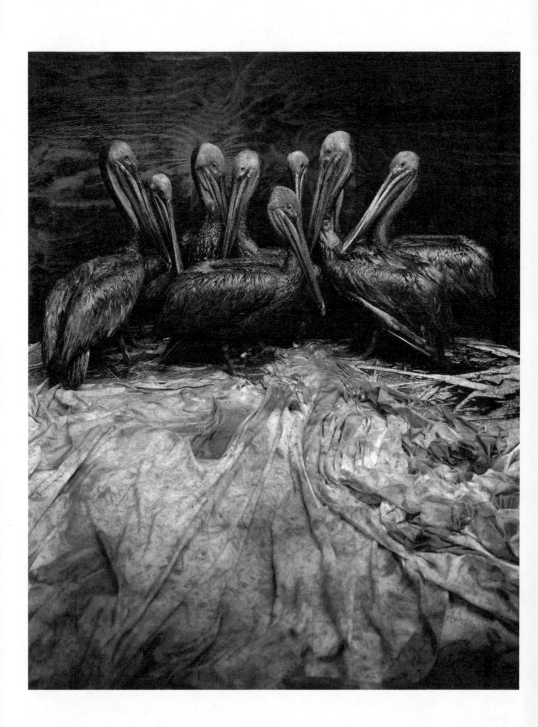

I T FELT FIVE YEARS TOO LATE. On July 2, 2015, the oil giant British Petroleum announced an $18.7 billion settlement to be made to all federal, state,
and local claims against them for damages incurred from the Deepwater
Horizon oil spill in the Gulf of Mexico in 2010. It was the largest environmental settlement in our nation's history, bringing to a close thousands of legal
cases brought by the Gulf states, which were ravaged financially, socially, and
ecologically by the millions of gallons of oil spewed into their coastal waters.
In the settlement, BP admitted they were at fault, and that environmental
crimes had been committed. And that in fact, ultimately, when the claims are
met and penalties are paid, the costs for the oil company may actually run as
much as $54 billion.

It is easy to hail this as good news. And this, too:

In 2012, Congress passed the Resources and Ecosystem Sustainability,
Tourism, Opportunities, and Revived Economies of the Gulf Coast States Act
(also referred to as the RESTORE Act). Tom Kiernan, past president of the
National Parks Conservation Association, wrote to their members: "This bi-
partisan legislation ensures that 80 percent of the Clean Water Act penalty pay-
ments stemming from the BP oil spill will be directed toward environmental

restoration and economic development in the Gulf region, including national parks like Gulf Islands National Seashore, Jean Lafitte National Historical Park, and Padre Island National Seashore, where the health of the Gulf is directly linked to the health of the parks."

But then one remembers the magnitude of the devastation. The Gulf Island National Seashore, with its barrier islands and surrounding waters, was affected by the BP oil spill in inexplicable ways. And so were the other seven national parks located in the Gulf of Mexico: Biscayne National Park (FL), Everglades National Park (FL), Dry Tortugas National Park (FL), Big Cypress National Preserve (FL), De Soto National Memorial (FL), Jean Lafitte National Historical Park and Preserve (LA), and Padre Island National Seashore (TX). And if we look at how many of our national parks, monuments, scenic rivers, and seashores are vulnerable to oil spills, it is worth reflecting back to the BP oil disaster as a cautionary tale.

I went to the Gulf Coast during the spill as a reporter in July 2010. Before I arrived, all I knew about the spill was what we'd been told:

- April 20, 2010: The Macondo Well blowout occurred approximately five thousand feet below the surface of the Gulf of Mexico, causing the BP-Transocean drilling platform Deepwater Horizon to explode, killing eleven workers and injuring seventeen others.
- Five million barrels of crude oil were released into the sea from the BP blowout. An average of sixty thousand barrels a day were escaping from the well until the gusher was capped on July 15, 2010.
- Six hundred and thirty-one miles of the Gulf Coast shoreline had been oiled: 364 miles in Louisiana, 110 miles in Mississippi, 69 miles in Alabama, and 88 miles in Florida.
- There had been 411 controlled burns on the surface of the sea to get rid of the oil, killing thousands of sea turtles and dolphins, with the number of deaths greatly underreported.

- Four hundred species of wildlife were threatened by the spill, including marine life such as plankton, whales, dolphins, sea turtles, tuna, and shrimp; dozens of species of birds including brown pelicans and piping plovers; land animals such as gray fox and white-tailed deer; and amphibians, the alligator, and the snapping turtle.

- Eight million feet of absorbent boom had been used to contain the oil spill in the Gulf of Mexico. Four million feet of containment boom had also been set around islands and shorelines for protection.

- Two million gallons of a dispersant called Corexit had been applied on the surface of the sea and below to break up the oil. It was produced by Nalco Holding Company, a corporation with ties to BP and Exxon. On May 10 the EPA gave BP twenty-four hours to find a less toxic alternative. Corexit's known toxicity, acknowledged following its use in the *Exxon Valdez* oil spill, was refuted by BP. The EPA's request was ignored.

- On May 25, the EPA gave BP a directive to scale back their spraying of the sea with dispersants. The Coast Guard overlooked the EPA's edict and granted BP seventy-four exemptions in forty-eight days, essentially rubber-stamping their continued routine use of Corexit 9500.

- An army of individuals paid by BP and the U.S. government were deployed in the Gulf of Mexico to protect and clean up vital shorelines: 17,500 National Guard troops and 42,500 BP workers. More than 5,300 private boats with their own captains registered with BP and were being paid to look for oil. The beginning rate for a twenty-foot vessel was $1,400 a day, $200 per crew member.

- August 3–5: BP officials reported that a permanent stop to the spill was now in place. Crews plugged the gusher with drilling mud and then concrete. Two relief wells at depths of 17,864 and 15,963 feet were then being drilled to ensure a secure and final closure of the well.

- Amid claims that the oil in the Gulf was nearly gone, an article in the August 19 issue of *Science* reported the presence of a plume of hydrocarbons at least twenty-two miles long and more than three thousand feet below the surface of the Gulf of Mexico, a residue of the Macondo Well blowout. The plume was described as moving in a southwesterly direction at a rate of about 6.5 kilometers a day.

I was angry. Living in the American West, I understand the oil and gas industry, both its political power in states like Utah, Wyoming, and North Dakota and its lack of regard for the safety of workers. Broken necks and backs are commonplace injuries. So are lost fingers. And when blowouts occur—just like Deepwater Horizon, only on land, not water—people die from exploding rigs. Production is paramount, at the expense of almost everything else.

And I have seen the environmental degradation that results from collusion between government agencies and oil companies. Federal regulations are relaxed or ignored, putting the integrity of our public lands at risk. Ecological health is sacrificed for financial gain. This sense of entitlement among oil companies supported by Congress has direct results on the ground: burning slag pools; ozone warnings; contaminated water wells flushed with benzene; and loss of habitat for sage grouse, prairie dogs, and pronghorn antelope. The scars on the fragile desert of southeastern Utah, from endless road cuts to the sheared oil patches themselves, will take decades to heal.

After months of watching the news coverage of the blowout and the subsequent oil spill, I did not trust what we were being told by BP or the Obama administration. Nor did I believe this was simply a local issue. I had to go to the Gulf of Mexico to see for myself what I felt from afar: this catastrophic moment belonged to all of us.

On July 28, 2010, I traveled to the Gulf Coast with two friends: Avery Resor, a recent graduate of Duke University who majored in environmental science, and Bill Weaver, a seasoned filmmaker from Montgomery, Alabama, who now lives in British Columbia. Avery grew up on her family's cattle ranch in Wilson, Wyoming. She was twenty-four years old then and biked wherever and whenever she could. Her name tied her to a deep family history rooted in Louisiana: Avery Island, famous for Tabasco sauce. Bill has dedicated his life to making films that illuminate issues of environmental and social justice. He is quiet and nimble; when he rolls his camera, you don't know it.

We arrived on the hundredth day of the oil spill and stayed until the "static kill" was complete. We sniffed out stories and followed them. We listened and we engaged. I took notes. Avery took pictures. Bill filmed. We smelled the oil in the air and felt it in the water. People along the Gulf Coast were getting sick and sicker. Marshes burned. Oysters were scarce and shrimp tainted; jobs were gone and stress was high. Meanwhile, 1 billion birds would migrate through the Gulf of Mexico that fall, resting, feeding, and finding sanctuary as they have done for generations. Seventy percent of all waterfowl in North America fly through the Mississippi Delta; their food would not be as plentiful, and they would be vulnerable to the toxic traces of oil and dispersants lingering in the marshes.

The only way I know how to grapple with the magnitude of this political, ecological, and spiritual crisis is to share the stories of the places we traveled and the people we met, and give voice to the beauty and devastation of both.

To bear witness is not a passive act. This is what I saw. These are the stories that were told to me.

Margaret and Kevin Curole

NEW ORLEANS, LOUISIANA

Kevin is working on his daughter's motor scooter, taking it apart in the middle of the sidewalk. I can't help but stare at the extravagantly colored tattoo on his back, Godzilla standing on a shrimping boat, battling other boats while oil rigs loom in the distance. He gets up, catches my eyes on his back, and shakes my hand. "It's a helluva good story if ya wanna hear about it," he says.

Margaret and Kevin Curole are Cajun shrimpers. They have lived along the bayous in Galliano all their lives. Today they are staying at their daughter's place in New Orleans, adjacent to a large cemetery. It's beyond humid, and the searing heat leaves me drenched. Margaret has agreed to talk to us about the Gulf crisis as both a resident of the region and an activist who serves on the executive board of the Commercial Fishermen of America. She also serves as the North American coordinator of the World Forum of Fish Harvesters and Fish Workers, an NGO that works with the UN's Food and Agriculture Organization to protect the rights of fishing communities around the world.

"It *is* a good story," she says, smiling at Kevin. "Let's get a couple of chairs and sit out back." She has a flower tattoo on her right breast, showcased by her low-cut black T-shirt. Her dark, shoulder-length hair accentuates her yellow-brown eyes. "Are you cool enough today?" she asks, smiling.

On May 16, 2010, Margaret Curole joined the aerial artist John Quigley and sent three messages spelled out with human bodies on the beach in Grand Isle, Louisiana, via their cell phones to BP, the federal government, Congress, and other officials, calling for immediate action to address the economic and environmental devastation from the spill.

Their message was simple and direct:

Never Again
Paradise Lost
WTF!!

The last line is where Margaret picks up with our conversation.

"Did you see that there was another spill today? A barge hit ground off Point Fourchon, not far from Grand Isle. That's in the Lafourche Parish, where we're from."

I'd seen the headlines in the *Daily Comet*: "New Oil Spill Sullies Locust Bayou Near Border of Terrebonne, St. Mary."

"About five hundred gallons of light crude. It's the second spill in southeast Louisiana this week," she says. "And they're happening all over the world."

Margaret's father was an oilman. In the 1950s he worked for Gulf Oil in Saudi Arabia. Both her parents lived in the oil compound in the Middle East before she was born.

"I was adopted. My birth mother was Cajun. I'm Cajun. The transaction was completed for the price of five hundred dollars and two new dresses for my mother. My parents are dead now, but I've lived in the same house in Galliano for fifty years."

"And your husband?" I ask.

"My husband shrimped all his life, until 2000." Margaret explains how the local shrimping industry crashed in the bayous since 2000 due to America "dumping" Asian shrimp into the market. "Our shrimp aren't worth anything, certainly not all the effort that goes into harvesting them. My husband used to sell a pound of shrimp all cleaned up and put on a bucket of ice for seven dollars. Then, after the Asian shrimp came in all covered with white blight and crowded out our own southern Louisiana shrimp, he'd get paid under a dollar. They treat our shrimp like trash. It's not just the money, it's our dignity. The ability to work hard is at the heart of Cajun culture.

"Ask Kevin about separating shrimp from a bucket for his grandmother when he was three years old," she continues. "It's in his blood. He was fishing those waters as a kid. Loved it. Lived for it. We all did. It's how we raised our daughter. You know why he quit in 2000? Cuz he was feelin' violent, violent toward the government, violent for them not valuing an honest day's work. He just left what he loved and went and worked for oil. At least we were one of the families who had options.

"For us Cajun folk, fishing isn't a business, it's a way of life. It's something beautiful. In these parts, you either fish or you work in the oil fields. So if you take away the oil job with the moratorium on deep-well drilling, and the fishing is gone, then we're down to nothing."

Margaret's speech slows. "And you've probably already heard about the dead zone in the Gulf of Mexico created by all the dumping of pesticides from farming, the nitrates from farms upriver?" Her eyes drop. "My sense of hope is fading fast."

She looks away and then her gaze becomes direct. "Don't believe seventy-five percent of what you hear about this blowout. Ask the people on the ground. People are not being allowed to talk. My husband has been working on the water for the past three months. Most of what is being done to clean up the oil is to make the American people think something is being done."

"So what's the story that isn't being told?" I ask.

"Two things: how much oil actually has gone into the sea, and the amount of dispersants used to make it disappear," she says. "The workers are getting sick with contact dermatitis, respiratory infections, nausea, and God knows what else. The BP representatives say all it is is food poisoning or dehydration. But if that's all it was, why were the workers' clothes confiscated? As we say in these parts, 'Answer me dat?'

"I never really got nervous until I got a call at nine thirty on a Sunday night from the BP claims office, who told me to back off. But I'm speaking out. I kid my friends and family and say I'll leave bread crumbs. The other day, two guys from Homeland Security called to take me to lunch. I'm a chef. They tried to talk food with me, to cozy up and all, and one of them told me he was a pastry chef." Margaret shakes her head. "But I knew what they wuz up to, I'm not stupid. They just wanted to let me know I was bein' watched.

"Here's the truth," Margaret says, now emotional. "Where are the animals? There's no 'too-da-loos,' the little one-armed fiddler crabs. Ya don't hear birds. From Amelia to Alabama, Kevin never saw a fish jump, never heard a bird sing. This is their nestin' season. Those babies, they're not goin' nowhere. We had a very small pod of sperm whales in the Gulf, nobody's seen 'em. Guys on the water say they died in the spill and their bodies were hacked up and taken away. BP and our government don't want nobody to see the bodies of dead sea mammals. Dolphins are choking on the surface. Fish are swimming in circles gasping. It's ugly, I'm telling you. And nobody's talking about it. You're not hearing nothin' about it. As far as the media is reportin', everythin's being cleaned up and it's not a problem. But you know what, unless I know where my fish is coming from, I'm eatin' nothing from here."

Margaret and I sit in silence for a long time.

I am suddenly aware of the shabbiness of the neighborhood, the cracking paint on the wooden slats, the weariness of the ivy in this dripping heat. We are sitting on dining room chairs Margaret brought from inside her daughter's house.

"I'm sorry," she says. "I haven't cried in a long time. I've been tough, I've been holding it all together, but it breaks me up." She looks at me with unwavering eyes. "Have you read *Evangeline* by Longfellow?"

I can't speak.

"Read it. Read it again," Margaret says to me. "It's our story as exiles. If I wasn't speaking out about this, I'd be havin' a nervous breakdown. I'll tell you another thing that nobody is talkin' about. At night, people sittin' outside on their porches, see planes coming into the marshes where they live and these planes are spraying them with the dispersant. That's the truth. But hey, we're Cajuns, who cares about us?

"I don't feel like an American anymore," Margaret says. "I don't trust our government. I don't trust anybody in power."

She leans forward in the heat as the pitch and fervor of frogs intensify. "We might not be the most educated people, school-wise, but we know more about nature than any PhD. We know. We know what's going on."

The Fin Bar

PORT FOURCHON, LOUISIANA

The sun, a bright orange orb, slowly sinks into the horizon of golden grasses. Flocks of great white egrets are flying to roosting trees, mostly dead cypress that have drowned from rising waters. We are stopped by the side of the road, struck by beauty in Lafourche Parish, "Gateway to the Gulf."

There is the sense that you are standing flush with the sea: wooden houses are on blocks above lawns, some on stilts. But though the sea is here, it no longer necessarily promises the blessed trinity of shrimp, crab, and oysters. In spite of banners advertising "Tails and scales for sale," seafood café after seafood café is closed. Shrimp boats named *Bywater Liberty* and *Daddy's Angels* remain docked on the sides of the canals, idle.

In small coastal communities like Golden Meadow and Larose, local artists have turned the sides of abandoned buildings into murals: "BP Took Our Arms, the Government Is Taking Our Legs, How Will We Stand?" Another features BP as the grim reaper, rising toward the statement "You Killed Our Gulf, Our Way of Life."

We drive over the marshes on a graceful freeway bridge that brings Fort Fourchon into full view. It is twilight, and the horizon of lights rising out of the wetlands reminds Avery and me of the oil fields in Wyoming, where one can read a newspaper at night in what was once a wilderness of stars at the base of the Wind River Mountain Range.

We stop at the Fin Bar for a drink. Once inside, we could be in Pinedale, Wyoming, or Rifle, Colorado, or Vernal, Utah. All oil towns breed the same kind of culture, hard-drinking drifters following the money. A circle of men are sitting on stools with pints of beer in hand.

Having grown up in the oil and gas industry, I recognize the men as kin. I walk over and ask if I might join them. Turns out they are boat captains working with the National Response Center, hired by BP as skimmers. They follow the oil spills wherever they occur worldwide. Some had been in Kuwait, others had worked the *Exxon Valdez* spill in Prince William Sound, and others had been in South America last year. They came from Seattle, New Jersey, Texas—from all over the United States.

"Do you think BP is doing a good job?" I ask them.

They look at one another. One captain says, "They're sure throwing a lot of money at it." The men begin talking among themselves about all the bogus boats in the Gulf registered under the "vessels of opportunity" that are supposed to be collecting oil.

"What they're collecting is a hefty paycheck for driving around in circles," says another captain, laughing. "They've got nothing to do."

"Where is the oil?"

"We sank it," one of them says matter-of-factly.

"How?"

"Dispersants, above and below."

"Carpet-bombed the whole fuckin' ocean," says another captain, who by now is drunk.

"Yeah, above and below and deep, man, I mean way deep," says the man sitting next to him.

"It's called Corexit. 'Corrects-it,' get it? Wonder how many millions some asshole in corporate America got for coming up with that one."

"Is it safe?" I ask.

"Who in the hell knows, but it got rid of the oil, at least on the surface. We just got told by BP that they'll be sending us home in another week or so."

"But don't count on it," says another. "We'll probably get called right back for duty after the first hurricane dredges up all the oil sitting at the bottom of the ocean and throws it inland."

The captain seated across from me seems troubled. He doesn't say much. He tells me later, when we are at the bar alone, that he worked on the *Exxon Valdez* spill. He says he had watched fish eat the dispersant as it gathered along the tide line in Alaska. He said he had seen the mullet doing exactly the same thing out in the Gulf.

"They're probably just eatin' the microbes that are eatin' up the oil after the dispersants have broken it up," he says. "But it can't be good for 'em. I don't know . . . I think that stuff really fucks up the food chain. The herring never did bounce back in Prince William Sound. Almost killed every last one of them."

Comfort Island

BRETON SOUND, LOUISIANA

The marsh grasses are burnt. The mudflats hold an iridescent sheen and it looks as if a painter came to shore with buckets of oil and dipped his brush in it, then spattered the island with drops, not black or brown, but red drops like blood. Comfort Island looks like the scene of a crime.

Jumping off the boat, I sink into the muck. It is my first look at an oiled beach. Shells are strewn across the shore—angel wings, whelks, and tiny hinged sunrise shells. Brown pelicans and royal terns stand three, four deep on the edge of the island. One pelican stands on the yellow boom, now a broken circle.

"Amateur hour," grumbles the boat captain, Danny Diecidue, who has fished these waters for more than thirty years. "The boom is fucked. It absolutely does no good. The island's too big and the workers have gotten it all wrong. At least the pelicans get a perch to fish from out of this incompetence."

I bend down and touch the oil, spread it over the pages of my journal so I won't forget. It burns my finger. White curled feathers cartwheel across the beach until they become heavy with oil. I find a small bed of oysters saturated in crude.

"The oil comes in with the high tide," says Danny, a native of Hopedale, in the St. Bernard Parish, an hour from New Orleans. "That would have been around two o'clock this morning."

Farther down the beach, a television reporter from the *CBS Evening News* stands with perfectly coiffed hair, sporting a flak jacket. He wants a shot of the yellow boom in the background. He is about to interview Dr. Paul Kemp, vice president of the Louisiana Coastal Initiative for the National Audubon Society. He asks his cameraman whether he is ready. The cameraman gives him the go sign: "It's Day 100 and I am on Comfort Island in the Breton Sound with Dr. Paul Kemp of the National Audubon Society. Dr. Kemp, would you agree this is not the environmental disaster we were all expecting?"

"It's too early to tell," says Dr. Kemp. "We just don't know what the effects of the dispersants are going to be on the overall ecosystem."

"But wouldn't you agree that the oil spill isn't as bad as was initially predicted?"

"No, I don't agree. It's just too early to tell."

"What do you know?"

"What we do know is that the Mississippi Delta is the only world-class river delta we have in North America. It really requires our attention. People think this will be here forever, but that is not the case. The system is in collapse. It will not survive another generation unless we change our point of view and move it to one of restoration. We need to restore the Mississippi River and engage in something as large in scale and vision as the Marshall Plan, so it can deposit the sediments it once did into the Delta and is meant to do. These extraordinary marshlands cannot afford to be cut up by canals to serve the oil industry or covered in oil when a spill occurs."

The CBS anchorman is getting frustrated. This is not the story he wanted. He tries again.

"So, what is the impact of oil on this system?"

Dr. Kemp: "No one can say. We can see that this system will come through it, but if we don't change the way we manage these wetlands, this is the beginning of the end."

"You are saying this is 'the beginning of the end'?"

"Yes. Not because of the oil disaster, but because of the navigational canals. They are fragmenting marsh grasses and creating more erosion. And coastal erosion is the issue. Since 1930, we have lost more than twenty-three hundred square miles of land. In 2010, we are losing one football field of land every thirty minutes. If we do not change the way we think about the Mississippi Delta, it will all be underwater very soon." He pauses. "America's Gulf Coast is in cardiac arrest."

"That's a wrap," the newsman says to his cameraman.

If only it were that simple: take a few pictures, speak a few words, end of story. Meanwhile, oil reaches the beach, the mud, the grasses, sullying the feet of birds, now preening their feathers with oiled beaks, ingesting the oil that will weaken them.

The system is breaking down, not from one thing but everything.

Dr. Kemp and I walk along the edge of the wetlands. Where we step down, oil oozes up.

"This oiling extends across six hundred square miles," he says. "Nobody knows. Nobody knows what these oil particles that are hanging just below the surface will do. Nobody knows how this will affect the animals living in the mud or the spawning of species in the sea or the planktonic absorption of oil or how the toxicity levels held in coral reefs will impact their health. Nobody knows what this means to the whole ecology of the Gulf Coast and the Delta that has already been compromised from decades of erosion.

"We need actions going forward, not incremental steps, that will change our whole outlook of how we see the Mississippi River. We have to start implementing this plan to restore the river now and get the Army Corps of Engineers on board—today."

I look at him and smile. "You know what you are advocating . . ."

"What?" he asks quietly.

"You are basically calling for a complete restructuring of Western civilization."

He doesn't flinch.

Gulf Islands National Seashore

PERDIDO KEY, FLORIDA

Voluminous thunderheads are building themselves into a vertical column against a deep indigo sky with god-streaks breaking through the clouds. Lightning bolts cut into the sublimity of the moment and it is hard to know whether to stay or flee.

We stay. Avery and I face the ocean on the white sand beach at Perdido Key, while Bill photographs clouds. A plane flies over the abandoned coast, carrying a red streamer that reads, "Thank you for visiting our beaches."

The sea is translucent, the color of emeralds. There is an orange boom farther out. Sanderlings forage along the beach, scurrying in and out of the wrack line.

Earlier we were at Gulf Shores, now a ghost resort with high-rise hotels, one after another, empty. Even so, there were a half dozen rainbow-colored umbrellas staked in the sand, mothers reading novels while their children were playing in the surf. A few couples walked hand in hand, ignoring the posted warning signs. A large cross of weathered wood had been erected in front of the red flag raised as a danger alert. Our eyes were burning. We had moved on to Perdido Key, part of the Gulf Island National Seashore, with the naïve hope that it might be safer.

Gulf Island National Seashore spans more than 135,000 acres that include beaches on the mainland of Florida and Mississippi and seven islands in the Gulf of Mexico. Of the seven species of sea turtles in the world, four of them nest here, including the endangered Kemp's Ridley sea turtle, the rarest of the sea turtles in the Gulf and the smallest sea turtle on Earth. The white quartz sands are numinous.

"We are sweating our prayers," says Bill as he continues to photograph the unfolding storm. It is 104 degrees without the heat index. We wear the humidity as wet clothing.

Clouds erupt into white-masted schooners—light in the presence of shadow, shadow in the presence of light. Nothing is as it appears. What is true and what is not? The white of these sands is true. Pelicans gliding over an oiled sea is true. Oil dispersed and out of sight is also true. Lightning strikes very close. I half expect to see the ocean burst into flames.

Just as we get up to leave, a BP bus pulls up. It is five o'clock. Forty workers in yellow and green vests rush onto the beach. They are met by a convoy of dune buggies and backhoes poised to dig in the sand.

We learn from two of the workers that the night before from sundown to sunrise, two thousand pounds of oil was recovered from the beach in a hundred-yard swatch.

The oil is buried in the sand—a buildup from Bonnie, the tropical storm that came through a couple of weeks earlier. On a hot day, the tar balls, some of them too big for a man to carry, will start to soften and melt, turning into something like gooey peanut butter that percolates through the sand. The workers dig it up.

When we ask two of the workers, both African-American, what happens with the ton of oil they collect in a night's work, they say, "We truck it away."

"BP says they're going to cook it, turn it into asphalt to pave roads, but if you ask me, I think it's just sitting there in some landfill, hot as hell," one of the workers says. "I've got kids. They like building sand castles. What's going to happen when they run into buckets of oil on the beach down there?" He points toward Gulf Shores. "Are they safe? I think about that."

We watch the two men walk down the wooden plank to the white beach where they will be digging throughout the night with thunder and lightning flashing all around them.

Platform 23051, BP-Transocean Deepwater Horizon

MACONDO WELL, GULF OF MEXICO

Tom Hutchings is flying barefoot over the open sea. We are flying to the source, the Macondo Well, ninety miles south of the mouth of Mobile Bay, Alabama. Coordinates: north latitude 28°45'12", west longitude 088°15'53". Destination time: forty-five minutes.

Avery and Bill are positioned in the rear of the small, agile Cessna 182, ready to take photographs from the open baggage door. I'm seated in front with Tom; we're all able to talk to one another through headsets.

"I don't use the word 'evil' often, but what's going on here in the Gulf is evil," Tom says.

This is the twenty-eighth flight since April 20. Hutchings has clocked in more than ninety hours in the air as a volunteer SouthWings pilot, taking public officials, photographers, and journalists to the site of the blowout to witness for themselves the magnitude of the calamity.

Hutchings's most recent trip was twelve days ago; he's interested in seeing how things have changed since then. "Given all the reports, I won't be surprised if we just see a lot of beautiful ocean today, which would be fine by me," he says, looking out the window. "But if there's oil to be seen, we'll see it."

Tom Hutchings is a Gulf Coast native who grew up spending summers near the water, in Josephine, Alabama. His father and brother were both lost at sea when Tom was nine years old. "We suspect pirates, although nothing was ever certain." His fierce sense of responsibility toward his remaining family has never left him. Married, divorced, and married again, but his devotion to his daughter, Brinkley, has been a constant. She is now a student at the University of North Carolina at Wilmington.

"When I flew Brinkley to the source in the early days of the blowout, she didn't say a word, not a word. A couple days later, she looked at me and simply said, 'Dad, get out of the way. Your generation screwed it up and we are going to have to fix it.' She's now working for Greenpeace. I told her, 'Look, you're twenty years old, you've got a long life ahead of you. Be careful.' But she's angry and I don't blame her. I'm angry, too."

I look down and see the wrinkled skin of the sea, blue-gray. Early-morning haze creates a mesmerizing illusion that there's no horizon. An orange boom floating on the water appears as script, a free-form writing exercise in futility. We pass Fort Morgan and Dauphin Island, where the infamous water sample that exploded on television was taken.

Tom points out the huge rafts of sargassum floating on the surface of the sea. "This seaweed is a critical habitat for aquatic larvae of all kinds, myriads of fish and juvenile turtles, and resting platforms for marine birds. They're like floating islands of life. The oil is killing it, breaking it up."

We fly over shallow-water rig platforms, one after another. We are now twelve miles off shore, seventy-eight miles from the source.

"It's disconcerting to hear one thing on shore and then fly out here and see something completely different," Tom says. "It's important to trust what you see, not what you hear. The plane for me is my own personal ground truthing."

Tom runs a consulting firm called Eco-Solutions, which helps various organizations and agencies come to better decision making through collaboration. But he is a known and respected agitator, one who isn't afraid to speak his mind. I recognize him as Coyote, a trickster. I am glad he is on my side.

"What seems unnatural to me is the wave action. Can you see what I'm talking about?" Tom asks. "There are usually peaks to the waves. But see those rolling waves? Normally, you'd say they belong to the wake of a boat, but they don't, they're just long rolling folds in the sea. I've never seen them before. There's got to be oil on the surface here—" He pauses.

And now we see it. Oil. Lots of it. Sickening sheets of iridescent sheen with sargassum floating inside. We are thirty-two miles from the source.

The oil now appears like miles of stretch marks on the pregnant belly of the sea. What is below we cannot tell, but surface stress is apparent. We see dead fish and birds on the sargassum mats. Trash, as well.

Tom continues to read the ocean. Oil. Oil. Oil. The headphones I am wearing become heavy hands pressing against my ears, reminding me of Edvard Munch's *The Scream*. I cannot track the disturbance in me. This is new territory.

The plane continues south by southwest. We are eighteen miles from the source.

I turn to Tom, my rage erupting. "Why is this not being reported? Why aren't there more planes out here filming these huge sheets of oil? How can anyone say this is over?"

"Shore-based reporting, I assure you," he says. "See what I'm talking about, the laziness of the waves? It's like the ocean is drugged."

Avery, sitting cross-legged on the floor of the plane, points below. "What is that?"

Tom banks the plane and circles the gray-white body. "Looks like a dolphin. Dead." I strain to see the animal over Tom's shoulders. Next, we see three large pods of dolphins.

Tom tells us of flying with the photographers John Wathen and J. Henry Fair, filming the oil burning. "It was apocalyptic," he says. "But the image that continues to haunt me was the group of dolphins facing the fires, perfectly lined up on the edge of the flames, together, watching."

Silence envelops us again. Enormous mats of oil-soaked sargassum hold our gaze in the midst of the oil shoals and swirls.

Finally, the source comes into view. The familiar television images do not match the reality. The BP-Transocean Deepwater Horizon rigs look like LEGO constructions surrounded by a child's collection of orange-bottomed barges and ships. After the shock and weight of oil stretching as far as one can see, as wide as one can look, these man-made platforms are anticlimactic. The irony that something that seems this small and tenuous has put an entire ecosystem at risk is difficult to fathom. We have entered a corporate play zone that kills.

As Tom circles the two remaining rigs, I have this eerie sense we are seeing something we are not supposed to see, that I am being robbed of an innocence I would have wished to preserve in order to go about my life as usual, unaware of the consequences of my actions. This place, this is the place where eleven men loved by their families were catapulted into a fiery hell; only some of their bodies were found. Five thousand feet below is the source of the violent blowout that created a geyser of oil for more than a hundred days, fouling the seas, floating onto shore, into the wetlands, into the food chain, into our bodies. Here is the source of our unconscious privileged lives where we remain blind to the harm we are causing to all that is alive and breathing and beautiful.

We circle the petroleum complex for the sixth time. Our eyes are red and burning. The stench of gasoline is strong. I have a headache and hold some pressure points on my right hand for relief.

Some scientists believe there is leaking beyond the Macondo Well. That there just couldn't be this much oil coming up from one opening. That pressure from the rogue well could have caused a fracturing of the sea floor, creating more fissures, extracting more oil.

"That would make sense," Tom says. "Nobody knows. That's the bottom line. Nobody fucking knows anything. We're in the middle of a goddamn science experiment."

We circle the source one last time. The brown-red crude is a deadly seam along the tide lines, where it congregates as poison. Smaller pools of crude have attached themselves to the sargassum, now dark as honeycombs. A film of oil floats along the surface of the sea. We are seeing rivers of oil as wide as the Mississippi braiding themselves into the currents, creating their own morbid shorelines. A striated sea drenched in a psychedelic sheen reflects a blinding light back to us.

I keep hearing the captain's declaration at Port Fourchon, "We sunk it."

"There is still oil on the surface, Omaha Ninety-Nine," Tom reports over his radio to the air traffic control aircraft circling overhead. "I just want to make sure the government aircraft working this event knows that someone else is seeing what is actually going on," he says to me.

Tom picks up speed and gains elevation. "Let's go see some beauty!" We fly off toward the Mississippi Delta.

"Frigate birds," Tom says. "And two pelicans to our right. We are entering the great marshes of the Mississippi."

I watch the magnificent frigate birds soar below like black crossbows.

The scenery changes dramatically. Now we are flying over vast wetlands, a tapestry of greens and yellows woven into the sea. The Mississippi Delta comes into full view like a great nurturing hand smoothing the edge of the continent.

"The untold story," Tom says, "is that this beauty is still here, in spite of hurricanes, oil spills, and a sinking landscape. We're looking at the most productive system of wetlands in North America."

White lilies are blooming in ponds. Miles and miles of spartina—marsh grass—shimmers in shallow water, creating a different kind of reflective mirror. Enormous flocks of gulls fly over the buoyant landscape. This is a perspective of grace and I feel my soul lighten.

"Verdant," Tom says. "I have probably used that word once in my life, but since I've been flying these past three months, I bet I've used it a hundred times. The contrast is stunning."

We cross over the tip of Louisiana's boot. If Tom is thinking about the word "verdant," I am holding the word "resilient." The resiliency of these wetlands is a testament to the enduring strength of wildness. But we can't continue to count on it.

Outside my window, there is a windswept island beaded with birds. "That's Breton Island," Tom says.

"Can we circle it?" I ask.

Teddy Roosevelt visited Breton Island in June 1915. It was the only refuge he ever visited, and the second one he committed to the refuge system. Piping plovers nest here, as do least terns, both threatened species. This critical nesting site is also home to thousands of brown pelicans and royal terns. There is still boom draped around one of the promontories for protection.

Tom circumnavigates the island, giving us a closer look at the pelican population. The numbers are large, which is reassuring.

We fly toward the Chandeleur Islands, also part of the Breton National Wildlife Refuge, which stretch across the Gulf of Mexico for fifty miles, forming the eastern point of the state of Louisiana. This vast matrix of freshwater marshes adjacent to the sea appears both enduring and fragile at once.

Heading back toward Alabama, we take a turn over Cat Island and Horn Island, part of the Gulf Island National Seashore, each of whose seven islands have been affected by the spill. But on this day we can see through the emerald waters to crystalline sands. I realize it is not the devastation of the oil that has undone me, but the beauty that remains. Constellations of cownosed rays speckle the sea with brown-red diamonds. Pods of dolphins race ahead of us. Tom sees a large shark that we miss. And schools of shimmering fish congregate in the shallow turquoise waters closer to shore.

"This is good," Tom says. "If the bait fish are doing well, the whole system will do well." His mood is shifting. "This is good, this is really, really good. I've not seen this much wildlife in the water since this whole mess started." Tom's eyes flash a joy recovered from the past weeks of gloom. "What a day."

Tom tips the wing of the plane abruptly and makes a sharp turn. My stomach drops. "I think I just saw a manta ray." He circles back around. "Yes, right there." I lean over his shoulders. Avery and Bill can see it through the opening. Then I see it, too. Even from the air, it is enormous. A manta ray can be as large as twenty-five feet across and weigh up to three thousand pounds.

"That is grace," Tom says as we watch its black wings undulate in blue waters.

Tom circles one more time so we can all get a good view. This time, I see its white horns. As the plane moves ahead, leaving the ray behind, he points, smiling. "There's two dolphins. They're mating."

He turns the plane around again and sure enough, as he banks the wings, we see two dolphins as one, a yin and yang of gray-white, an equipoise upon the waters.

BP Decontamination Unit

GRAND ISLAND, LOUISIANA

"Welcome to Grand Oil!" announces a freshly painted sign in the coastal community of Grand Island, Louisiana.

Grand Island was among the first shorelines to take the hit from the blow-out. Brown pelicans were drowning in oil; oysters were saturated. Real estate signs now read "Oil Spill Special," with $150,000 homes slashed to $115,000. Most of the vacation homes on stilts are shuttered. We park our car on the edge of the public beach. It, too, is empty, cordoned off by an orange plastic fence. "Authorized Personnel Only."

Since Doug Suttles, the chief operating officer of BP, just went on national television and said he would feed Gulf shrimp to his children and then de-clared all Louisiana beaches now open, we ignore the airy fence. The beach feels desolate, stamped by enormous vehicle tracks. Gulls and terns stand on the sand, and it's hard to tell whether their dark color was caused by oil satu-ration or not.

Avery goes in one direction and I go in another, each of us appreciating a rare moment of solitude. Bill films terns hovering above the surf. I walk along the edge of the sea; there is no wrack line, no seaweed. Dead blue crabs roll in the small waves as if communicating a secret. I touch the water. It's oily. A silky sheen emanates off the water, made more extreme by the severity of the heat. The stench of oil hangs in the humid air. Even so, the lure of the long, empty expanse propels me forward.

I stop to pick up a few broken shells and continue walking, still weak from having gotten violently ill following our flight the day before. I wretched my guts out while Avery drove us from Alabama to Mississippi to Louisiana. Each time I was on my knees by the side of the road, I wondered whether this was dehydration or what it feels like to be poisoned from too much intake from oil fumes during our four-and-a-half-hour flight over the sea. For weeks, we had been saturated in a toxic hell and we were just visitors. What were the residents experiencing?

Suddenly I see a vehicle with a red flashing light and hear someone yelling. A man dressed in head-to-toe black gets out of his truck and motions me toward him.

"Is there a problem?" I ask.

"Yes, ma'am. You are contaminated."

I begin to walk past the fence. "Step back, ma'am. You are now contaminated, I cannot allow you to step out from the fence."

"Who do you work for?" I ask, seeing the "Talon Private Security Guard" insignia on his black sweatshirt.

"No comment."

"Where are you from?"

"The United States of America, ma'am." He pauses and looks past me. "Louisiana."

Avery starts to cross the imaginary line as well. "Step back. Stay on the beach. You're contaminated and we are going to have to take you to the BP Decon Unit."

"The Decon Unit?" I ask.

"To be decontaminated, ma'am."

"And what are we contaminated with?"

"I am not at liberty to say, ma'am."

"Dispersants?"

"No comment, ma'am."

"Why isn't there a warning posted?"

By now another man has joined the Talon guard. "Didn't you see the sign?"

"I did see the sign," I say, "but since Doug Suttles announced this morning that all Louisiana beaches were open, we took him at his word."

We are marched, in military fashion, a half mile down "the contaminated beach," the Talon guard and the BP worker leading us onward from the other side of the fence as the stifling afternoon breeze blows hot sand across their footprints, erasing them. Up ahead, we see two men dressed in full-bodied white Tyvek coveralls, with gloves and boots secured with duct tape. They stand stoically near two kiddie pools filled with a clear, bubbling liquid.

"Welcome to the BP Decontamination Unit," one of the HAZWOPERs says as the other unwinds a roll of white paper towels. He tears off six sheets and places them carefully on the blue tarp, one for each of our feet. He puts the towels down and grabs a metal brush, asking for our flip-flops, which we dutifully take off. It seems that our hands ought to be contaminated as well now, but that doesn't appear to disturb them. He dips our sandals in the fluid and scrubs them hard.

"Please step in the pool," the other HAZWOPER instructs.

"What's in the water?" Avery asks politely.

"Don't worry, it's all natural," he says.

"Looks like it, especially the bubbles," Avery says, laughing.

I am next and as I step into the water my feet begin to burn.

"Is this about dispersants?"

"Yes, ma'am."

Bill is standing on the edge of the tarp, quietly filming the whole thing. When it's his turn they ask him to put the legs of his tripod in the liquid. He remains quiet and continues the washing and rinsing with his camera running.

As we wipe our feet on the paper towels and step off the tarp, a BP worker asks for our names and phone numbers.

I write down my name and number, figuring they have both since I've already received two unsolicited phone calls from BP representatives while traveling in the Gulf. Each left a message with his name, requesting I get in touch with their public relations department. When I returned their calls, one of the men said curtly, "I'm busy right now, about to go into a meeting. I don't have time to talk to you." It was clear their calls were for intimidation, not information.

Bill gives his name and a bogus number.

Avery surprises both of us with her acerbic rebuttal, delivered in utter cheerfulness. "I'll give *you* my name and number, but I'm not giving either to BP."

The worker, charmed, whispers, "Just give me another name and some numbers for me to write down. It doesn't matter." And so she does.

Across from the Decon Unit is a white tent where a dozen or more cleanup workers are taking a forty-minute break from the heat. Amused by what we were just put through, they ask whether we want some water or Gatorade. We take them up on their offer, sit down, and join them at the extreme displeasure of the Talon security guard. He disappears.

What we hear for the next fifteen minutes are tales of oil on the beach and of more oil to come. Dispersants dominate the discussion, how they were used repeatedly. Again, the phrase "carpet-bombed" is used. Fear for their own safety emerges. They share BP's instructions, given to them a few weeks ago, that should tropical storm Bonnie materialize, the whole island would be evacuated because it would turn into "a hot zone." The workers were told there was a high probability of huge amounts of oil being dredged up from the deep and deposited on shore.

"We were on high alert," one worker says.

The Talon guard returns with his radio in hand and says sternly, "You need to go—now."

I look at him and want to ask by whose authority.

While in the Gulf, my friend Becky Duet, who ran a convenience store in Galliano, very near Grand Island (that she lost in the spill), sent me this email:

> I have a deeper and different feeling now. It's hard to explain—the bayous, the boats, the people, and all our lives. I always said if you starved down here it was because you were lazy. Well since April 20, 2010, we are starving. An

act caused by humans changed our lives . . . I have not felt like a Cajun lately.
When you see boats with oil booms instead of shrimp nets, crab cages on
the banks, oyster boats with port a let on them and bait shops empty,
we have lost our freedom.

This is not just Becky's story. This story belongs to all of us.

On our way back to New Orleans, Avery, Bill, and I stop at the edge of the
marsh to get our bearings before entering the city. Tree swallows are in a
feeding frenzy and white egrets are returning to their nightly roosts along the
bayou. It is twilight. The sky is crimson. My eyes focus on a large oyster bed
where each shell is poised upright in the black tainted mud. I see them as
hands, our own splayed hands, reaching beyond the oil.

CANYONLANDS NATIONAL PARK,

UTAH

⤙⤚

We are in some strange wind says the wind

WE ARE IN SOME STRANGE WIND SAYS THE WIND and it has always been that way in southern Utah. Downwind from nuclear testing. Downwind from the state lawmakers who want to sell public lands to the highest bidder so they can develop them. Downwind of shale oil and gas extraction that threatens to erode the very beauty that defines America's red rock wilderness.

This is the place I call home.

What do I do?

I write letters. Lots of them. I write letters to editors, newspapers, magazines, to people who are dead and people who are living. I write letters to my family and friends.

I write letters to my students with questions. I have even written letters to myself so I will remember what I never want to forget, that this landscape is what keeps me sane in a world that would have me believe that I am mad.

I write letters and rip them up, burn them, bury them. There is no end to the missives I write that are never read, because they were never sent.

My most powerful letters are written at night in the hours when I can't sleep. They are my spoken letters to the dark, unretrievable.

But when I wake up in the desert, I keep writing. It is my incurable disease. In the desert, it is amplified because like time, words become lost in the canyons.

Canyonlands National Park is an open letter to time, deep time. This is broken country—twisted, turned, cracked, baked, uplifted, warped, compressed, cut, collapsed, fallen. It is the most beautiful place on Earth. It is also the most vulnerable. The red rocks deserve our correspondence.

Letters

Edward Abbey, writer
Anne Milliken, neighbor
Opinion, *Los Angeles Times*
Matthew Rothschild, editor, *The Progressive*
Lyn Dalebout, friend
Editor, *Salt Lake Tribune*
Matthew Rothschild, editor, *The Progressive*
Carl D. Brandt, literary agent, friend
John Wesley Powell, explorer
Sally Jewell, Secretary of the Interior
Tim DeChristopher, climate activist

14 FEBRUARY 2006

Dearest Ed,

I miss you. We all do. I'm sending you a cartoon that appeared recently in the *Salt Lake Tribune*: A grandfather and his granddaughter are standing on the rim of Dead Horse Point, overlooking Canyonlands and much of the Colorado Plateau. With his arm around her, he says, "One day, none of these public lands will be yours."

Right now, Ed, the cartoonists are the bravest among us. They are the truth tellers, the ones fearlessly drawing the lines between a free society and a society for sale. Evidently, selling off America's public lands is not only good for democracy, but good for the economy. It will pay the bills for building more roads and make up for the losses in the decline of timber sales. It will also help pay for the war in Iraq, a war predicated on lies. The outcry is faint. The streets are empty. We are comfortable here in the United States of America. We the People seem to be asleep, numb, and dead to the liberties being lost.

I wonder what you would be saying right now, and more importantly, what you would be writing. *Desert Solitaire* was published in 1968—an antiwar credo written straight up, no fiction. It is a book of civil disobedience, or more to the point, wild obedience—a guide to finding one's whole self in relationship to wildness, not one's fragmented self through war. You celebrate Arches National Park, one of the essential "democratic vistas" that your brother Walt Whitman urges us to embrace.

It's not hard to imagine what you would think of America's current "War on Terror." Your views on Vietnam are well documented. In a letter to your hometown paper, the *Arizona Daily Star*, you wrote on December 29, 1972:

> After winning the election with the fraudulent promise that "peace is at hand," the Nixon-Kissinger team have now revealed the true depth of their intellectual dishonesty and moral corruption. Through the tangled cobweb of official lies comes the thunder of bombs falling on the people of Vietnam. After eight years of defoliating forests, poisoning rice fields, burning villages, napalming civilians and torturing prisoners, our Government is now engaged in an apparent effort to obliterate the cities and destroy the population of the northern half of the little peasant nation of Vietnam. Nothing in American history, not even the wars against the Indians, can equal the shame and brutality and cowardice of this war.

But this war in Iraq is different. We started it. And now we don't know how to end it. "Insurgents" (I can hear your voice interrupting, "Wasn't George Washington an insurgent to the British?") are blowing up trucks, tanks, and buildings daily. Our colony in Iraq has seen several thousand soldiers killed and close to twenty thousand wounded—with tens of thousands of Iraqis dead. But we never hear about the Iraqi civilians. Nor do we see the flag-draped coffins of our own coming home weekly. And if mothers of the fallen speak out, we call them fanatics, hysterical liberals, "pawns of the failed femi-Nazis," and we arrest them at the State of the Union for wearing black T-shirts with the body count painted in white.

The projected cost of the Iraq War is said to top $2 trillion, given the health care costs for the wounded. To date, we have spent $173 billion, roughly $4.5 billion a month.

These figures provide some context for understanding the madness of the George W. Bush regime that has grandparents lamenting to their grandchildren that our public lands are now for sale.

At this moment, the Bush administration plans to sell more than three hundred thousand acres of national forests, our public commons, to pay for rural schools in forty-one states. Who could be against educating our children? The stories are spinning. The government certainly doesn't want to admit to selling off pieces of America's heritage to pay for a bloody war.

Gale Norton, the secretary of the interior (or depending on your point of view the secretary of oil and gas development), says the land sales could yield more than $1 billion. The BLM, which you lovingly referred to as "the Bureau of Livestock and Mining," also plans to pawn their lands to raise a pitiful $250 million.

And if this is not fantastic enough, a charismatic congressman named Pombo, a character akin to those you created in your fiction, has come up with the idea of selling fifteen of our national parks. He lives in California near Disneyland.

Forgive my rant, Ed, but you encouraged this, you taught us the difference between anger and rage—how anger turns in on ourselves while sacred rage creates something useful and at times even beautiful—the art of healthy discourse with humor, always with humor. I can hear your words:

> Anger! I'm foaming at the typewriter again. But of the seven deadly sins, wrath is the healthiest—next only to lust. *Pop!* Goes the pop-top. A can of Coors will calm me down.

So here's a story you will love—something you inspired but didn't live long enough to witness: The Glen Canyon Institute. They took your dare. Under the leadership of a Mormon physicist named Richard Ingebretsen, these conservative conservationists have created a legitimate movement to restore Glen Canyon by draining Lake Powell. In *The Monkey Wrench Gang,* your cast of characters blows up the dam. Ingebretsen sees this not so much as metaphor, but a mandate. Glen Canyon dam must be removed. They have stated their case. Figures project the silting of Lake Powell in the next fifty years, and now they are asking why this man-made pond is necessary and at what cost. Congress has taken them seriously enough to hold hearings. Earth First! may have held up the monkey wrench in defiance, but the Glen Canyon Institute has turned the wrench into a microphone, giving voice to all that has been destroyed and what must be restored.

A young Mormon activist named Chris Peterson, with glacial blue eyes, has been talking with Navajo medicine men, and just last summer filled a houseboat with elders so they could witness Lake Powell for themselves. The Rainbow Bridge Religion, thought to have drowned, surfaced once again in that revolutionary patience only Native People can know—and a lawsuit is under way declaring these tribal lands sacred.

The irony of Nature is already in play. Lake Powell is being drained by drought. Elves Chasm is exposed once again and Cathedral in the Desert is awash with light. Again, your words:

> Action, there's the thing. Action! When I grow sick with the buzzing of the brain, I like to go climb a rock. Cut down a billboard. Disable a bulldozer . . . Climb a mountain. Run a rapid . . . "Be true to the earth," says Nietzsche. I like that.

So, here is my question to you, Ed. In this era where the war on terror is used as an excuse to exploit and plunder, and sell off our public lands, in this new world where the World Bank and World Trade Organization honor corporate rule over local enterprises, and where environmental issues are being usurped in the favor of more jobs and a robust economy, *Where is the place for wilderness?*

Writers like you and me, Ed, are viewed by some as akin to colonialists, part of an American-made system that continues to see wilderness as a frontier apart from the human community—something separate, outside ourselves. We have not conveyed our view of a larger community in the Leopoldian sense well enough—a community that includes plants and animals, rocks and rivers, whole communities, not fragmented ones—a community of other species that is indifferent to us but that we are not indifferent to. Wilderness is not a place of privilege, but rather a place of probity, where the evolutionary processes of life are free to continue.

I wonder what will become of us as a species, Ed, if we lose this ecological balance within "the places we call home"?

The Hopi know. Vernon Masayesva, a Hopi elder, realized that every day for the past thirty-five years, 3.3 million gallons of sacred groundwater had been mined by Peabody Coal to run their slurry line, adding up to over 1 billion gallons. The aquifer was being drained. He saw that within a decade or so, the aquifer would be empty. Sacred springs were already drying up.

So Vernon Masayesva organized the Black Mesa Trust to protect the Hopi aquifer and expose this injustice. Spiritual values have become pragmatic ones. In the Hopi language, "Paatuwaqatsi" means "water is life."

Through the tribe's vigilance and in partnership with other organizations, the Mohave Power Plant was shut down in January of 2006, stopping Peabody Coal from operating on Black Mesa. The slurry line has been terminated. This action was not taken lightly and it was at great expense to the tribe. But in the end, water was found to be more valuable than the short-term subsidies the coal revenues provided. Daryn Melvin, a Hopi youth and part of the Black Mesa Trust, said, "We are nothing without water—the Hopi are water."

Water creates civilization. I see wilderness as water, our aquifer as human beings that ties us to the whole of this planet, the water that allows us to drink deeply from the source of community that comprises all life, not just the culture of our own species.

I wonder, Ed, at this point in time, especially in the United States of America, if we are creating civilization or culture. I suspect the true answer is that we are creating both, and our task is to learn the difference.

And so, dear Ed, I thank you. Thank you for leading us to the Maze, where "the heart of it remains unknown," where both "ecstasy and danger" exist side by side in Canyonlands. This is a landscape that should not be sold. Nor can this strange, difficult, complicated maze of human thought and action regarding the wild be quelled.

Your photograph is on my desk. Your books are on my shelves. Your presence has entered our bloodstream as a patriot with vision. We will carry your example of sacred rage with joy and perseverance, and remember your words, speak your words:

"I will not. I will never surrender. I will fight through to the finish, whatever the outcome. I will not quit. I will not betray and desert the best thing in my life. No, no, I will not surrender . . . Earth is the place for love."

This past summer, a group of ten students from the Environmental Humanities graduate program at the University of Utah participated in the class called "The Ecology of Residency." On a hot Sunday afternoon, the students met with Ken Sleight at Pack Creek Ranch. They sat in a circle in the shade of cottonwood trees and listened to stories about you and the Monkey Wrench Gang.

As Ken was speaking, one of the students interrupted him and asked what it meant to be an environmentalist. Ken paused and looked directly at the young woman. "To be an environmentalist," he said, "is to be engaged in life—" And then he told them stories of floating down Glen Canyon before it was dammed. He exhorted them to help him take the dam down with their monkey wrenches. The students smiled. They were witnessing "Seldom Seen Smith" from *The Monkey Wrench Gang*, in the flesh.

And then Ken said, "I'm almost eighty years old. I've got a lot of secrets. I don't want to die with them." He looked down at his dusty work boots and was quiet for a long time. "The monkey wrench is not a symbol of destruction. Ed told me right here on this ranch, the monkey wrench is a symbol of restoration. It's symbolic of your own talents. That's how you are going to fix the world—with your own gifts and talents."

Shortly before my brother Steve died on January 21, 2005, he gave me an old monkey wrench that he'd found in an antique shop. My brother was a pipeline contractor who worked the kind of backhoes, bulldozers, and trucks that the Monkey Wrench Gang sugared. But he was also an environmentalist, albeit a reserved one, who loved *Desert Solitaire* and the red rock desert of southern Utah. He also loved me, his sister, an activist writer. This gift was his acknowledgment that although we went about our lives differently, our hearts were in the same place, a shared love for all that is wild.

I tell you these last two stories, Ed, because your influence is an ongoing correspondence.

That your words can be read and reread and read again by each generation is more than hopeful. It is revolutionary.

With love,

Terry

12 JULY 2007

My Dearest Anne:

I saw that Lady Bird Johnson died yesterday. I am so sorry. I know Mrs. Johnson and your mother, Susan Mary, were great friends and that you knew her when you were living in Washington. Imagine what history died with her. She was truly a woman with a greatness of spirit, savvy, intelligence, and restraint.

I must have told you that I met Mrs. Johnson and her press secretary, Liz Carpenter, at the Austin Lake Spa in December 2000. It was one of those writer scams where if you show up and give a reading, they will comp you for three days of spa bliss. The only requirement was that you give your reading in one of their white terry-cloth robes. Ann Tempest joined me and we had a ball.

The night I gave my reading only two women showed up. Both were elderly in wheelchairs, but very attentive. I read loudly and enthusiastically from a work in progress that would later become *Red: Passion and Patience in the Desert.*

At the end of the reading, I asked if they had any comments or questions. One of the two women leaned forward and said, "Thank you, Mrs. Williams, that was a lovely piece of writing. But now, can you tell me again, in your own words, why I should care about your desert?"

I was completely caught off guard. I thought that is what I had just done, waxed eloquently about why America's red rock wilderness mattered. I didn't know how to respond. And then, in her measured Texas drawl, she said:

"Make me see it, make me feel it. Tell me, how are you going to translate those words for real people in real places in real time." And then she said—"I'll never forgive Lyndon's boys for turning my environmental agenda into a beautification project. But I went ahead and talked about wildflowers so as not to scare anybody, because I knew if the people came to love wildflowers they'd have to eventually care about the land that grew 'em."

It was at that point I realized who was speaking—these were not two elderly women, this was Lady Bird Johnson herself and the formidable, sharp-tongued Liz Carpenter, who covered stories including press conferences with Eleanor Roosevelt.

"Beautiful language isn't enough," she said. "You have to be very smart about what you are doing when talking about the environment. You have to reach people where *they* are—not where you are. You must find out what they care about and build relationships with them, involve them in your cause. Then, you can speak like a writer, but until then, you must speak like one of them. That was Lyndon's gift. He figured out what people wanted and what they were afraid of and then, convinced them how he could help them."

We ended up sharing a pot of tea into the wee hours of the morning, talking politics and women's rights and all things environmental. It was during the time when we still didn't know who would be president, Bush or Gore. Neither one of these political women minced any words. I was taking notes like mad. I didn't want to forget any of it.

Lady Bird was eighty-eight years old at the time and Liz was eighty. They were very funny about their spa treatments. "Now, what on earth can the 'Queen of Sheba' be?" Mrs. Johnson said. And then, Liz Carpenter replied, "That's not the one that interests me, I'm going for 'the Tour of Texas.'"

We all agreed that the spa was trying to starve us and the former First Lady said that if we needed anything, she could send out the Secret Service men for some extra food.

I fell in love with her, Anne, and I see why you have always spoken about her with such fondness and respect. It was interesting when she said that President Johnson never got over how his southern Democrats abandoned him after the civil rights legislation. "It wasn't the Vietnam war that killed Lyndon, it was civil rights," she said. "He knew it was the right and moral thing to do, but it cost him many, many of his closest friendships."

Forgive me for going on, I just wanted to acknowledge her passing, knowing you were a part of her circle. I wish I could have asked Susan Mary more questions about the Kennedy-Johnson years when she was alive. What a history you hold, Anne.

I love you so much. I sense you might be in Maine savoring time with John and the girls.

Please give them my love. One day we must plan an overlap.

xxx

Terry

7 DECEMBER 2008

Dear Editor of the *Los Angeles Times*

On election day, the Bureau of Land Management in Utah quietly announced its last round of oil and gas lease sales for the year. On December 19, close to four hundred thousand acres of America's red rock wilderness—much of it adjacent to Arches and Canyonlands National Parks and Dinosaur National Monument—were to be sold for drilling to the highest bidders.

Public outcry was fierce. The National Park Service had not been consulted, as it usually was, and much of the land listed for auction had long been proposed for wilderness protection. The BLM succumbed to the pressure and met with the National Park Service, which asked that ninety-three oil and gas leases be removed from the list. The BLM backed off twenty-two parcels, and then later deferred other leases in sensitive areas.

From a cynical perspective, the lease sale announcement could be seen as a fire the BLM set intentionally around the edges of Utah's most precious natural treasures, knowing it could extinguish the flames, emerge as a reasonable land steward, and still get what its current boss, the Bush administration, wants—more and more public land in the American West to exploit.

George W. Bush and Dick Cheney, riding bareback and backward in the last gasp of their fossil-fuel governance, are holding fast to their dictum that what is good for the oil business is good for the country. In the interior West, we know this is a lie. Just look at Wyoming, Colorado, New Mexico, and Utah and see how they have been laid to waste, a wide-open wound in America's failed energy policy.

The long horizon, emblematic of our wide-open spaces, is disappearing. Thousands of oil and gas rigs interrupt the sea of sage. Public lands are pumped and pimped. Pronghorn antelope, known for their agility and speed, are no longer running but sitting in the midst of a cobweb of roads— an act of defiance or resignation, it's hard to know. When you walk onto an oil patch, instead of a night sky of stars, oil derricks are lit up like marquees in Las Vegas, and you can forget you are in Boulder, Wyoming, or Vernal, Utah, or Rifle, Colorado.

Consider the Jonah Field, an oil and gas development in southwestern Wyoming where, this year, the town of Pinedale experienced its first ozone alert and where water wells have been found to be contaminated, some with benzene. Or the Powder River Basin, just outside Gillette, Wyoming, where a knock on your ranch-house door may be followed by the news that while you own the surface rights to your land, the federal government has the mineral rights, and it just sold them to an oil company. Within days, a road is cut, drilling begins, and the wellheads, compressor stations, and processing plants are constructed, regardless of your sentiments, livelihood, or well-being.

Among many westerners, the consensus is this: We are not against oil and gas development. We are against the greed, speed, and scale of it. This is not about energy independence but the oil and gas industry's dependence on an oil-loyal administration to do its bidding. The integrity of our public lands depends on the integrity of our public process within the open space of democracy. This process is being abused and violated.

The December 19 lease sale in Utah is just the latest symptom of the problem. The parcels were chosen under the cover of new BLM management plans that will guide the state's land policy for the next twenty years. To witness these plans is to witness a governing mind wedded to fragmentation, not wholeness. According to such environmental groups as the Southern Utah Wilderness Alliance, the plans were finalized in October and November with an eye to fast-tracking the lease sales before Bush's term runs out. In addition to allowing oil and gas drilling, they open twenty thousand miles of backcountry trails to off-road vehicle use, putting in jeopardy wildlife habitat, rivers and streams, and important cultural and archaeological sites. Once parcels are leased, a new administration would find it hard to undo the deals. And once parcels are developed, their possible wilderness designation would most likely become moot.

These acts of greed would come at the expense of a geography so stark and arresting that it renders one mute. The hands of erosion cut windows in sandstone; a spire, an arch, or a natural bridge framing a sunset. The curvature of the Earth is not only seen but felt. Burnished and bronzed through time, this geologic architecture has inspired our American character, where self-reliance is predicated on humility, not arrogance.

The BLM has been forced to curtail the December 19 lease sale, but 275,000 acres are still slated for the auction block, and the new management plans are still in place. "Deferred" leases can just keep appearing on quarterly sales for decades, and the fight over Utah's wild lands will go on unless we, the people, act. We should see to it that Congress passes

America's Red Rock Wilderness Act in 2009. It would once and for all put 9.4 million acres of Utah red rock wilderness in reserve, where it belongs.

The last-minute land grab in Utah's spectacular desert must be seen for what it is: not a boon for business but a bankruptcy of the imagination. What is actually being sold is the soul of a nation, one public parcel at a time.

Terry Tempest Williams

Castle Valley, Utah

30 MARCH 2009

Dearest Matt:

It was the kind of lede I dreamed of as a Utah resident but could never have imagined appearing on the front page of the *Salt Lake Tribune*: "He didn't pour sugar into a bulldozer's gas tank. He didn't spike a tree or set a billboard on fire. But wielding only a bidder's paddle, a University of Utah student just as surely monkey-wrenched a federal oil and gas lease sale Friday, ensuring that thousands of acres near two southern Utah national parks won't be opened to drilling anytime soon."

His name was Tim DeChristopher. He was twenty-eight years old. The date was December 19, 2008. And for those of us living in Utah, in particular, who had been battling the Bush-Cheney oil regime for close to a decade, it was a very sweet moment in the protection of public lands.

As you know, much has been written about the economics student from the University of Utah who walked inside the Bureau of Land Management auction on that snowy day. When asked if he was there to participate in the BLM auction he said, "Why, yes," and became Bidder 70, spontaneously raising his paddle and the prices of oil and gas leases on Utah public lands. Within minutes, DeChristopher found himself the winning bidder on fourteen parcels of land, totaling 22,500 acres, many of them adjacent to Arches and Canyonlands National Parks, for a price tag of $1.8 million.

He had successfully interrupted the auction. In a brave and imaginative act of civil disobedience, one young man with a love of wilderness and a message from his generation on how fossil fuels are contributing to climate change, thus robbing them of a livable future, not only exposed the cozy relationship between industry and government, but challenged it.

Tim stated clearly and eloquently that he could not in good conscience sit by and let these illegal leases on America's public lands be sold to the highest bidder, that his act was one of civil disobedience in protest of the Bush-Cheney energy policies that were contributing to global warming.

Two months later, on February 4, 2009, Secretary of the Interior Ken Salazar "shelved" the sale of seventy-seven lease parcels due to improper and rushed land reviews during the previous administration, including the parcels that DeChristopher had won. The BLM oil and gas lease sale was deemed illegal by the U.S. Department of the Interior.

On April Fool's Day 2009, Tim DeChristopher was indicted on two felony charges for violating the terms of the auction as outlined in the Federal Onshore Oil and Gas Leasing Reform Act and making false statements. Tim pleaded not guilty on both charges, and faces up to ten years in prison and $750,000 in fines if convicted. Ronald J. Yengich, DeChristopher's attorney, said, "Bush and the BLM should be on trial here, not Tim DeChristopher."

U.S. District Judge Dee Benson denied DeChristopher the opportunity to argue in court that he tried to sabotage the auction to combat global warming. Now the trial has been canceled indefinitely. Many speculate the oil and gas industries do not want their past privileges granted by the Bureau of Land Management aired in the courts and called into question by this high-profile case.

For some, Tim DeChristopher is a folk hero. For others, he is more than a bogus bidder, he is an intentional felon who should go to jail.

For me, he bravely and brilliantly exposed the Bureau of Land Management's complicity with the oil and gas industries for what it is: a wholesale giveaway of America's most beautiful wildlands. The integrity of our public lands depends on the integrity of our public process. DeChristopher showed, with the raise of his hand repeatedly, how the auctioning of these commons had become corrupted and abused.

In December 1982, Edward Abbey said this in a television interview: "I think a lot of people are going to become very angry, and they're going to resort to illegal methods to try to slow down the destruction of our national resources, our wilderness, our forests, mountains, deserts. What that will lead to I hate to think."

Whatever you think of Tim DeChristopher, he is now a leader within the climate change community who should not only be taken seriously, but seen as an emblematic member of his generation, smart and strategic, who is tired of business as usual.

The challenge becomes how to act when there is a widespread belief in America that climate change is a hoax, a conspiracy led by socialists, atheists, and, yes, eco-terrorists to "control world population and destroy capitalism." Consider the Utah legislature, which proudly passed early this year "House Joint Resolution 12," a resolution that not only denounces climate change but calls it "a trick." By the time you get through the fifteen declarative "whereas . . ."es you finally reach: "NOW, THEREFORE, BE IT RESOLVED that the Legislature of the State of Utah urges the United States Environmental Protection Agency to immediately halt its carbon dioxide reduction policies and programs and withdraw its 'Endangerment Finding' and related regulations until a full and independent investigation of the climate data conspiracy and global warming science can be substantiated."

HJR 12 is sponsored by the state representative Kerry Gibson, a dairy farmer. He says he's afraid that if the federal government goes forward with cap and trade, it might lead to a "cow tax," causing his own cows to be measured for "belches and other gases." Another state rep, Mike Noel, added: "We need to have the courage to do nothing."

I am relieved that for now, Tim DeChristopher's trial in Utah is postponed. God knows who might be serving on the jury.

Tim and I have been keeping in touch. In a letter dated February 10, he wrote me about the film *Freedom Riders* he'd seen at Sundance the week before.

"I feel like *Freedom Riders* represents everything that the climate movement is missing: commitment, sacrifice, boldness and confrontation," he wrote. "We're always told that people need to feel personally threatened by the climate crisis in order to act, but some of the key figures in the film were white students in Tennessee who were not threatened in any way by the status quo. Yet they made a bold commitment to ride into certain danger in the Deep South. They dropped out of school during finals and literally signed their wills and last testament before they left."

He went on to say, "The Freedom Riders weren't trying to change any minds in the South. They were using the closed-minded antagonists in the South to escalate the tension until the federal government had to intervene. Those today who try to get the Utah State Legislature to understand climate science are using the tactic of trying to get Bull Connor to really love black people.

"This really puts our movement in perspective," he wrote. "I don't know of a single one of us in this movement who have committed anything close to the level of sacrifice that the Freedom Riders did. We have more than enough people in our movement to force the changes we seek. A small group willing to throw themselves into the gears of the machine really can stop the machine."

Tim wasn't afraid to acknowledge his despair. "We must let ourselves be shattered by the hopelessness of the crisis," he wrote. "When we abandon the hope that things will work out, the hope that we will be able to live the easy and comfortable life which we are promised, the hope that someone else will solve this problem, then we are free to act . . . The opposite of hope is empowerment."

He signed his letter "with love and desperate action, Tim."

Tim saw a crack in the system and realized he could widen it with an action. I hope one day we can all act that quickly, that bravely, and with that kind of conscience and serious mischief should another opportunity arise in the name of environmental justice. Tim DeChristopher shouldn't have to serve time in prison, even though he says he is prepared to pay the consequences for his actions. I can think of better candidates who have oil on their hands and greenbacks lining their pockets.

As you know, we lost dear Stewart Udall a few days ago. Another hero.

As ever,

Terry

24 SEPTEMBER 2010

My Dearest Lyn:

We are losing our elders. I loved Stewart Udall. He passed away last spring, but his spirit remains. He was an elegant man who wore his silver hair often pulled back in a small ponytail. I recall his crisp white shirts accented with a Hopi bolo tie, black pants, black boots. He was a westerner to his core, tied to the American Southwest through his Mormon roots in St. Johns, Arizona, where he was born, to New Mexico, where he died on March 20, 2010. He was ninety years old. He lived, as T. S. Eliot describes in *Four Quartets*, "a life of significant soil."

Did you see that on September 21 the Department of the Interior building in Washington, D.C., was rededicated and now bears his name? He was the one who carried a vision of what "the open space of democracy" looked like as secretary of the interior, from 1961 to 1969, under the Kennedy and Johnson administrations. His vibrant leadership helped to protect federal public lands for future generations.

That both the spring equinox and autumn equinox are marked this year by Udall's passing and placement in perpetuity is a testament to his commitment to balance—a balance of power with a balance of nature.

Consider his legacy: In 1964, the same year Canyonlands National Park was established, Udall was a driving force in both the writing and passage of the Wilderness Act that included the protection of 9.2 million acres of public lands. Today, more than 100 million acres of wilderness have been protected. Under his leadership, sixty additions were made to the National Park Service, including the creation of Canyonlands, North Cascades, and Redwoods National Parks, eight National Seashores, nine recreation areas, twenty national historic sites, and fifty-six wildlife refuges preserving critical wetland habitats for migratory waterfowl.

Udall was also a key player in creating the Wild and Scenic Rivers Bill, the National Trails Bill, the Land, Air, and Water Fund, and the National Historic Preservation Act. He was a fierce advocate for Indians. When he died, LaDonna Harris, the president and founder of Americans for Indian Opportunity, told *Indian Times Today*: "Native Americans have a special place in our hearts for the first secretary of the Interior to recognize American Indians as contemporary, self-determined peoples." Harris, a member of the Comanche Nation, added: "He was a real hero for his tireless fight for justice for the many Navajo and other tribal members who were contaminated by uranium mill tailings."

A champion of diversity throughout his life, Udall changed the face of the National Park Service. Robert G. Stanton, the first African-American to head the National Park Service in 1997, credits Udall for his career.

"Stewart Udall came in and took a look at the face of his workforce and there was a noticeable absence [of African Americans] in the professional and technical areas," says Stanton in his oral history. "So Secretary Udall went to the bureau heads and raised the question, 'How many do you have on your staff?' We were called Negroes at the time. 'How many Negroes do you have on your staff?' And he was not satisfied with what he learned. In 1961 the National Park Service had only one African American ranger, Noble Samuel, who was in the Virgin Islands National Park."

According to Stanton, Udall then said: "What I will do is pull together in my immediate office a cadre of recruiters to go into places where Interior has never gone before, at least on a large scale, to recruit from the historically black colleges and universities."

Udall sent one of his recruiters to Huston-Tillotson, where Stanton was a student. The recruiter told the college president: "It's a new day. We realize Interior has not recruited among your student body before and we want you, Mr. President, to recommend among your students those who you think will represent the college well and will represent themselves well in a new environment."

Robert Stanton was one of the two students recommended by his college president. He became the first black park ranger in Grand Teton National Park, Wyoming. This story carries a particular poignancy when set against the backdrop of Udall's personal history. As a Mormon missionary in 1940, he was well aware that "negroes" were not allowed to hold the priesthood of his own religion. And in the Book of Mormon, Indian people are referred to as "Lamanites," carrying a curse of their rebellious forebearers.

Part of Udall's greatness of spirit resides in his sense of an inclusive justice. Like Aldo Leopold, he understood that people of all races had a contract with their community, both human and wild. Udall recognized that social issues and environmental issues were issues of justice whether he was sitting on the Central Arizona Water Conservation Board or the Arizona Supreme Court or serving as secretary of the interior.

The last time I saw Stewart Udall was at his home in Santa Fe, a couple of years ago. His son Tom (now a U.S. senator from New Mexico) was with him. Brooke and I wanted to pay him a visit. We had just read his op-ed in the *Denver Post* honoring the centennial of Rachel Carson's birth. He had been a close friend of Carson's and was one of the pallbearers at her funeral. Both Carson and Udall had written landmark books that had become national bestsellers: *Silent Spring*, published in 1962, and *The Quiet Crisis*, published in 1963. Known as a great orator, Stewart was preparing his talk that he would deliver at the JFK Library to honor Rachel Carson. After sharing some memories of his friendship with the great conservationist, he quoted Carson from memory:

"Man's attitude toward nature is today critically important simply because we have now acquired a fateful power to alter and destroy nature . . . but man is a part of nature, and this war against nature is inevitably a war against himself."

"A war against ourselves," he repeated. He paused as he stood before the three of us. Our eyes met and I'll be honest, mine were filled with tears. "Will we acknowledge this in time?" he asked.

In a letter to his grandchildren on Christmas Eve 2009, he spoke of the great challenges of our time: peak oil and climate change. "Whether you are a person of faith who believes the Earth is the Lord's and the fullness thereof, whether you are an individual who has had mystical experiences that link you to the network of eternity, or whether you are a fervent conservationist who wants to leave a legacy for your progeny, the Earth needs your devotion and tender care," he wrote. "Go well, do well, my children! Support all endeavors that promise a better life for the inhabitants of our planet. Cherish sunsets, wild creations, and wild places. Have a love affair with the wonder and beauty of the Earth!"

Stewart Lee Udall and my own great-grandmother Vilate Lee Romney shared the same middle name of a common ancestor. They would have both known and quietly held this Mormon Article of Faith:

We believe in being honest, true, chaste, benevolent, virtuous, and in doing good to all men . . . We believe all things, we hope all things, we have endured many things, and hope to be able to endure all things. If there is anything virtuous, lovely, or of good report or praiseworthy, we seek after these things.

Stewart used to tease me, saying we come from "good pioneer stock," as they say in our part of the world. We were relatives. And so I take his counsel personally and recommit myself not only to his communal vision, but to his loving, passionate embrace of a personal justice that he created so powerfully in his practice of the wild.

I wish you were here in Castle Valley where we could walk among the golden chamisa and flush out meadowlarks between sage.

Kiss the Tetons for me and your beloved bears.

Love, Terry

27 JULY 2011

Dear Editor of the *Salt Lake Tribune*:

Judge Dee Benson was right in determining that Tim DeChristopher is dangerous. He was right in delivering a stiff sentence in a federal prison to try to silence him if what the judge fears is an evolving democracy. And we can all thank him for showing us how terrifying civil resistance is to the power structures of the United States of America, when a citizen, especially a student, steps forward in an act of courage when justice is being denied.

But Judge Benson was dead wrong when he reprimanded DeChristopher for speaking out after his conviction in March. He stated during the sentencing hearing that DeChristopher might not have faced prosecution, let alone prison, if it were not for that "continuing trail of statements."

DeChristopher spoke on the steps of the federal courthouse after being convicted on two felony charges after being denied the right to tell his story in court about how public lands fell prey to industry cozy with the BLM and why a fossil fuels future endangers all of us. This "continuing trail of statements" is called freedom of speech, Your Honor, not "anarchy." We are all shamed by this sentence. The criminal is not DeChristopher but our justice system.

Terry Tempest Williams

Castle Valley, Utah

1 AUGUST 2011

Dearest Matt:

You asked for an update: On July 26, 2011, Tim DeChristopher was sentenced to two years in a federal prison and three years probation by Judge Dee V. Benson in Salt Lake City, Utah. He was taken away in handcuffs and so was any sense of justice in the United States of America.

On March 4, 2011, Tim DeChristopher was convicted of two felony violations of the Federal Onshore Oil and Gas Leasing and Reform Act and making false statements. I witnessed that trial of four days inside Judge Benson's courtroom.

It was a shattering display of politics on the bench beginning with jury selection, whereby the judge delivered a lengthy lecture on the importance of impartiality, after which he said to the entire jury pool, "And there should be no discussion between you and the 'kumbaya' crowd in the courtroom."

I realized sitting through this painful partisanship day after day, where Tim was repeatedly silenced and the defense consistently overruled, that the only proper way to convey the trial proceedings would be to act out the transcript as though it were a Shakespearean tragedy with corresponding roles through comedy or satire.

Not only was Tim never allowed to tell his story, nor voice what his motivations were for committing civil disobedience in the name of climate justice, he was cast as an imposter, an anarchist, an ecoterrorist, and a threat to American democracy.

The most surreal moment of the trial came in the closing arguments. Scott Romney (a cousin of mine) in closing arguments of the trial likened DeChristopher's behavior to that of a customer pulling up to a fast-food restaurant and ordering seventy hamburgers, throwing them in the trash, and then driving away without paying for them.

I didn't understand the analogy either, except that we were nearing lunchtime.

Judge Benson actually stated during the sentence hearing, "The offense itself, with all apologies to people actually in the auction itself, wasn't that bad."

One has to ask why then was he convicted?

On July 28, 2011, Pat Shea, DeChristopher's defense attorney (former head of the Bureau of Land Management under President Bill Clinton), filed documents to appeal Judge Benson's edict. Meanwhile, Tim DeChristopher, twenty-nine years old, is serving time in the Davis County Jail before being transferred to a federal prison camp.

I have saved an email Tim sent me on the spring equinox, March 21, 2011, shortly after his conviction:

Terry,

I woke up at 4am and couldn't get back to sleep because I realized that Judge Benson and I have never spoken.

He has never asked me a question, and I have never asked him one. He has never looked me in the eye. In all the time I spent sitting across from him in the courtroom and in his chambers, he has never made eye contact. The only time I was allowed to speak was when he was sitting behind my right shoulder.

I met with the sentencing officer at the courthouse last week. His name is Glen and his office is actually across the street. The first thing he said when we sat down was, "Essentially, it's my job to get to know you." The terrifying thing I realized this morning is that he is the only one who is expected to do so. He was the first person in the Department of Justice to look me in the eye or call me by my first name. After our morning together, he knows far more about me and what I've done than the judge or the prosecutor, but he has no authority to decide about my fate.

This is what Americans need to know about our justice system. While decisions are made among the regalia of the courtroom, down the stairs and across the street there is a man whose job is to look me in the eye.

Tim

To look another human being in the eye. It is such a simple thing; to be seen, to be heard; to feel the respect and regard of another. Democracy is a fraud without this kind of direct action. And that is what I have come to love most about Tim DeChristopher. He is a man of action. He will not avert his gaze, even in prison, especially in prison, for it is through our eyes being met that we remember what it means to be human.

If we fail in this century, it is because we are too timid.

If we lose our way in America, it is because we are too complacent.

And if we allow the law to dictate what is fair as in the case of putting Tim DeChristopher behind bars for committing civil disobedience in the name of a livable future while raising a paddle to expose corruption between industry and government—then we are not just prisoners but slaves to the corporations in bed with the courts.

There is a tradition of courage in our country and we must exercise it now.

Tim was given one opportunity to speak directly to Judge Benson before he received his sentence and he looked the judge in the eye: *"The people who are committed to fighting for a livable future will not be discouraged or intimidated by anything that happens here today. And neither will I. I will continue to confront the system that threatens our future. Given the destruction of our democratic institutions that once gave citizens access to power, my future will likely involve civil disobedience. Nothing that happens here today will change that. I don't mean that in any sort of disrespectful way at all, but you don't have that authority. You have authority over my life, but not my principles. Those are mine alone."*

My last image of Tim was standing on the sidewalk in Telluride, Colorado, after a week at the Mountainfilm festival with a big grin on his face. He was purposeful and at peace. We hugged each other for a long time. I gave him my copy of *Sal Si Puedes (Escape If You Can): Cesar Chavez and the New American Revolution* by Peter Matthiessen, published in 1969. He later called, saying how much he loved it, and wondered how he could get a hundred more copies for activists.

Matthiessen writes, "I feel that the farm workers' plight is related to all of America's most serious afflictions: racism, poverty, environmental pollution, and urban crowding and decay—all of these compounded by the waste of war."

These words would resonate with Tim's message in 2011, be it the farm workers, the freedom riders, or climate change activists. "In a damaged human habitat, all problems merge."

Cesar Chavez wrote during one of his hunger strikes, "When we are really honest with ourselves, we must admit that our lives are all that really belongs to us. So it is how we use our lives that determines what kind of men we are. It is my deepest belief that only by giving our lives do we find life. I am convinced that the truest act of courage, the strongest act of manliness, is to sacrifice ourselves for others in a totally non-violent struggle for justice."

This is the sacrifice Tim is making with his life. True civil disobedience comes with a cost. It is "the vitality of the struggle." He is giving us a contemporary story of resistance and insistence born out of America's history of social justice. And he is doing it with his body, mind, and soul in place, in prison.

To not act on behalf of social change and ecological justice is our greatest risk.

Tim DeChristopher's closing sentences before the court inspire me to participate in more direct actions, equally bold and beautiful. "At this point of unimaginable threats on the horizon, this is what hope looks like. In these times of a morally bankrupt government that has sold out its principles, this is what patriotism looks like. With countless lives on the line, this is what love looks like, and it will only grow."

A flock of piñon jays just blew through the valley, Matt. I miss you.

Abrazos,

Terry

20 JUNE 2013

My Dearest Carl:

It is raining and my heart is with you. I pray your health is steady. In the desert, when the winds pick up and clouds roll in, a sweet, pungent aroma arrives, sharp and fresh. There is a word for this smell: petrichor.

Lightning strikes. Nitrogen and oxygen molecules split and separate into atoms. Some of these recombine into nitric oxide, and dance in the atmosphere, sometimes producing a molecule made up of three oxygen atoms—O3—ozone. I love the science of this pleasure. The scent of ozone heralds a storm because in the frenzy of a thunderstorm, call it a downdraft, winds carry O3 from higher altitudes to nose level.

So when the desert smells like rain it is ozone. Petrichor. There is another level to petrichor and it has to do with oils exuded by certain plants especially, in times of drought. When it rains, these oils that have been absorbed into the dry soil and rocks are released into the air with another compound known as geosmin.

This phenomenon added to the flash of lightning that creates ozone creates the sweet smell of rain when it is needed most.

Scientists believe this aroma has a purpose beyond pleasure. As the smell follows rain into the desert, turning arroyos into creeks that run into rivers, certain fish may receive aromatic cues that alert them that this a good time to spawn. Other information supports this smell as a messenger. Camels will follow their nose to water.

Paying attention to what appears to be peripheral—This is what interests me. This is what I want to write about. What is peripheral eventually moves to the center. What rabbits know. What pronghorn know.

What we have forgotten with our predatory eyes facing forward.

What is peripheral is petrichor, the unmistakable scent of rain before it falls.

We are warned by side knowledge of what is to come and too often, we discount it.

> the whispering of
> "the still small voice"
> that when ignored
> comes in on a storm:
> sheet lightning, thunderbolts
> deluge—derecho

When we hear someone say, "It is the calm before the storm," we feel it. We ignore it. Sometimes we act. Most often, we move on. But the directives that save us are the subtle exchanges with our soul. It's what mountaineers know, if one person in the group has an instinct to stop and continue no further on the designated route, the whole group turns back, no questions asked.

Instinct. Intuition. Peripheral vision.

I feel this storm coming.

We are evolving faster than Darwin could have imagined. I can imagine that children in the future will be born with wider-set eyes becoming closer to a prey species, pray species, either way it is to our species' advantage to develop peripheral vision, including prayer. I can also imagine our own eyes slowly migrating toward our ears as we choose to listen more fully beyond words. A child once drew me a picture of an owl flying at night whose wings were ears. The world is changing and so are we.

What is being asked of us?

What am I asking of myself?

My beloved Carl, this desert, these Canyonlands, are becoming sites of disturbance. I think back to the day last fall when we were standing at the overlook at Island in the Sky and could see the Needles and into the Maze all the way to the bitten horizon, and you said, this was your peace.

I wish I was at peace now, but the desert has become my heartbreak. Perhaps that is the nature of deserts—to break us open, wear us down to bedrock. Castle Valley has been reconfigured by flood, a flash in the night that came with such force, such ferocity, I heard it before I saw it, the thunderous roar.

That night, that roar, lives inside of me.

I opened the front door—the desert was a vast and shining sea, a mirror reflecting stars. I didn't know where I was. The turbulence didn't register, only the strangeness of water in the desert. The only thing separating the water from me was a dike built in anticipation of a deluge such as this. I walked up to the dike and witnessed the water moving sideways with such velocity that rolling boulders became a parade passing by with uprooted junipers and cottonwood trees, hundreds of years old, being flushed down the valley, through every widening arroyo parallel to our house.

I stood on the dike alone and watched my known world being washed away. There was nothing I could do.

And then, as quickly as the flash flood came, it was gone—

In the morning, the desert was returned dry. I walked to the place of my midnight dreaming and knelt down to touch the red sand. It was damp, that was all. By the end of the day, that same sand was running through my fingers like sand in an overturned hourglass. I walked back to the house and picked up a rake. I returned to the site of disturbance and began raking sand.

I am at home in the desert raking sand.

Sixty miles north on the banks of the Green River is the site of a proposed nuclear plant. East of Green River, plans are being made for the first tar sands development in the United States to be placed in the heart of the Book Cliffs, one of the wildest areas in Utah, where mountain lions stalk the tops of mesas and wild horses are commonplace. And now, when you traverse the plateau that leads you to Dead Horse Point, where the curvature of the Earth can be viewed, you see more oil rigs and gas flares than ravens rising from branches of junipers. These are the changes I cannot abide. Canyonlands and Arches National Parks are becoming annexes for oil fields. America's red rock wilderness is under siege.

Just like the rest of the world.

What do we do?

My friend Trent Alvey makes art. A wedding dress she fashioned from plastic bubble wrap hangs from a whitewashed branch of a disembodied tree. It is a fourteen-foot shimmering cascade of fossil fuel dreams where the bubbles of our own illusions are about to pop. "The Very Large Wedding Dress" dares to ask the questions, "What are we married to?" and "What is the nature of our commitments?"

If Alvey allows us to witness marriage as a prison that ties us to a ball and chain of our own making, be it to a person or an ideology that tethers us to our own oppression, how are we then to change and move forward toward a sustainable life? Or are we left hanging like a perversity from a dead limb of our own family trees.

We must divest from our current future. We must slip the bubble-wrap dress off the branch and make something of it.

We have never been here before.

Climate change. Will we change?

You and I may disagree on our capacity as human beings to change.
Your first gift to me, after all, was Gibbon's *The History of the Decline and
Fall of the Roman Empire.* It is your belief that it is in our nature to destroy.
I believe it is in our nature to change if we are to survive the disturbances we
have created.

And then, there was the day we read Genesis out loud in the Garden of
Eden in Arches. You asked me to write you a story that is needed now. I am
searching for that story.

So for now, dear Carl, I stand on our dike in the desert, this beloved
desert of red rocks and ravens that bears a history of erosion, be it wind or
water or my own human presence. It is over 112 degrees with a hot, dry
breeze blowing through our valley. There is no contentment here, only the
truth and terror of more disturbances to come.

For now I will continue to rake sand in the desert.

Love, Terry

13 SEPTEMBER 2013

Dearest Major John Wesley Powell:

It has been fifty years after the last bucket of concrete was poured in the
construction of the Glen Canyon Dam, creating "Lake Powell" named in
your honor, a Civil War veteran, an explorer of the Colorado River, and
director of the United States geological survey. It is an unfortunate irony
perpetrated by bureaucrats who have little knowledge of history.

I write to you on the banks of the Colorado River at a time when the
landscape before me feels much like the political landscape in our nation's
capital. Both are collapsing. Both are experiencing a state of drought: one
involves a lack of water; the other involves a lack of vision.

Almost 150 years ago, as a prophet overlooking the future of America's western lands, you predicted this collision of mind and matter. You recognized that the matter of aridity in the desert southwest was a matter of identity. You adopted that identity as a man who was bathed and baptized in the wild waters of the Green and Colorado Rivers. Your lips were parched, your skin was dry and your body was stretched by each mile you muscled through, rapid after rapid, as you explored the beauty and brutality of this unknown territory, these blank spaces on our country's evolving map. And in the process of your wanderings, you became even more passionate about "creating a society to match the scenery," as your biographer Wallace Stegner described the measure of your character in *Beyond the Hundredth Meridian.*

When you returned to the political mirage of Washington from the wilderness of red rock canyons and dry heat that animates the stone stillness of the desert, you said courageously to minds accustomed to green, that rain does not follow the plow. And you advocated for the dissolution of state boundaries seeing them for what they were, a geometry of power that had little to do with the realities of nature, and you argued vociferously for the adoption of boundaries based on rivers and watersheds. This was not just a pragmatic statement in your hope of creating an enlightened public policy regarding our public lands, your "Report on the Arid Regions of the United States, with a More Detailed Account of the Lands of Utah" written in 1876 was nothing short of a spiritual manifesto. Your vision was a call for connectivity in a country in love with compartmentalism. You saw the need for cooperation within communities laced together through water.

I can imagine your ire in 1893, as you put aside your planned speech and spoke from your radical heart to the International Irrigation Congress in Los Angeles, California, after hearing them proudly praise their delusional dreams of irrigating the millions of acres of federally owned lands in the arid West as though the myth of the garden could simply be reclaimed through water. You called them mad, you said, "I tell you gentlemen, you are piling up a heritage of conflict and litigation over water rights for there is not sufficient water to supply the land." And you were right, drought right, to the last drops of water we find ourselves protecting a century later. But on that day, those in attendance and power, heckled you, booed you, and disregarded your words.

In 1894, you resigned from your post of director of the United States geological survey after thirteen robust years of geographic reform. You not only led the geologic mapping of the American West, but you led an intellectual revolt in understanding a region where erosion and drought would inspire a philosophy of restraint. You never forgot your fidelity to sound science and not only fought for but supported a myriad of disciplines such as history, anthropology, and art to color our perceptions of what it means to be human.

No, you were not listened to then, but you are heralded now, revered by those of us living in the American southwest today. We honor your prudence and prescient intelligence born out of the fullness of your explored experience of these vast wild spaces, still incomprehensible to dandies in Washington, still discounted by politicians who denounce and deplore science in favor of religion. Your lifelong project to integrate the "science of man" with the "science of the earth" is ongoing in our colleges and universities and remains part of our public discourse, be it in the value of wilderness or how our communities can sustain unbridled growth.

With my trembling pen, Major Powell, this is what I can tell you: Our rivers are shrinking. Our lands are blowing away. And our lawmakers from our president to our legislators, both federal and state, are in denial of this one hard fact: We must change our lives, our politics, our beliefs, our actions, if we are going to survive.

Three things you should know from the grave, Major Powell:

1. There has been a tear in the ozone. The planet is heating up. The level of carbon in the atmosphere due to our exhaustive use of fossil fuels (used to support our rising human population of seven billion people) is increasing causing the seas to rise, storms to escalate, and droughts to expand. Extreme weather is now the norm. Glaciers are melting. Islands are disappearing. People are being displaced. The story of aridity in the American West is becoming the narrative of the planet.

2. A new epoch is upon us. The Holocene that you were so familiar with as a geologist which began after the last ice age, some 11,500 years ago, is being replaced by a new epoch, marked by the force of our own species. We now live in the Anthropocene. Scientists and geologists alike are coming to see our press on the planet as its own geologic force that will one day write its rapid and destructive history in the stratigraphy of the Earth. Surprisingly enough, it will not be the laying down of our cities or the removal of our forests or even the plowed scars of agriculture that will mark this moment through time. It will be the effects of what is currently invisible, the changing composition of our atmosphere, that will describe the demise of diversity on the planet. The burning of coal, the fracking of natural gas, and the extended dependence on oil to heat our homes, fuel our cars, and run our factories will blacken the record of our existence. Bleached corals in the increasingly acidic seas will tell our story of this sixth extinction that is upon us.

3. The Grand Canyon appears to be much older than we thought. Data unearthed by researchers at the California Institute of Technology suggests that the conventional geologic models that have placed this wonder of the world to be five to six million years old, are much too conservative. Clarence E. Dutton's *Tertiary History of the Grand Cañon*

District, so painstakingly researched and elegantly drawn 130 years ago by the hands of Thomas Moran and William H. Holmes, is now more of an aesthetic document than a scientific one. The Grand Canyon, Major Powell, that you, sir, respectively put on the map, with all its blessed layers of deep time explored, expressed, and catalogued through your leadership of the U.S. Geologic Survey, may in fact be 70 million years old.

What are we to do with these revelations? How do we integrate and incorporate the harsh and horrifying facts of today with the wisdom and beauty held and recorded in the stratigraphy of the Earth exposed in the Colorado Plateau, be it Canyonlands National Park or the Grand Canyon?

I return to your wisdom on the importance of a "home-grown education," of being wedded to a place through our wanderings and fighting for it. I have learned from your history, Major Powell, that it is only through the power of our own encounters and explorations of the wild that we can cultivate hope because we have experienced both the awe and humility in nature. We can passionately enter in to the politics of place, even the realm of public policy and change it, if we dare to speak from the authority of our own residencies.

I hear your words on the banks of this mighty river rich with the sediments of time and honor them:

We have an unknown distance yet to run, an unknown river to explore. What falls there are, we know not; what rocks beset the channel, we know not; what walls ride over the river, we know not. Ah, well! We may conjecture many things.

Respectfully yours,
Terry Tempest Williams

21 DECEMBER 2014

Secretary of the Interior Sally Jewell
Department of the Interior
1849 C Street, N.W.
Washington, D.C. 20240

Dearest Sally:

It is the longest night of the year. There is a clarity to the desert in winter, especially on a starlit night like tonight. I wish you were here to share the light of these candles here in Castle Valley. Forgive my informality, but I view you not just as our secretary of the interior, but a fellow sister in conservation.

Thank you for your leadership and the tremendous energy you embody that is inspiring us. As I mentioned to you in Washington, D.C., Valerie Naylor, former superintendent of Theodore Roosevelt National Park, so appreciated your visit to Medora, North Dakota. You came without fanfare and touched the community not only by your leadership but by your authentic presence. I can't imagine the weight you are carrying on your shoulders and in your heart as you review, respect, and respond to all points of view.

I have heard you speak eloquently on the essential nature of our public lands: why our national parks matter to the soul of America; why the Gettysburg National Battlefield can be a healing not a wound; and why wilderness is a breathing space for all of us in the twenty-first century.

This is a transformative moment. I honor how you are widening the dialogue and advocating for the participation of diverse audiences within our national parks. I am seeing your impact firsthand in Grand Teton National Park, where a group of Latino students recently volunteered in the park, opening doors for the local Latino community to participate more fully. And they are. Everyone benefits from greater inclusivity.

The public sphere you inhabit is a sphere of power. But there is another kind of power. I want to share with you a story from my own home ground in Castle Valley, Utah. Forgive me if this story takes time. Time, here in the red rock desert, is what has created this erosional beauty.

In November, fifteen students gathered in our living room with Jonah Yellowman, a Navajo-Diné spiritual leader from Monument Valley. He and our friend Gavin Noyes came to talk to our graduate students from the University of Utah's Environmental Humanities Program on a Sunday morning in the desert.

When Jonah arrived, coyotes began howling, a rarity at nine o'clock in the morning. He entered our home with his large presence, the students sat near him, and he began his remarks with a blessing. After the blessing, he spoke about how one learns. He shared stories about how his father taught him as a young boy to bring in wood and water at night, so that in the morning when you awaken, you will have dry wood to make a fire for warmth, and water to boil a cup of tea. These practices ensure you will not be caught short in a blizzard.

He shared with us how he became a medicine person, how the ashes spoke to him, how if one holds a crystal up to the stars for guidance and then peers back into the ashes, one can see into the soul of the person in need. He went into great detail about these matters of the spirit. One of the students, a bit uncomfortable, asked Jonah why he was sharing this personal knowledge.

"It is time," Jonah said.

Jonah and Gavin then laid down their maps to share with us the Diné Bikéyah proposal for the protection of Bears Ears National Monument. The day before, the students had seen other maps from the National Park Service, from the Greater Canyonlands Coalition, from the advocates from

San Juan County who are supporting Congressman Bishop's forthcoming wilderness bill.

Jonah spoke about the power of voice and why these lands remain sacred to the Diné people.

"I have dreamed of being in this place before," Jonah said. "They told me that this canyon where the great river flows was created by the bison from scraping the Earth with his hoof."

"It is time to go outside," he said.

We walked outside onto the stone porch to stretch our legs when to our amazement a horizontal rainbow spanned from Parriott Mesa to Castleton Tower. We watched the colors radiate above the red rocks, flush with the horizon. I turned to Jonah and quietly asked if he sees horizontal rainbows frequently.

"No," he said.

"What does it mean to the Diné?" I asked.

"It is the pathway of the Twins, how they travel."

The Twins Jonah was referring to are Child-Born-of-the-Waters and Monster Slayer, the sons of Changing Woman in the Navajo creation story.

We had been visited.

A few weeks later, the Saturday after Thanksgiving to be exact, Brooke and I had a dinner party for twelve. Jonah Yellowman sat at the head of the table. To his right was Scott Groene from the Southern Utah Wilderness Alliance, to his left was Bill Hedden from the Grand Canyon Trust.

The rest of the table looked like this: Gavin Noyes from Diné Bikéyah was seated next to Scott Groene. Next to Gavin was Walt Dabney, former superintendent of Canyonlands National Park, with his wife and daughter. I sat at the other end of the table facing Jonah, with Walt on my left and Josh Ewing from Friends of Cedar Mesa to my right. Eleanor Bliss, our neighbor who also works for the Grand Canyon Trust, sat next to Josh. Sue Bellagamba from the Nature Conservancy and advocate for the Dugout

Ranch sat next to Eleanor. Brooke Williams sat between Bill Hedden and Sue. Heidi Redd from the Dugout Ranch and San Juan County Commissioner Bruce Adams sent their regrets due to travel and illness.

Anna Brady, a student who had been present on the day of the horizontal rainbow, offered to make the meal for the dinner party. Her menu was simple, thoughtful, and local: lamb stew with winter squash; cornbread; a southwestern coleslaw; and for dessert, apple slices with a communal caramel sauce for dipping. A Castle Rock cabernet was served with the dinner.

Jonah gave a blessing on the food. We broke bread together as neighbors and friends. Politics were set aside. The conversation was lively and spirited, full of wit and affection and stories.

After dinner, maps were laid out on the living room table. Four maps became close to one map. What we quickly recognized was that we all wanted the same thing and that the boundaries we had drawn separately were closer together than anyone knew once we gathered around one common table of concern.

Several hours of honest conversation and at times heated discussion over our differences ensued.

And then, Jonah spoke: "These lands are our medicine cabinets. We know that where the fog falls on a particular mesa is where one plant will be found to cure a cold, we know where each herb is located that will heal us in very particular ways. This is where our food comes from—We are deer. Whatever the deer eats, we eat also, as we partake of deer . . . This is where our wood comes from to heat our homes. Who will we become if we lose these lands? This is what I ask my people. Can we come together as one?"

Scott Groene from the Southern Utah Wilderness Alliance asked Jonah how he felt about the north boundary being extended up through Canyonlands.

"The more land the better," Jonah said. "We are with you."

It was a transformative moment for the Utah conservation community and its leadership.

And so, Madame Secretary, to have the Navajo contingency travel to Washington to share their vision of Diné Bikéyah, now known as the "Bears Ears" proposal, which is increasingly a shared vision not only within the Utah conservation community, but most importantly among the Indian communities within the American Southwest, Hopis and Utes among them, was a landmark moment. To then have them leave knowing that the United States secretary of the interior counseled them not to work with the Southern Utah Wilderness Alliance, was more than disheartening, it was an unexpected fracture line being drawn in the sand by Washington. The Navajo leadership returned home with a perceived directive from the Department of the Interior to disengage from a local, collaborative vision.

As a board member of the Southern Utah Wilderness Association who shared this seat with Wallace Stegner for more than a decade, and one who continues to watch this organization grow and deepen in its approach to protecting Utah wilderness, this saddens me deeply. What would Wally say?

Here's what Stewart Udall did say on the edge of Canyonlands National Park at Grand View Point on July 26, 2006: "If I was young enough, I would work to expand Canyonlands National Park to its original million acres." He paused. "I have been saying for decades, the most beautiful scenic area in the world is the Colorado Plateau."

We have a chance for the first time in Utah's conservation history to move forward with a united proposal, a shared map, led by Native People, to protect some of the most significant wild lands in North America. It is a beautiful and bold proposal, one we hope President Obama will support by establishing the Bears Ears National Monument.

I would ask for your support in this united effort—not your disparagement.

People within the environmental community in Washington write off Utah as an impossibility and too often see SUWA as an impediment rather than an advocate for protecting America's red rock wilderness. I would argue that if we can come together in Utah, and we are, we can come together anywhere.

Here is what no one sees: Tonight on the Winter Solstice, a community gathered in Bluff, Utah, to watch a Paleo-Bison burn built by resident hands. Arrows tipped with fire were hurled into the heart of this beast from ancient atlatls. Together, we circled these regenerative flames with the constellation of Orion above us. There were cowboys and Indians, environmentalists and county commissioners, locals and visitors, alike, paying our respects to this burning bison as a stay against darkness with great joy and faith in this moment of turning.

Please join us, Secretary Jewell. This conjoined map led by a native vision that could lead to tribal governance within a national monument for the first time in history has the makings of a magnificent moment not only in the beating heart of America's red rock desert, but within the National Park Service. A revolutionary moment. A moment of healing grace.

I look forward to this continuing conversation.

Respectfully yours,

Terry Tempest Williams

17 NOVEMBER 2015

Dearest Tim:

Thank you so much for sharing this month with our students, both in Vernal and in Castle Valley. You are a beautiful and gifted teacher. When you and Dylan began the class by stating that "this is not a safe place," you spoke the truth. With infant mortality rates tripling in Uintah County due to what appears to be the result of toxic emissions from the oil and gas industry, just one of the hazards associated with the recent energy boom, it couldn't have been more sobering. That you chose to attach plastic baby dolls to your pant legs as your Halloween costume without ever acknowledging their existence only added to the level of student discomfort.

I think you will appreciate Kathleen Metcalf's response to your action in her paper:

> Often, things are not actually about what they seem to be about. Such as Tim's Halloween impersonation. He consistently fended off questions and comments all day about the dead babies hanging out of his pockets. Whenever anything was mentioned to him about the dolls, he either coldly ignored the questions, or pleaded ignorance to their existence. He didn't actively deny their presence, or refuse to talk about the dolls. He did nothing and said nothing that he could be quoted or accountable for. Tim's consistent eschewal of the subject of the dolls became intimidating, and as I felt uncomfortable mentioning them, it created such compunction and embarrassment for my enquiries that I stopped asking him. I don't know if he ever openly talked with anyone by the end of the weekend, but I experienced the dynamics he created with his role-playing as a brilliant version of how effectively deceitful and misleading a person (. . . or corporation) can be without ever specifically lying or acknowledging association for a crisis they have responsibility for. He successfully turned a blatant, disturbing reality that he was associated with into a nonissue.

I believe the students traveled far in their understanding of issues of climate justice and why stopping America's first tar sands mine in Utah's Book Cliffs matters to the health of the region, including its water. The proposed

"National Park Highway" that would complete the paved "superhighway" from Vernal to the mine site on top of PR Springs down to Moab is nothing more than a ruse to gain local support so that the state can fund an efficient thoroughfare for moving the fuel and water needed for the operation.

It was fascinating that the oil shale and natural gas push we witnessed in the Uintah Basin outside Dinosaur National Monument and on the boundaries of Canyonlands National Park was in stark contrast to the political changes we witnessed during this same time period in Washington, D.C. Within a matter of days, examples such as President Obama's decision not to approve the Keystone pipeline; Shell Oil's announcement to forego drilling in the Arctic Ocean; the revelation of Exxon's climate change cover-up, that they not only knew about the dangers of global warming but chose to lie about it, now under investigation; to the bill just introduced in Congress by Senator Jeff Merkley and Bernie Sanders that would bar new leases on coal, gas, oil, and tar sands extraction on public land—all show dramatic shifts in climate justice and public policy.

Don't you love that this bill is called the "Keep It In The Ground Act" (which also prohibits offshore drilling in the Arctic and Atlantic Ocean, as well as the renewal of leases that have not yet yielded oil) was inspired by the #keepitintheground movement that you and other activists have begun? When Senator Merkley announced on the steps of the United States Capitol, "This bill is about recognizing that the fossil fuel reserves that are on our public lands should be managed in the public interest, and the public interest is for us to help drive a transition from fossil fuels to a clean energy future," I could hardly believe my ears.

The world is truly changing. This is the good news in the midst of the hard facts.

Could you have imagined, Tim, that in 2008, after you shut down the BLM's oil and gas lease auction in Salt Lake City through your act of civil disobedience, that seven years later, an army of activists would be ready and willing to be arrested at another BLM oil and gas sale in the same city? And that it, too, would be "postponed" due to another kind of protest, this one calling for fossil fuels to be left in the ground? This national and local campaign to stop oil and gas development on our public lands appears to have real momentum with Utah as ground zero.

The statistics are staggering as you pointed out to our students up on Big Flat near Dead Horse Point—that the oil, coal, and natural gas taken from federally owned lands and waters are responsible for more than 20 percent of the country's total greenhouse emissions. It's hard to imagine that if the unleased fossil fuels remaining under federal lands were to be developed, 450 billion tons of CO_2 would be released into the atmosphere.

Thank you for sending me your essay "Transcending Paradigms." I was struck by the following paragraph:

> *Like any paradigm shift, the alternative will only become conceivable when the status quo becomes untenable. That's why the groups committed to this campaign will be grinding the whole system of fossil fuel development on federal lands to a halt. Civil disobedience has the potential not only to directly disrupt circumstances, but through the power of our own vulnerability, it also has the potential to psychologically disrupt perspectives and worldviews.*

I just read in a recent report by the Center for American Progress that forty-two national parks are threatened by oil and gas development—with twelve of them currently affected: Arches, Canyonlands, Grand Teton, Yellowstone, and Glacier among them. This deserves not only our attention, but our resistance.

As I write to you, Paris is now in a declared state of war for the next three months after the terrorist attacks and the climate talks are about to begin next week with all public demonstrations halted.

The world is not a safe place. Perhaps it never has been, but it is still a beautiful place. This is the disorienting truth of the Colorado Plateau: We stand on the edge of a great erosional landscape. The silence before us translates into deep time. We look out not simply toward a linear horizon but a curved one where the planet becomes a globe spinning toward change.

Thank you for your generosity of spirit and for inspiring us once again; for both your impatience and patience with all we discussed. It seemed appropriate given the tumultuous nature of these times, that we ended the course with a formal tea ceremony performed under blue skies and golden cottonwood trees surrounded by the sanctity of burning red cliffs. Not a bad thing to think about doing before any future actions, should we choose to cross the line at the tar sands mine this summer after your parole is lifted. . . .

Have a great Thanksgiving, my friend.

Love, Terry

ALCATRAZ ISLAND, GOLDEN GATE

NATIONAL RECREATION AREA,

CALIFORNIA

❧

the bodies are all gone from it, the purchases have been made

O N NOVEMBER 25, 1894, nineteen Hopi men who were considered "hos-tiles" from the Arizona Territory were arrested by U.S. military forces. They were seized and incarcerated on Alcatraz Island for refusing to oblige government policies that ranged from forcing them to abandon traditional farming practices to taking their children and shipping them off to boarding schools in far-off cities. From the archives:

Traveling by foot, horse, train and boat, Heevi'ima, Polingyawma, Masatiwa, Q'tsventiwa, Piphongva, Lomahongewma, Lomayestiwa, Yukiwma, Tuve-hoyiwma, Patupha, Q'tsyawma, Sikyakeptiwa, Talagayniwa, Talasyawma, Nasingayniwa, Lomayawma, Tawalestiwa, Aqawsi, and Q'iwiso would arrive in San Francisco over a month later. On Alcatraz they were to be "held in confinement, at hard labor, until . . . they shall show . . . they fully realize the error of their evil ways . . . until they shall evince, in an unmistakable manner, a desire to cease interference with the plans of the government for the civilization and education of its indian wards." They would be held on the Rock from January 3 to August 7, 1895.

"The Rock" is Alcatraz Island, located in San Francisco Bay, about a mile and a half from the city itself. It has been a military garrison in various incarnations since 1850 when President Millard Fillmore purchased it for military use. During the Civil War it imprisoned Confederate soldiers held for treason. From 1933 through 1963, it was a federal penitentiary saved for "the worst of the worst" because of its isolated location surrounded by the sea. Prisoners included Al Capone, George "Machine Gun" Kelly, and Robert Franklin Stroud, known as "the Birdman of Alcatraz." It was eventually closed because it was too expensive to run, and its structures were being eroded by wind, water, and salt.

Once abandoned, "the Rock" was left to the birds after which the island was named "La Isla de los Alcatraces" (The Island of Pelicans) by Juan Manuel de Ayala, who first came to the island in 1775. This is home to countless colonies of seabirds—gulls, cormorants, and pelicans. Alcatraz is haunted by a dark history and even darker memories, which you can hear in the relentless cries of gulls circling the West Coast's first lighthouse, alerting travelers of the treacherous cold-water currents.

But on November 20, 1969, the history of Alcatraz would return to the Indians. In the wake of the formation of the American Indian Movement, seventy-nine Indian activists—men, women, and children, many of them college students from Berkeley—literally came in waves, by boat, to "the Rock."

This group—among them Richard Oakes, Mohawk; Adam Fortunate Eagle, Red Lake Chippewa; Shirley Guevara, Mono; and John Trudell, Sioux—took their stand on Alcatraz Island in the name of justice and civil rights for all Native American people.

"As the ship drew within 250 yards of the island, Oakes, not content to make a symbolic claim, shouted, 'Come on. Let's go! Let's get on!' And jumped overboard," the historian Troy R. Johnson recounted. "Jim Vaughn, Cherokee; Joe Bill, Eskimo; Ross Harden, Winnebago; and Jerry Hatch followed."

"It was the first time I'd seen Native People willing to . . . say this is our land and we're going to stand up for what we believe is right. We're going to take control of our own lives," Wilma Mankiller, Cherokee, said.

The United Indians of All Tribes claimed Alcatraz Island by right of the 1868 Treaty of Fort Laramie, between the United States and the Sioux, which promised "to return all retired, abandoned or out-of-use federal lands to the Native peoples from whom it was acquired." The activists also enacted their "Right of Discovery" as indigenous peoples who had claim to "the Rock" thousands of years before any Europeans had come to the Americas.

"The occupation of Alcatraz was in reality an issue of law," John Trudell said. "The American government signed 300 to 400 treaties with different native tribes in this country. We were taking the legal position . . . saying to the American government and the American people that your government must obey that law . . . When I got off that boat and got on that island, here's all these Native People. I didn't know any of them, but yet, I did. It was like going home."

They issued an "Alcatraz Proclamation," written on buckskin:

We invite the United States to acknowledge the justice of our claim. The choice now lies with the leaders of the American government—to use violence upon us as before to remove us from our Great Spirit's land, or to institute a real change in its dealing with the American Indian. We do not fear your threat to charge us with crimes on our land. We and all other oppressed peoples would welcome spectacle of proof before the world of your title by genocide. Nevertheless, we seek peace.

The Indian activists occupied Alcatraz Island for nineteen months and made it their home, an intertribal community with Indians coming and going freely, engaged in weekly council meetings, conversations, and ceremonies. Alcatraz ceased to be an island imprisoned by its history and instead became a homecoming.

———

When we step off the ferry, "INDIANS WELCOME" is the first thing I see. It is painted in bold red letters against the white face of a building on Alcatraz Island. It has been here since the Indian occupation, an open invitation to all Native people.

I am here with two friends, Tim DeChristopher and Dylan Schneider. Tim is on parole, having spent two years in a federal prison for disrupting a Bureau of Land Management auction in Utah. With time served as a climate activist, call him a political prisoner. "Bidder 70" (as he is affectionately known by his friends) is now a graduate student at Harvard Divinity School on a presidential scholarship.

But Tim is not one to play it safe, even on parole. In a speech at the Massachusetts State House during the legislative season in 2015, DeChristopher said, "Divestment is a truly radical movement that challenges the core of capitalist values, the duty-free right of the rich to get richer with no responsibilities to the rest of the world . . . We know that those at the top of the power structure in this country are scared of this movement and you should be because we're coming for you, we're coming for your power and we're coming for your privilege and we are here to undermine the concentration of wealth that is oppressing the planet and at the same time, oppressing people across the globe in so many interconnected ways. We are here to dismantle the status quo. We can't play a small game anymore."

Dylan is also a graduate student, getting her master's degree in public administration from the University of San Francisco with the Jesuits. She's been a community organizer in Peaceful Uprising, a nonprofit group that emerged in support of Tim during those difficult years while he was awaiting trial. Their guiding principles are simple to articulate but difficult to carry out. In their words, "We are committed to defending a livable future through empowering nonviolent action. We seek to change the institutional and social status quo at the root of the climate crisis, and move toward a just and healthy world." Dylan remained close to Tim during his incarceration, not only as one of his closest friends, but as his liaison between prison life and public life.

I love both Tim and Dylan. They challenge me. If Tim was a pastor, I would go to his church. I wish Dylan would run for president of the United States.

We had come to Alcatraz to see the art show *@Large: Ai Weiwei*, which has been constructed through the various buildings of the former federal prison, now part of the national park system.

Ai Weiwei is the Chinese conceptual artist known for his dramatic gestures that question tradition and power, like filming himself shattering pots from the Ming Dynasty; or haunting antique markets for ancient artifacts, and then painting them in garish colors; or taking pictures of himself giving the finger to the White House, the Eiffel Tower, and Tiananmen square.

Ai Weiwei is a dissident artist, now a prisoner in his own country. Throughout the duration of this show (from the fall of 2014 to the spring of 2015), he could not leave China; the government had confiscated his passport. On April 4, 2011, Ai Weiwei was arrested for "suspicion of economic crimes." He disappeared from the public for eighty-one days.

It's hard to know which of his actions the Chinese government found most offensive. Chief among them was the Internet campaign he launched to expose the fatal consequences of what he called the "tofu architecture" the government had allowed to be built for student housing and schools, resulting in the deaths of more than five thousand young people in the 2008 earthquake in Sichuan Province—deaths that were never reported or acknowledged by the Chinese government. This public accusation waged by Ai Weiwei and denied by those in power inspired hundreds of young volunteers to research the names of the dead and publish them as both an act of public shaming of the government and as a way to bring dignity to those lost. Transparency is what the activists wanted. The government wanted Ai Weiwei to know there are consequences for speaking out. But Ai Weiwei refused to keep silent, kept pushing, finally demanding that the government admit to sending thugs to his hotel room to beat him, causing serious brain injury that required emergency surgery a few days later.

Each one of Ai Weiwei's projects is a middle finger raised to power.

"I see myself not as a leader but as a somebody who initiates things or finds the problem and provokes a discussion," he says. "You have to always be ready to engage, willing to participate. When events or history happen, you just have to be aware and respond."

Not long after Ai Weiwei's detainment and release, Cheryl Haines, a friend of his and the founding executive director of the FOR-SIGHT Foundation in San Francisco, visited him at his studio in Beijing.

I asked the artist what small thing could I do to assist him after this experience. He said that he hoped that I could bring his ideas and art to a broader audience. I had been asking myself what kind of artist would be well suited to create work on Alcatraz. At that moment, I suddenly realized that this artist was the answer. Here was a remarkable opportunity to engage someone who lived through the Cultural Revolution—a time when his father, the renowned poet Ai Qing, suffered terribly for his artistic stance; an artist who is not only an outspoken human rights activist but someone who has personally experienced being detained for his beliefs. I asked, "What if I brought you a prison?" His immediate response was, "I would like that."

The National Park Service and the Golden Gate National Parks Conservancy quickly signed on as enthusiastic partners. The relationship between artists and the National Park Service has a distinguished history. Thomas Moran was part of the Hayden Geological Survey of 1871 that explored the region of northwestern Wyoming. As a painter, he rendered the Grand Canyon of the Yellowstone River as a surreal landscape of pastels and preternatural light.

A decade later, William H. Holmes, an illustrator, created stunning nuanced topographical maps using a chromolithographic technique for the geologist Clarence E. Dutton's *Atlas to Accompany the Monograph on the Tertiary History of the Grand Cañon District in 1882.* To this day, Holmes's artistry, married to accuracy, remains the pinnacle of scientific and artistic collaborations. Chiura Obata's haunting watercolors of Yosemite, painted from the 1930s through the 1970s, interrupted only by World War II, when he was interned as a Japanese prisoner of war at Topaz Mountain in Utah, hold an emotional depth and delicacy that is singular. Photographers like Carleton Watkins, Timothy O'Sullivan, George Masa, Dorothea Lange, Ansel Adams, Lee Friedlander, Mark Klett, and Sharon Harper have repeatedly shaped public perceptions of our national parks by bringing these "exotic" landscapes home into the hearts of Americans. And writers such as John Muir, Marjorie Stoneman Douglas, Sally Carrighar, Nancy Newhall, Ann Zwinger, and Edward Abbey painted word portraits of Yosemite, the Everglades, the Grand Tetons, the Grand Canyon, and Arches National Park as forcefully as any visual artist.

Ai Weiwei comes to Alcatraz as part of this tradition. Frank Dean, the superintendent of Golden Gate National Recreation Area, believes that although this particular exhibition doesn't celebrate a natural landscape, it "invites visitors to examine some of the more provocative and harder edges of society. Ai Weiwei joins the ranks of other political prisoners at Alcatraz including 'anarchists,' conscientious objectors (Quakers, among them), and Hopi who were incarcerated for refusing to send their children to government boarding schools."

He adds, "The exhibit *@Large: Ai Weiwei at Alcatraz* . . . bolsters and supplements the interpretive story of this challenging, multi-layered national park site—confinement and liberty; repression and release; despair and hope; and the role and responsibility of the individual to drive social change."

For two years, from afar, Ai Weiwei familiarized himself with America's most feared penitentiary. *Break the law and you go to prison. Break the law in prison and you go to Alcatraz.* Through maps, photographs, and sophisticated technology, Ai Weiwei could virtually walk the haunted halls of Alcatraz. Each of his seven installations is site-specific, designed to illuminate and interpret each particular space—the cell house to the hospital to the dining hall to the New Industries Building, rarely open to the public. He used habitats of incarceration and confinement to evoke and provoke notions of freedom.

"I think restrictions are an essential condition in the fight for freedom," Ai Weiwei says. "It's also a source for any kind of creativity."

The New Industries Building

A dragon greets us, long and sinuous, flying through the austere concrete quarters of the New Industries Building. The dragon is a kite made of paper, elaborate and expressive, cut, folded, stretched, and enlivened with the hues of a rainbow. His mouth is open, teeth bared, his eyes are focused, ears are raised. For the Chinese, the dragon is power, strength, and protection. It is fire on four legs, ancient and commanding.

Tim asks me to take his picture beneath one of the dragon's round scales made of silk. "Every one of us is a potential convict," it reads. The words belong to Ai Weiwei; this truth belongs to Tim. As a twenty-eight-year-old economics student at the University of Utah, could he have imagined that his life would have taken this turn from a lover of wilderness to a felon? His work, like Ai Weiwei's, is now the work of freedom and justice. Both men understand the best response to intimidation is joy and resolve.

On Alcatraz, work was a privilege, an escape from the boredom of the Cell House. Within the confines of the New Industries Building, built in 1939, located on the opposite end of the island from where the prisoners were held in their six-by-nine cells, a prisoner was offered a view of the seabirds circling above in the breeze as he walked to work.

The prisoners' work orders were to wash, dry, iron, and fold the clothes of the military. The entire floor of the New Industries Building was basically a dry cleaning operation, the largest in San Francisco. Prisoners also engaged in sewing projects, making military uniforms.

And so, filling this space with a dragon, Ai Weiwei's symbol of personal freedom, accompanied by handmade kites in the shapes of hawks and owls flying left and right, reminds us of the power of our own free nature expressed outside, when inside we face the constraints of a system that surveils us.

To be kept in check is to be kept in fear.

When I saw Tim for the first time after his two-year sentence, in a halfway house in Salt Lake City, he said, "We are all in prison—civilians just don't know it."

Traces

In Iran, Shiva Nazar Ahari, a journalist, is arrested on charges of waging war against God; she is serving a four-year prison sentence. Lolo, a Tibetan singer, arrested for recording an album that called for Tibet's independence and the return of the Dalai Lama, is sentenced to six years in prison. Agnes Uwimana Nkusi, a Rwandan and editor of the independent newspaper *Umurabyo*, was arrested on grounds of corruption after publishing opinion pieces criticizing the government; she is now serving a four-year prison sentence. Mikola Statkevich, a politician and presidential candidate from Belarus, was sentenced to three years' labor for organizing mass protests against lifting presidential term limits. Amnesty International called him "a prisoner of conscience."

On the concrete floor in the room adjacent to the dragon, we find portraits of prisoners. Some we recognize—Nelson Mandela, Aung San Suu Kyi, Edward Snowden, Chelsea Manning—others are largely unknown to us. There are more than 175 here. And the portraits are made out of LEGOs.

Dylan, Tim, and I wander in silence through the faces that seem more like pixelated images on a television screen than portraits constructed from a child's plastic building-brick set. Had this exhibit occurred two years earlier, Tim's face might have been among them.

"These are nonviolent people who have lost their freedom simply because they expressed their ideas . . . In truth, they are heroes of our time," Ai Weiwei writes.

Two LEGO bricks, comprised of eight dots each, when put together form a block of sixteen dots, creating a raised surface. Other LEGOs can build on that foundation, creating surprising structures. What is the relationship of the individual to the collective? Ai Weiwei picked his medium well. For the artist, form becomes the message. Each portrait is a compilation of choices, decisions, fated in an act of liberty that caused the prisoners' incarceration, even death. Each portrait is a person, a life, a story known and unknown. Is it courage these political prisoners share? Or is it love, a sustained focus and insistence on justice?

I find the portrait of Liu Xiaobo, the Chinese writer still in prison for calling for political change in an online petition called Charter 08. In 2009, he received an eleven-year sentence for "inciting subversion of state power." In 2010, he received the Nobel Prize in Literature: an empty chair was placed on the stage in Stockholm, symbolic of Liu's absence.

On December 10, 2014, *The New York Times* reported that a friend of Liu Xiaobo's living in Berlin received an unexpected letter from the Nobel laureate, the first time Liu had been able to make outside contact since his incarceration in Jinzhou: "I am O.K. Here in prison, I have continually been able to read and think. In my studies, I have become even more convinced I have no personal enemies. The nimbus around me is shiny enough by now. I hope the world could pay more attention to other victims who are not well known, or not known at all!"

I make a small bow to this writer I have never met and wonder how my pencil might become sharper.

Trace. Why did Ai Weiwei choose this word with these images? Without a trace. Leaving a trace. I am tracing my own path of resistance. It is not enough.

Refraction

From the ground floor of the New Industries Building, we walk outside in blinding light with a view of Angel Island before us. Three Canada geese fly overhead and low, so low we hear a cracking sound from their wings. A small hollow bone lies on the path before we enter the building, most likely belonging to a gull. I slip it into my pocket. We open the door to the New Industries Building and walk up the steep stairs to the gun gallery, where we walk single file along a narrow corridor, taking larger steps to miss the floor grates that draw your eyes down to the floor below.

Ours is the vantage point of guards watching every move of the prisoners, only this time the prisoners are portraits made of LEGOs. Their eyes are following us. In a prison, there is no such thing as privacy. Someone is always watching.

We walk farther down the gauntlet and look through the broken panes of window, rusted and opaque. It is hard to know what we are seeing—the hillside garden behind us reflected in jagged triangles of glass, or the large steel wing visible below, too heavy to fly, yet positioned as if it might.

Ai Weiwei has created a bird wing from Tibetan solar cookers. Each reflective panel has been repurposed as a feather. Seeing them together, one can almost believe in their collective power to propel the wing. "Trace" was assembled by more than ninety volunteers at the Palace of Fine Arts at Golden Gate State Park who put together each portrait just as Ai Weiwei had conceived them. Similarly, this five-ton wing was shipped across the ocean to be assembled in place, in this dark, damp room illuminated by refracted light, capable of trickery.

Tea kettles are perched precariously on the metal shafts of each feather. It is easy to imagine that with enough heat reflected off the solar panels, the water will boil, and the kettles will one day scream like the voices of the oppressed—in Tibet, in China, and elsewhere in the world. The tea kettle becomes every whistle-blower who dares to tell the scalding truth. And with so much latent energy, when the time is right this wing will rise, regardless of the body politic that is missing from it.

Inside. Outside. Freedom and constraint. Earthbound. Airborne. What we see and what is reflected back can imprison us. Refraction. Do we ever see anything clearly without our own reflection getting in the way?

For prison guards, authority is an illusion. For prisoners, the dream of flight is not. There is power in an idea that can move us.

How can a hollow bone and a wing made of steel speak to each other? My hand surrounds the wing bone in my pocket, reminding me of a bird bone flute I once held at the Utah Museum of Natural History, where I worked. In a private moment, I blew the whistle. It was the high-pitched cry of owls, capable of piercing darkness.

When air is stale as it is here, sorrow seeps into the walls like mildew, breaking down cement until it looks like the exposed honeycomb of bees, void of honey. The walls of Alcatraz are crumbling. A prison anywhere has the stench of prisons everywhere. Incarceration is an olfactory offense. One smells hopelessness. Nothing moves but the imagination.

Between the New Industries Building and the Cell House is the morgue. A photographic exhibit shows how the bodies of dead prisoners were disposed of. In a graphic image of what appears to be a prisoner dying, wracked with pain, an unrelated byline of the National Park Service appears below the photograph: "Experience your America."

The Dining Room

We enter the prison dining hall, where you can still see cans of mace bolted to the ceiling in case of riot. For years, Alcatraz followed "a strict rule of silence" in the Cell House that only increased the severity of a prisoner's isolation. In the dining hall, a few perfunctory words whispered to pass the food along was the full sum of one's verbal contact with another.

Visitors to @*Large: Ai Weiwei* at Alcatraz enter the dining room and are invited to engage with political prisoners around the world by writing them a postcard. Each card bears a photograph of a particular country's national flower or bird on one side, a political prisoner's address on the other. Pencils are available on the long, narrow tables.

Each of us picks a postcard, sits down at the table, and begins writing. The name on my card is Natnael Mekonnen, who is serving time at Kilinto Prison in Addis Ababa, Ethiopia. I will later learn he is a politician, a member of the opposition party known as Unity for Democracy and Justice. He was arrested in 2011 on terrorism offenses that brought a sentence of eighteen years. In 2013, he went on a hunger strike to protest inhuman conditions in the prison. He had not been allowed to see his family when they visited and had been tortured repeatedly.

My pen pauses above the card. I want to say the right thing. Then I realize it is the gesture that matters. To receive mail in prison means you have not been forgotten. A piece of your humanity is restored. Isolation is momentarily suspended.

I look up and see Tim writing easily without any self-consciousness, his pen rapidly moving across the card. How many times did I write Tim De-Christopher in prison? Not enough. How many times have I answered letters I received from inmates? Not many.

Each of us drops our postcard into the mail bin when we finish.

"I wrote to Chelsea Manning," Tim says.

"Was that by coincidence?" Dylan asks.

"No, I looked through all the postcards until I found the one with her name on it. She's at Leavenworth in Kansas."

"Did it make a difference when you received letters?" I ask.

"It did. But I had a hard time answering them."

"Because?"

"Not a lot goes on in prison. Didn't have much to say."

We walk over to the kitchen at the other end of the dining room. Tim leans into the barred gate and scans the countertops, the pots and pans, and comments on the menu posted in plastic letters on the wall.

Dylan reads the menu out loud:

21 MARCH 1963

ASSORTED DRY CEREALS

STEAMED WHOLE WHEAT

1 SCRAMBLED EGG

2 MILK

STEWED FRUIT

TOAST

BREAD

BUTTER

COFFEE

"I think that was the last menu on the last day at Alcatraz before it closed," she says, and she is right. The prison on Alcatraz officially closed on March 21, 1963. Frank Weatherman was the last inmate transferred to Alcatraz, and he was also the last inmate to leave. Most of the prisoners were transferred to the military prison in Leavenworth, Kansas, where Chelsea Manning is now.

Tim told stories of working in the kitchen at Herlong, the federal correctional facility he was at just outside Susanville, California. He had previously been in a prison in Nevada and before that in a county jail in Davis County, Utah, which was "the worst," he says.

"See those cutouts for the sharps?"

"The sharps?" I ask.

"Yeah."

On the counter was a white wooden box with what appeared to be a cut-out form for knives. Each knife fit into a corresponding outline according to its size and function. If the knife was not put back, the black empty space revealed it was missing.

"Before we could be dismissed from our kitchen duty, each 'sharp' had to be put back in its place like a completed jigsaw puzzle." Tim pauses. "I haven't thought about any of this stuff since I've been out."

Illuminations

If each national park possesses a "soft spot" like that found on top of a baby's head before the plates of the skull close, exposing where vulnerability lies and the tender point of power can be found, the hospital at Alcatraz is where metal touches bone. It is here where a doctor could determine whether an inmate was fit to associate with other prisoners in the cell block; whether one was healthy or insane—free to return to the prison population or kept in isolation, and they weren't immune to pressure from the warden.

It is here where Robert Stroud, "the Birdman of Alcatraz," a notorious criminal with a string of murders behind him, landed in the insane asylum of the hospital after the doctor diagnosed him as a psychopath. Some say it was a way of keeping his disruptive presence away from the general prison population. Some say he warranted it.

Before he was transferred from the Leavenworth Penitentiary to "the Rock," Stroud made quite a name for himself through his love of birds. In 1920, while in the prison yard, he found an abandoned nest with three sparrows inside and raised them. This altruistic act turned into a passion that became his profession as a respected ornithologist, publishing books in the field of avian pathology, based on his observations from his own menagerie of more than three hundred canaries he was allowed to keep in his cell. He was known as a bully among inmates, with the growing perception outside that he was being given unearned privileges inside with his canaries.

In 1942, Stroud was busted for making alcohol with his lab equipment and transferred to Alcatraz. Out of the fourteen years he was in prison on the island until his death, eleven were spent in the small, dark room of the asylum with no birds in sight.

Of his own eighty-one-day detention in China, Ai Weiwei writes, "You're in total isolation. And you don't know how long you are going to be there, but you truly believe they can do anything to you. There's no way to even question it. You're not protected by anything. Why am I here? Your mind is uncertain of time. You become like mad. It's very hard for anyone. Even for people with strong beliefs."

Tim DeChristopher is a man with strong beliefs, both political and spiritual. While he was at Herlong, he was reprimanded for writing a particular email that the prison management deemed a violation of his sentence. How they secured this email is another story. Nevertheless, he was placed in what inmates call "The Hole," solitary confinement, for three weeks.

"It was just like this," Tim says, as the three of us stand in one of the two tiled chambers designated as "observation rooms" for prisoners thought to be mentally ill. They were known on Alcatraz as "the bug rooms."

Dylan and I listen as Tim describes "The Hole"—how little light there was, how stark it was, how hours would pass without sound, even the movement of air. As he speaks, the light deepens around us as if to underscore his description.

Freedom is a word like "love" or "health" that teeters on the edge of cliché until you don't have one or the other and you wish like hell that you did.

I think about Breyten Breytenbach, who was jailed in South Africa. He tells the story of a ritual that developed in his prison. The night before an execution, the prisoner about to die would sing and his voice could be heard by the other prisoners. "The quality of our listening changed," Breytenbach said.

There are Hopi chants being piped into this chamber of nightmares. Ai Weiwei had sound recordings from the Hopi Eagle Dance installed in one room, while next door, and simultaneously, emerge Tibetan chants from the Namgyal Monastery in Dharamsala, India.

The Hopi chants wash over us like rain in the desert.

Often subjugated people, marginalized people, indigenous people from around the world have been viewed as insane when their views, and their voices, are simply different from those in power.

This cell. This music. The Hopi voices rise and fall in the asylum like breath, like wings—an eagle circling above the prison. This is my definition of resilience when the penetralia of a people emerges in place as a prayer.

The light deepens further; we find ourselves standing in darkness, touching what feels melancholic and sublime. The longer we stay, the more hypnotic the chants become. They seep into our bloodstream; they slow our pulses down until I feel myself back home in the desert. My headache is gone.

I have been to the Hopi mesas. And I have witnessed Crow Mother on the morning of the Bean Dance, walking among the pueblos, holding out her basket of corn as an offering to the dawn, keening for the sorrows of the world.

The Cell House

As I step into the Cell House, a large red handprint on the white stucco wall above the doorway registers like a pictograph in the desert. It marks the moment of the Indian occupation of Alcatraz, an occupation that would last nineteen months and nine days before the Native occupiers were forced to leave Alcatraz by U.S. marshals. But the Indians had won.

"It was body and spiritual politics," John Trudell said. The Indian occupation of Alcatraz ushered in a new era of Indian laws, resulting in significant legislative acts and reform. The federal government ended its official policy of terminating Indian tribes in favor of Indian self-rule and determination.

"Alcatraz is not an island but an idea," said Richard Oakes, the chosen leader of the occupation.

"Alcatraz was a spiritual awakening of our people," Wilma Mankiller said, and that is true, but it is also true that it changed non-Indians, as well. No longer could people ignore the unfairness of our relations with Native people. No longer could the government pretend Indians didn't exist.

In 1972, just a year after the occupation ended, Alcatraz Island became part of the national park system. That same year, *Bury My Heart at Wounded Knee*, by Dee Brown, a history of Native Americans in the American West in the late nineteenth century, became a national bestseller. And Vine Deloria Jr., a Standing Rock Sioux who was a theologian and historian activist, was about to publish *God Is Red: A Native View of Religion* on the heels of *Custer Died for Your Sins: An Indian Manifesto*. There is an art to making history, and it has everything to do with storytelling, and good storytelling is personal, layered, symbolic, and complex. The Indians told their stories on Alcatraz.

Perhaps this is what our national parks hold for us: stories, of who we have been and who we might become—a reminder that as human beings our histories harbor both darkness and light. To live in the United States of America and tell only one story, from one point of view, diminishes all of us.

Ai Weiwei interprets his history through art and it is always political.

"I think all aesthetic judgments, all the aesthetic choices we are making— are moral choices," he says. "They cannot escape the moral dimension in the broader sense. It has to relate to the philosophical understanding of who we are and how so-called 'art and culture' functions in today's world."

I would echo and amplify Ai Weiwei: all *environmental* judgments, all the *environmental* choices we are making are also moral choices. They cannot escape the moral dimension in the broader sense. It has to relate to the philosophical understanding of who we are and how so-called *ecology* and culture functions in today's world.

"When visitors come to Alcatraz, they ask two questions: Where's the bathroom and where's Al Capone's cell?" the park ranger shouts through his megaphone. He is more ringmaster than interpreter, the setting more circus than prison, as he greets tourists at "the Rock." His message reaches us on top of the island, in line for the loo outside the Cell House.

"What's your impression of Alcatraz?" I ask the woman next to me.

"Disturbing."

"How so?"

"I wasn't expecting an art exhibit."

"Had you heard of Ai Weiwei before?"

"No."

"What do you make of it?"

"It's scary. I wanted to see what Alcatraz was like in the past. He made me think about what it means to be in prison now. I didn't want to think about that. I have enough on my mind. I'm glad I saw it, but—" She disappears into the next available stall and locks the door.

Overhearing our conversation, another woman says, "I liked it. I wasn't expecting it, either, but I thought it was really neat to sit in a particular prisoner's cell and listen to the music or poetry they created there." She smiles. "I hadn't heard the lyrics of Pussy Riot before. Can you imagine singing that in Russia?"

In Cell Block A, Ai Weiwei invites visitors to "stay tuned" and explore twelve six-by-nine open cells, each one with a stainless steel stool placed in the center of it. Each becomes the open receptacle for a poem, a song, a speech, or a symphony composed while the artist or activist was incarcerated.

I walk into the first cell and sit down. Here is the voice of Fela Kuti, the Nigerian musician known for pioneering the Afrobeat. Fela was arrested more than two hundred times for his protest lyrics opposing Nigeria's oppressive regime in constant violation of human rights. I marvel at the conviction of his voice in "Sorrow, Tears, and Blood." It moves me.

Hey, yeah
Everybody run, run, run
Everybody scatter scatter
Some people lost some bread
Someone nearly die
Someone just die
Police dey come, army dey come
Confusion everywhere
Hey, yeah

I want to dance with Fela, not sit.

Hey, yeah
Everybody run, run, run
La, la, la, la
My people self dey fear too much
We fear for the thing we no see
We fear for the air around us
We fear to fight for freedom

A few cells down, Tim sits facing the wall, listening to the Reverend Martin Luther King Jr. deliver his April 4, 1967, speech at New York City's

Riverside Church in protest of the war in Vietnam. *Some of us who have already begun to break the silence of the night have found that the calling to speak is often a vocation of agony. But we must speak. We must speak with all the humility that is appropriate to our limited vision. But we must speak.*

A few minutes later, I find Tim and Dylan, engrossed in conversation outside the cell. Tim turns to me. "I was just telling Dylan that I've been studying Dr. King's speeches and I'm amazed how far down he takes his congregations into the dark realities of that time in America before he raises them with hope. He just keeps descending into the tragedies occurring in the country, the beatings, the killings, the failings of democracy in the struggle for civil rights and the ongoing lies plaguing America's involvement in Vietnam. He was unapologetic in his realism, some may call it his pessimism, but the audiences stayed with him. We forget the place of anger in the work of love."

Anger in the work of love.

"Today, everyone thinks we need to stay positive and hopeful and not be completely honest about what we are seeing, what we know to be true. Whether we're talking about climate change or what's occurring on the streets in Ferguson, we are so afraid of offending people," Dylan says. "And then, we only talk to our own constituencies and it's the same rhetoric over and over again until the words become bloodless."

I find this unsettling and accurate. "It was interesting to hear Angela Davis speak at the Cathedral of St. John the Divine after Trayvon Martin's death," I say. "Davis stood before a largely black audience and responded to a man's question about what should be done. 'I would ask for your compassion,' she said. 'This is our greatest form of activism now.' The audience didn't move, it was a hard message to take from someone aligned with the Black Panthers."

"We have to tell the truth, otherwise, we're betraying not only ourselves in this moment in time but those who will come after us," Tim says. "Truth leads to authentic action." He pauses. "I hear a lot of cheerleading. I don't hear a lot of truth telling."

We disperse into our different cells of choice. I keep thinking we have to listen to one another and in that act of listening, unexpected truths will be revealed. King's line returns to me: "The people who sat in darkness have seen a great light."

This time, I sit down and listen to the Chilean singer Victor Jara. Jara was central to the Nueva Canción Chilena—the New Song Movement—that incorporated traditional folk songs with leftist politics during the cultural renaissance of the 1960s. He was a strong supporter of Salvador Allende's Popular Unity government. Jara was arrested the day after Allende's government fell to the U.S.-backed military coup on September 11, 1973. He was taken as a prisoner along with thousands of other political activists by the Pinochet regime to the Chile stadium where he was murdered by the military, his body discarded outside the arena like a sack of garbage. Listening to his song "Manifesto," I am brought to tears.

"When everything gets stripped away, the truth sings," Victor Jara declares through the power of his singular voice, as his fingers strum the strings in solidarity with his guitar.

I wonder about the relationship between incarceration and creativity; confinement and freedom; oppression and expression. I keep thinking the essential gesture is to act, to respond, to remain true to our core beliefs, and not be afraid to give voice to our anger.

Ai Weiwei says: "If you don't act, the danger becomes stronger."

What is the danger? For me, the danger is silence and it multiplies into complacency and consent. My question remains, how do we take our anger and transform it into sacred rage?

Dylan comes and finds me. We enter the cell where Pussy Riot is performing their "Punk Prayer," the song that bought the three young women a ticket to Siberia, "Virgin Mary, Put Putin Away." We listen to the lyrics tossed between a reverential choir and a damning beat. Both Dylan and I are speechless, shaking our heads. Pussy Riot's bravery is breathtaking. We can see them, in Moscow's Cathedral of Christ the Saviour, protesting the Russian Orthodox Church, which was supporting Vladimir Putin in the presidential election:

The head of the KGB, their chief saint,
Leads protestors to prison under escort
In order not to offend His Holiness
Women must give birth and love

Shit, shit, the Lord's shit!
Shit, shit, the Lord's shit!

(chorus)
Virgin Mary, Mother of God become a feminist!
Become a feminist! Become a feminist!
(end of chorus)

. . . Mary, Mother of God is with us in protest!

Virgin Mary, Put Putin Away!
Put Putin Away! Put Putin Away!

On August 17, 2012, the three members of Pussy Riot were charged with crimes of "hooliganism motivated by religious hatred." This came with a two-year sentence.

But on October 22, 2012, *The New York Times* reported that two jailed members of the all-female collective, Nadezhda Tolokonnikova, twenty-two, and Maria Alyokhina, twenty-four—both mothers of young children—had been sent to penal colonies to serve their sentences.

A lawyer for the two women confirmed the news to Agence France-Presse, saying, "Nadya Tolokonnikova has been sent to Mordovia, and Maria

Alyokhina to Perm." The group's brief statement described Perm and Mordovia as "the harshest camps of all the possible choices."

Feminism supported by Pussy Riot, an anarchist collective committed to women's and LGBT rights, is seen by the Russian Orthodox Church as something "that could destroy Russia."

In 2014, at the Women of the World Summit in New York City, Hillary Clinton called Pussy Riot "strong and brave young women" who "refuse to let their voices be silenced."

I am staring at the wall, my back to the bars where the door is open. The wall is deteriorating. The chipping away of various coats of paint has created the shapes of a cross and a female figure, rounded in the hips with a circle around her belly. Above her right shoulder, there is a black line on the wall like a bolt of lightning being hurled at her; a blow of fate. Does any artist know where a creative act will lead them?

What I know is that the place where I write is a cell of my own making.

The Sudanese poet Mahjoub Sharif wrote the poem "A Homesick Sparrow" while in his cell, jailed for his politics. He was able to get this poem out to the world by repeating it aloud to others.

> *So long as I have a voice in my cords,*
> *What prison—or even death—can silence me?*
> *No. We will never succumb.*
> *They have no say,*
> *In our destiny. No they don't.*
> *We are the ones who bring life,*
> *To the dead pores of dormancy.*

"A prisoner is always fantasizing about escape," Tim says quietly behind my shoulder in Sharif's cell. "Always." I turn. "Do you see where the source of the music and poems is coming from in each cell?"

I hadn't given much thought to where the voices originated.

"It's the vent," Tim says. "The sounds are coming out of the vents. The vent of voice and music is the escape. Ai Weiwei is showing us the way out of our own oppression, self-imposed or otherwise."

In Block B, just around the corner from where we are, visitors are shown in elaborate detail how Clarence Anglin, John Anglin, and Frank Morris, on June 11, 1962, removed the grates of the vents in their rooms and dug a tunnel with a fork (stolen from the dining hall) that led them to the outside world and freedom. On the night of their escape, the men placed papier-mâché heads in their beds as foils to fool the guards into thinking they were asleep, then they burrowed their way out. The men are said to have left the island in an inflatable raft, the only three prisoners ever to successfully escape from Alcatraz. Even though the men are presumed to have drowned, their story is legendary.

"It's all about escape," Tim repeats. "The minute I walked in here and saw the cells, my eyes went straight to the vent. Somewhere inside the vent there is freedom."

We have been inside long enough. As the three of us walk back down the hill, the water tower, the tallest structure on the island, advertises in emblazoned red letters from the occupation, "Free Indian Land."

Back on the ferry for San Francisco, we climb the stairs to the top deck tier, where the view is clear. We are wrapped in our own thoughts. "Liberty is our right to question everything," Ai Weiwei writes.

Western gulls veer in and out of our wake, the view interrupted by fellow passengers using selfie sticks to capture their moment.

A photograph of the three of us standing in front of a fake backdrop of Alcatraz is waiting for us to purchase. It was snapped while we were in line to get the last remaining tickets to board the ferry in the wee hours of the morning.

"Don't even think about it," Tim says.

GLACIER NATIONAL PARK,

MONTANA

⊰⊱ ⊰⊱

it is so extreme this taking-the-place-of, this standing-in-for,
this disappearing of all the witnesses—

FOR MY FAMILY, Glacier National Park is a landscape of fire, not ice.

The summer of 2003 is known as "the pinnacle year of fire," in the history of Glacier National Park breaking all records: twenty-six fires were burning in the park, consuming more than 145,000 acres in three months. It was also the summer the Tempests decided to take a family vacation to celebrate our father's seventieth birthday.

On July 23, 2003, we had reservations for twelve at the Granite Park Chalet for one night, and the Sperry Chalet for another, with campsites reserved in between. My father wanted to duplicate the backpacking trip we made in 1982 (the same trip where I met Doug Peacock on the trail), hiking sixty-six miles in six days from the Sperry Chalet to the Granite Park Chalet, over Swiftcurrent Pass, culminating at Many Glacier. This time we were hiking the route in reverse, beginning with the Highline Trail.

More than any other park I know, Glacier embodies the majesty of alpine landscapes, surrounded by rock castles and slow-moving rivers of ice with secret lakes the color of turquoise. The hike into Granite Park Chalet, beginning at Logan Pass, is a glory of wildflowers: red paintbrush, sticky geranium, larkspur, and the flowering stalks of bear's grass appearing as white globes lighting up the meadows. Our family spaced themselves evenly along the narrow trail beneath the Garden Wall, with the strongest hikers in front led by my brother Steve and his wife, Ann, followed by their family, Callie and Andrew (newly married), Sara, and Diane. My father and his companion, Jan, walked with them; my brother Dan and his wife, Thalo, followed behind. And Brooke, perhaps the strongest among us, stayed in the rear with me, gathering bones.

There is something soul-satisfying about carrying what you need on your back: water; food; a cook stove; a sleeping bag, pad, and tent; rain gear; a down vest or parka; hat; gloves; a change of clothes; camp shoes; sunglasses; sunscreen; bug dope; a first aid kit; a good book and headlamp to read by; a journal; pens; binoculars; camera. And then, with a topo map in hand, you chart your course and walk.

Some of the miles you may talk to your hiking partner, some of the miles you remain quiet, observant to the world embracing you. And there are other miles when your mind not only wanders through a labyrinth of thoughts but climbs the steep hills of obsession, be it love or loss or laments. "Walking it off" is not just a phrase but a form of reverie in the religion of self-reliance, where every mile is registered in the strength of calf muscles.

Eight miles later, Granite Park Chalet greeted us with an opaque view of Heavens Peak. Visibility is obscured due to the smoke. The Robert fire was raging in a far-off drainage that we could see with our binoculars; and the Trapper fire, with plumes of smoke visible to our naked eyes, had begun earlier in the week. But we had been assured by rangers at Lake McDonald, who carefully checked our itinerary, that the current fires would pose no threat to us.

The Granite Park Chalet is full of alpine charm, a largely stone building that sits at the base of Swiftcurrent Pass with the Grinnell Glacier Overlook just a short, steep hike above. The chalet was built by the Great Northern Railroad between 1914 and 1915 to attract more American tourists with a hut-to-hut trail system like those found in Europe. Of the nine alpine chalets that were built in that era, two remain.

Each of us settled into our designated cabins, furnished with a set of bunk beds that we completed with our sleeping bags. Half the party stayed at the chalet, while the other half hiked up Ahern Pass for a wider view.

My brother Dan and I sat at the picnic table on the chalet's porch and talked about Jim Harrison's novella *Legends of the Fall*, set in Montana.

"Do you think fathers and sons are fated to destroy each other?" Dan asked.

"I can't answer that—" I said. "But I remember hearing a psychologist talk at a conference on boys. He said, 'If you want to see a man cry, ask him about his father.'"

Our conversation changed to our mother.

"Do you think we'd all be different if Mother had lived?" Dan asked.

"No question."

"How?"

And that conversation carried us into the late afternoon.

We all cooked dinner together inside the chalet, having been warned by a large handwritten sign not to touch the shrimp in the freezer. Rumor had it the shrimp had been flown in as a special surprise for First Lady Laura Bush, who, with some of her girlfriends, was arriving at the Granite Park Chalet toward the end of the week.

We watched the sun burn through the smoke and stare at us like the red eye of a demon. And then a blue haze settled on the valley.

That night, I dreamed a spiral of bats flew out of the forest followed by flames. I woke up anxious.

The next morning, we all noticed the smoke had thickened. As we ate breakfast on the porch of the chalet, fire was on everyone's mind. Chris Burke, a Park Service employee, appeared anxious as well, his worry heightened by the discovery that the water pump at the chalet was broken. He hiked out to meet a maintenance worker on the trail to get a new part as a safety measure.

About midday on July 24, the flames from the Robert fire appeared to be coming closer. Dad walked down to the edge of the chasm, a sizable rock-faced cliff that separated us from the forest, to calculate the distance from the fires to the Granite Park Chalet.

"It's a fair distance," he said. "But if the winds change, we could be in trouble."

Just then, a helicopter hovered above us and landed on flat ground. To our surprise, a captain from the smoke jumpers, stationed out of Los Angeles, stepped out of the chopper looking like Cool Hand Luke. He had been instructed to stay with us in case the fires escalated. He found a canvas director's chair, carried it to the top of the knoll, sat down, and crossed his legs as he gazed toward the burning horizon, offering us a relaxed image, the epitome of calm.

The other guests at the chalet began to gather, also alarmed by the smoke and the fires that seemed to be advancing. Chris was back with the new part needed for the water pump and installed it, and quickly, with the help of Brooke and Steve, began wetting down the roof of the chalet.

Suddenly a spiral of bats flew out of the forest just like I had seen in my dream. They rose in a black column of wings against the gray sky and just as quickly disappeared. My heart began to race. I looked at my watch: 4:30 p.m. The smoke was increasing. The fire was escalating, with spot fires gaining momentum ahead of the blaze, igniting all around us. The captain stood up from his chair. Several deer emerged from the trees and ran behind the chalet. Chris was on his cell phone, talking to the fire lookout. What we didn't hear from the woman on the other end of his conversation was this: "We can't calm the beast of Trapper fire . . . it looks like it's making a run for the Granite Park Chalet!"

Chris and the fire captain called us together.

"We seem to be at the center of a perfect storm," the fire captain said. "The Robert fire, the Trapper fire, and a new fire unnamed seem to have merged into one crown fire they're calling the 'Mountain Man Complex.' It's all blown up in the last four hours—and it appears to be heading our direction."

"We must prepare ourselves," Chris added. "Keeping the chalet wet will help, and we need to get rid of whatever could burn on the porch. I could use some help."

Brooke, Steve, and Andrew worked with Chris, throwing the picnic tables and chairs off the porch down the hillside so there would be nothing burnable next to the stone walls of the historic chalet.

The propane tank nearby was a concern. The winds were picking up dramatically; it was increasingly hard to hear. Chris and the captain passed out particle masks. We stood on the porch bathed in an eerie orange glow, watching in disbelief as firs and pines exploded into flames with pieces of charred bark raining down on us. We could feel the waves of heat as the flames roared from all directions.

Thalo and Dan ran down to their cabin and returned with their backpacks strapped on.

"We're leaving," Dan said. "Does anyone want to come with us?"

"I'm gettin' the hell out of here, before we burn up!" Thalo said, her blue eyes bloodshot and frantic. "I saw what happened to the people who listened to the authorities inside the World Trade Center on September eleventh and thought they'd be rescued."

"You're better off staying here with the rest of us," Chris said. "Don't panic—I don't think you'll make it up to Grinnell, the fire's moving too fast."

Thalo was already gone.

"I'm going with Thalo," Dan said. And we watched them disappear into the smoke—the Grinnell Glacier Overlook, still a steep mile and a half away.

"Do something, John," the captain said to my father.

"He's a grown man, he's going to do what he's going to do," Dad said. "I can't stop him."

"The next person who leaves is under arrest," the fire captain said. "Everyone needs to put on their hiking boots and make sure you have your personal ID with you. Go—now—hurry! I want to see everyone inside the chalet as fast as you can get there."

Flocks of birds were flying helter-skelter into the chaos of the crosswinds. More deer were running out of the woods ahead of the burn. Heat singed my eyelashes. Our eyes were red and our faces were flushed. Everyone wore masks. I had two extra and put one on each breast for comic relief. Sara and Diane laughed.

Dad, Jan, and I rushed down to our cabin to get our necessary gear, fear accelerating with the advancing fire. Chris had run down to the campground and brought other hikers back to the chalet for safety. He mentioned that two former Bureau of Land Management employees from Alaska who had registered at the chalet earlier in the day had disappeared.

Walking briskly back to the chalet with the heat chasing us, I kept looking up the mountain to see whether I could see Dan and Thalo, but it was consumed in black smoke. The spot fires increased as flames jumped over trees like banshees; the wind howled like a speeding train. I turned to see the blaze, now an inferno, racing up the mountain toward us.

Ann was inside the chalet with the girls. Callie and Andrew were standing on the side porch, watching the flames behind us. Brooke and Steve were still working with Chris, getting rid of more flammables, including trying to move the propane tank farther away from the building, and then, with longer white canvas hoses screwed together, they continued spraying down the roof and porch of the chalet until the very last minute.

"Everybody inside, now!" the fire captain yelled.

A couple had been playing Scrabble. They quickly put away their game. Two women held each other's hands, crying. A young man, crouched in the corner, seeming a bit dazed or drugged, continued playing his guitar, quietly singing, "Come on, baby, light my fire," until Chris put his hand on his shoulder to get him to stop. I stared out the windows. All I could think of was my brother and his wife in the middle of the firestorm.

Chris made a quick count and turned to the captain. "Two others besides the two that left are unaccounted for. Everyone else is here."

Thirty-five of us stood in the center of the chalet, most of us coughing.

"Okay, everybody, listen up: I want the children sitting in the center. Everyone else sits in a circle around them. The fire is going to reach us in minutes. Stay calm—low to the floor. You're going to hear a loud roar coming closer and closer. It's going to get hot, real hot. The windows will shatter. The oxygen's going to be sucked out of the room—temporarily—and then, hopefully, the fire will quickly move over us, and shoot up Swiftcurrent Pass and we'll all be just fine. The Park Service knows we're here. Any questions?"

No one said a word, we just sat on the floor, children in the center, holding each other, waiting . . . some with their eyes closed, praying.

We would later learn that we had been taken for dead by the Park Service. Miraculously, we survived—as did Dan and Thalo, who watched the fire come within two hundred feet of the historic Granite Park Chalet, split around us, and rejoin its force as it roared up Swiftcurrent Pass. The windows didn't blow out, nor did the oxygen get sucked out of the room. The fire missed us. We were alive.

In Christopher Burke's words: "We could see that the crown fire that had been coming our way had arced around and above us, burning through Swiftcurrent Pass with two-to-three-hundred-foot flame lengths and seventy-mile-per-hour winds . . . At sunset the flames surrounding us lit up the chalet with an orange-pink glow and spot fires continued to burn above and around."

The two former employees of the BLM who had disappeared reemerged from the latrines before dark, where they had positioned themselves next to the pit toilets, ready to jump in the dark, nasty holes if necessary.

Our family stayed up all night and, from the porch of the Granite Park Chalet, we watched the fires burn. The intensity of our focus must have been tied to a delusional belief that if we just kept our eyes on the flames, we could keep them at bay. This kind of magical thinking soothed us, even though we all knew it was only the luck of the winds changing direction that had allowed the flames to split and burn around us instead of through us—leaving behind a charred heap of bodies, a circle of ash.

Early the next morning we "escaped" the continuing fires by hiking out the way we had hiked in—single file on the Highline Trail. Only this time, we were led by Christopher Burke, with the fire captain bringing up the rear. Three grizzlies walked out with us, slightly below the Garden Wall ledge, having also survived the historic Trapper fire of 2003.

On February 5, 2005, Secretary of the Interior Gale Norton presented the sixty-second annual awards for outstanding service and valor to government employees. Chris Burke, having just completed his twentieth season with the National Park Service, was among those honored:

> Christopher J. Burke—In recognition of his willingness to place himself at great personal risk in order to save the lives of 39 others.
>
> "At 3:30 p.m. on July 23, 2003, while Mr. Burke was working at the Granite Park Chalet, a historic high mountain chalet in Glacier National Park, he noticed heavy smoke coming toward them from the Flattop Moun-

tain area of the Trapper Fire. He radioed the Swiftcurrent Lookout for an update on the fire and was told that the wind had shifted. The lookout had been smoked out and was unable to see the fire activity. Mr. Burke and another co-worker scrambled to get pumps running and suppression sprinklers and nozzles charged and ready. Mr. Burke noticed that the drive belt had broken on the main water supply pump. With some very quick and resourceful modifications, he was able to switch to a different pump to supply water to the chalet fire suppression system. The wind was blowing approximately 70 miles per hour, knocking Mr. Burke and his co-worker to the ground. Mr. Burke ran for tools he needed to make emergency repairs to the pumps and water system. Returning, he was caught by thick hot clouds of smoke and had to feel his way back to the chalet. After hearing radio traffic talking about a running crown fire heading in their direction, he and his co-worker opened up all of their charged lines and began the defense of their lives and the historic chalet. Mr. Burke marshaled assistance of seven volunteers and assigned tasks to defend their position. They were being struck hard by burning bark, embers and ash as they wetted down the front of the chalet. Most of the chalet occupants huddled in the dark and smoke-filled room of the chalet, some praying and some crying. One of the men declared he was going to escape by hiking ahead of the fire over Swiftcurrent Pass. Mr. Burke quickly recognized that he had to establish firm control over the group. Mr. Burke explained that the safest place to stay was in the chalet and that their defense was strong and holding. Over the next several hours, the fire continued to rage around and past the chalet, finally dying down around 9:00 p.m. Mr. Burke and his co-worker had successfully defended the chalet and the lives of everyone in it. In the morning, Mr. Burke and his co-worker organized the group for the hike out to Logan Pass to safety. Before leaving, however, they received a standing ovation and personal thanks for their heroic efforts from each of the grateful survivors. For his heroic actions, courage, and professionalism, Christopher J. Burke is awarded the Valor Award of the Department of the Interior."

Glacier National Park is a landscape of change. Today if you hike into the Granite Park Chalet on the Highline Trail, you will see evidence of the Trapper fire in the standing forests of black-burnt trees now in a state of regeneration, marked by the magenta flares of fireweed. Hike up to the Grinnell Glacier and you will see more change from a different kind of heat.

In 1850, 150 glaciers were recorded within the boundaries of Glacier National Park. In 2015, only 25 active glaciers remain. After decades of research, scientists have concluded that the glaciers for which the park was named could be gone within fifteen years as a consequence of the burn of global warming.

Climate change is not an abstraction here, but real change in real time: the rapid retreat of glaciers. Rock once covered now lies bare. To touch warm granite beds once blanketed by glaciers is both a hard fact and a perversion. No longer do you see the chiseled high peaks defined by fields of snow. In the twenty years our family had been visiting Glacier National Park, from our first visit in 1982 to the fires of 2003, the absence of ice was disorienting and unnerving. A vital characteristic of the terrain is being erased by global warming. The geographic relief of the mountains was rendered monochromatic and bland. The "Crown of the Continent" is slipping. I wonder what the mountain goats are thinking, these "beasts the color of winter." In this part of the world, predicting the future is a foolish proposition.

No one knows this better than the Blackfeet Nation. They are the true witnesses of change. The Blackfeet Reservation borders Canada to the north and Glacier National Park to the west, what the elders call "the backbone of Mother Earth." The Blackfeet have been living in this landscape for generations, spanning hundreds of years and thousands more before that. With the knowledge of their ancestors still present through ceremonies and stories shared, contemporary Blackfeet are able to reach back through time and reclaim traditional wisdom, just as they are in the process of reclaiming the land that was once theirs.

When Glacier National Park was established in 1910, the Blackfeet were displaced and physically removed from their home ground where the men hunted bison on horseback and women gathered berries and roots for their families. It wasn't just their food that was derived from the land, but all their medicine, as well. Not only were they removed from their sources of subsistence, but they lost access to much of the land where their spiritual life took place. They were not only ripped from the land where they lived, but torn from their spiritual traditions, inhibiting songs, dreams, prayers, and ceremonies, especially those ceremonies and vision quests practiced within sight of Chief Mountain, a geologic formation central and sacred to the tribe. By the laws of another nation, foreign and disconnected from their own, the Blackfeet were not only displaced but deceived by the U.S. government, disregarded and dismissed as a sovereign nation with rights.

The first superintendent of Glacier National Park, William Richard Logan, was no friend to the tribes even though he was an Indian agent to the Assiniboine and Gros Ventre at the Fort Belknap Reservation. He wanted Blackfeet land for the minerals believed to be in the mountains and for the future economic value of tourism.

In 1895, the U.S. government initiated a deal with the Blackfeet Nation to trade the western mountains on their reservation rumored to be filled with gold in exchange for cash and the continued nonmineral rights to hunt and fish on their land as they had always done.

White Calf, one of the Blackfeet leaders, said, "I would like to have the right to hunt game and fish in the mountains. We will sell you the mountain lands from Birch Creek to the boundary, reserving the timber and grazing land."

Pressured to sign the agreement, the Blackfeet asked for $3 million. They were paid half that by the federal government. George Bird Grinnell was one of the government negotiators and an early advocate for Glacier National Park. He gave his word to the Blackfeet that they could retain their hunting and fishing rights as long as these lands remained public. But upon the opening of Glacier National Park in 1910, their native rights were revoked on the technicality that these were no longer public lands but park lands. It made no sense other than Indian removal. The Blackfeet were denied (with some Indians even being arrested) the previous access they had been promised.

Where is the valor in these actions taken by the U.S. federal government?

Much of the enduring valor of the Blackfeet Nation is drawn from fire. Between the glaciers that continue to hang in the high peaks above their homes and the slow rivers of ice that have carved the landscape around them, it is fire that helps to maintain their traditions and strength. Whether it is smoking the sacred pipe in ceremony or participating in sweat lodges with steaming stones and smoldering sage to purify the body and spirit, fire is a truth teller among the Blackfeet people. Even the Sun Dance, once practiced secretly for fear of government reprisal, imprisonment, or death, is now practiced openly in the name of prayer, sacrifice, and renewal, honoring the Sun that lights up the world, a force that both gives life and destroys it.

It is said that the Blackfeet get their name from their characteristic moccasins darkened by the ashes of fire.

Fire is akin to many tribes.

There is a long history of Indians as fire preventers and firefighters within the United States. In 1933, with the creation of the Civilian Conservation Corps under President Franklin D. Roosevelt, more than eighty-eight thousand Native Americans were employed in the Indian CCC Division to build fire lookout towers, fire cabins, and hundreds of miles of trails within remote forested terrain that provided access to firefighters should the trees ignite.

In 1948, the famed Mescalero Red Hats organized themselves to become the first Native American fire crew to fight fires in the Southwest. Most of them were World War II veterans. They were also the ones who rescued an orphaned bear cub after a large burn in New Mexico that later fostered the legend of Smokey the Bear, dressed in a ranger suit and advocating for fire safety in our national forests.

During that same period, David H. DeJong of the Native American Research and Training Center writes, "The Hopi Indians organized a trained firefighting crew; two years later, the Zuni Indians did the same. In 1954, the Red Hats and the Zuni Thunderbirds received meritorious service citations for firefighting from the U.S. Department of Agriculture. During 1953–55, Native American crews were formed in Montana from the Crow, Northern Cheyenne, Blackfeet, Flathead, Rocky Boys, and Forts Belknap, Peck and Hall reservations. In the mid-1950s, the Bureau of Land Management (BLM) also organized crews from among Alaska Natives."

According to the Bureau of Indian Affairs National Interagency Fire Center, close to 25 percent of all firefighters working today on wildfires on our public lands in the United States are Indians. In Montana, many are Blackfeet. The distinguished "Chief Mountain Hot Shots" are comprised of highly skilled Blackfeet crews who are dropped into dangerous fire zones to tame the flames. They are known as the "Fire Warriors."

I can't help but wonder how many Fire Warriors were fighting the "Mountain Man Complex" we witnessed in the summer of 2003.

Fire has been a traditional tool of warfare among the Blackfeet Nation for centuries, creating fire walls against enemies as well as using fire as a tool of restoration to rejuvenate land through intentional burns and fire management essential to the regenerative health of the prairies. It makes sense that the work of the "Fire Warriors" would be heightened in the twenty-first century as global warming is causing bigger and hotter fires due to the ravages of the pine bark beetle in western forests. Freezing temperatures during long, cold winters killed the beetles. Now, no longer. Now, due to higher temperatures in both summer and winter, pine bark beetles go through multiple breeding cycles that kill more trees.

The same climate changes that are creating more wildfires in the American West are creating the retreat of glaciers. Fire and ice are harbingers of change and both are found in the dynamic landscape of Glacier National Park.

A political fire is also burning in Glacier National Park. After more than a century of promises made and treaties broken by the federal government, the Blackfeet are challenging the status quo. They are demanding reinstatement of their reserved treaty rights to hunt, fish, and gather medicinal plants inside the national park boundaries. They are also asking for the voluntary closure of cultural sites essential to their spiritual practices. And their final ask is for joint management of Glacier National Park itself.

Here is one prediction that can be made: Soon, the Blackfeet will stand shoulder to shoulder in shared governance of these parklands with the National Park Service. After more than a century of being forced to retreat, the Blackfeet Nation is advancing like fire. The Blackfeet identity is rising from the ashes of national park history. Two-thirds of the Blackfeet live in Canada. Like the ecosystem of Waterton-Glacier, they have been divided by an international border. Today, their sky-blue flag flies high at the Lake McDonald Visitor's Center—flanked by the American flag on one side and the Canadian flag on the other—inside America's tenth national park. Three sovereign nations merge in an International Peace Park where Glacier National Park and the Waterton Lakes National Park create a contiguous boundary of faith.

It was at this intersection of nations that we celebrated John Tempest's birthday in Canada on July 26, 2003, across the border in Waterton Lakes National Park, a country away from the fires of northern Montana, but still within sight of melting glaciers.

In 1990, the writers Bill Kittredge and Annick Smith edited a thousand-page anthology of Montana literature including Native storytelling, the journals of trappers, poems, short stories, and essays from close to 150 writers, offering a mosaic of some of the finest writing past and present that had ever been written in the American West. The collection was called *The Last Best Place* and it became a regional phenomenon that both jump-started a western literary renaissance and captured a hard truth in one poignant phrase—the disappearing landscapes within the Rocky Mountains.

Darnell Davis, a Blackfeet elder, said recently, "The last best place is our first place."

CÉSAR E. CHÁVEZ NATIONAL

MONUMENT, CALIFORNIA,

AND THE FUTURE

-<-+-->-

I say to myself keep on—it will not be the end—not yet—

THE SOUND OF RUNNING WATER in the midst of drought is unnerving, a drought so brutal the curled leaves of the great oaks of California are crackling in the hot breezes. The soil is dry. Grasses are brittle. I hardly dare breathe for fear of starting a fire.

Brooke and I are visiting the César E. Chávez National Monument, established by President Barack Obama in 2012 in Keene, California. It is high noon, hot and dusty save for the sanctuary of this Peace Garden with its fountain flowing in the central plaza.

César Chávez, the great labor organizer and activist on behalf of farm workers, is buried in this garden of roses with a stone-carved statue of St. Francis of Assisi in one corner and La Virgen de Guadalupe in the other. Chávez lived and worked in this community of Nuestra Señora Reina de La Paz located in the Tehachapi Mountains, ninety miles northeast of Los Angeles. Together with Dolores Huerta, he founded the National Farm Workers Association in 1962, which later became the United Farm Workers (UFW), to secure basic human rights and fair wages for the largely Latino community of laborers.

His grave is simple. A cross made of barn wood with a welded crucifix stands behind a slightly raised piece of granite bearing the carved words:

CESAR ESTRADA CHAVEZ

1927–1993

Offerings have been left: a small American flag; two eagle feathers that hang on each arm of the cross; a weathered Mexican flag; one red rose; and at the base of the gravestone, a bobble-headed mariachi figure playing the guitar. Next to the toy musician is a pair of red and black clippers used to cut grapes.

These 187 acres of rolling hills were once a rock quarry, but in 1918, they became the site of the Stony Brook Retreat, a sanitarium for those suffering from tuberculosis. The hospital could accommodate fifty-five adults, while next door, in the "preventatorium," there was room for forty-four children. After Kern County shut the sanitarium down in 1967, locals believed the place was haunted.

Chávez didn't see it that way. He saw it as a perfect gathering place for the United Farm Workers; a place where they could organize and live in peace. The association had outgrown its national headquarters, Forty Acres, in Delano and had been looking for the right piece of property. When word reached César that Kern County was planning to auction off these 187 acres in the remote high desert of Tehachapi, close to Delano and Bakersfield, it sounded promising. Representatives from the UFW asked the county officers to show the land to them. The county refused.

César solicited the help of his friend Edward Lewis, a movie producer from Los Angeles. They hatched a plan: Edward Lewis would ask to see the land as an "interested party," accompanied by César's younger brother Richard posing as Lewis's chauffeur. The men returned with the report that the site was perfect, with a number of houses, office buildings, and a large community center already in place, ready to be renovated and reinhabited.

The plan worked. Kern County sold the property to Edward Lewis for $231,500. The state of California was stunned when Edward Lewis then turned around and sold the parcel to the United Farm Workers for $131,000. The UFW named it Nuestra Señora Reina de La Paz, and it became indeed a place of peace, a refuge not only for César and Helen Chávez and their eight children, but for many other members of the movement. It was both a home and a sanctuary for strategizing, organizing, and keeping the dream of farm workers' rights alive.

The history of our national parks and monuments is a history of subversion, shaped by individuals with either too much money, like John D. Rockefeller Jr., and held suspect in the cow town of Jackson, Wyoming, or by the too poor and too political migrant farm workers led by César Chávez, working the fields of reform in California.

On October 8, 2012, President Barack Obama designated the land at La Paz as one of our newest national monuments. The proclamation reads:

> *At La Paz, members of the farm worker movement celebrated such victories as the passage of the Agricultural Labor Relations Act of 1975, the first Federal law recognizing farm workers' collective bargaining rights. At La Paz, the UFW grew and expanded from its early roots as a union for farm workers to become a national voice for the poor and disenfranchised.*

Walking through the village, the spirit of collaboration remains among the empty buildings that once housed the conversations of struggle and reform. Emaciated California ground squirrels are barely moving in this land of little water and I am having a hard time separating the welfare of farm workers from the welfare of the biotic community who lives here now. I watch a black phoebe drink from the basin of the fountain and listen to the sound of water in this oasis surrounded by parched land.

Penance; paying penance. Chávez believed in penance, in part because he never felt he'd done enough. He led boycotts, strikes, and hunger strikes—gestures used to bring about greater justice and attention to the plight of the farm workers, who were demeaned and used, who battled desperately low wages and exposure to pesticides. Leaning against an oak tree for shade, I can't help but confront my own ignorance regarding these issues. I remember the grape boycott, but little else. It was not my struggle. That was my privilege. Now, I see it differently. Acts of injustice undermine all of us. The privacy of hypocrisy is corrosive.

What if our national parks and monuments became places of conscience instead of places of consumption? How many more T-shirts can we buy, let alone wear, that advertise where we've been? How many different forms of recreation must we create to assuage our adrenaline addictions from wing suits to pack rafts to roller blades? Is it not enough to return home with a fresh idea gleaned while walking in new territory? As I have been visiting our national parks, I keep asking myself: Who are we becoming?

In the end, it may be solitude that the future will thank us most for conserving—the kind of solitude born out of stillness, the stillness César Chávez and Dolores Huerta held for themselves at La Paz in the midst of their revolution. It is the kind of stillness that can still be found in each of our national parks where a quieting of the soul inspires creative acts.

The Organic Act is the United States federal law that established the National Park Service as an agency of the United States Department of the Interior. The act was signed into law one hundred years ago by President Woodrow Wilson; Congressman William Kent of California and Senator Reed Smoot of Utah co-sponsored the bill. Stephen Mather, who was assistant secretary of the interior at the time, had lobbied hard for a unified agency to oversee America's national parks, and so it was both logical and fitting that he became the first director of the National Park Service.

Mather was both an industrialist and a conservationist; a man who had become a millionaire through his family's Pacific Coast Borax Company. The singular image for Borax detergent, "20 Mule Team Borax," was Mather's brainchild. He applied his keen marketing skills to help promote the national parks in the early twentieth century.

Who could have imagined that the vision of our national parks, devised in 1916 by a privileged white businessman, could be transformed a century later to include the vision of a black president, a former community organizer, to establish a national monument to honor a Latino labor organizer and a community of farm workers who understood their privilege as the privilege of human dignity?

If our national parks are to remain viable in the future, they must become sites of transformation where the paradigm of domination and manipulation ends and a vision of unison begins.

We have opportunities to expand this vision of environmental and social justice by establishing more national parks and monuments. We can also enlarge the borders of the ones we have like Yellowstone and Canyonlands in the name of ecological connectivity in an era when the last desperate cries of the fossil fuel industry are threatening to destroy not only our most revered public landscapes but the planet. The Arctic National Wildlife Refuge is a shimmering example of a fifty-year fight for protection. Native voices are now forcefully calling for a resolution in the form of a national monument. The Gwich'en see these lands as the birthplace of caribou, "The Place Where Life Begins," that must be held for future generations. "This is a human rights issue," says Sarah James, a Gwich'en elder. "Oil development there would hurt the caribou and threaten our way of life."

Robert Thompson, an Inupiat guide and hunter in the village of Kaktovik, Alaska, on the border of the Arctic Refuge testified before the United States Senate on March 4, 2005:

I am honored to be part of this movement to save our land, our ocean and our culture . . . We are attempting to use the democratic process to save our culture. Before this it could be said and often was, that we wanted all that oil money. You are now facing a group of people who are saying that no amount of money is worth exchanging our culture for oil. However this goes, future generations of Inupiat can look back and say, those people who signed this petition to protect our lands tried to do the right thing. Somehow, I feel that it will be important to them to know that someone cared.

The idea of traditional knowledge being embedded within traditional land management is both a revolution and a healing between Indians and the National Park Service. This is the vision behind the Bears Ears National Monument proposal, led by the Navajo, Hopi, Uintah and Ouray Ute, and Mountain Ute Coalition, and supported by twenty other tribes in the American Southwest. Willie Greyeyes, chairman of Utah Diné Bikéyah, said, "The tribes are determined to see the cultural values in this landscape protected." Close to two million acres of ancestral lands adjacent to Canyonlands National Park would be secured through the Antiquities Act. "We can still hear our ancestors' songs being sung on the mesas," one of the elders told me. "Prayers have to be walked, not just talked," Regina Lopez-Whiteskunk said.

At the intersection of landscape and culture, diversity and inclusion, patterns of cooperation emerge in the name of community. The power of what binds us together, rather than what tears us apart, becomes a shared priority. A creative tension between needs, both human and wild, must be considered and negotiated. An unexpected harmony begins to emerge as something to be honored and safeguarded like water in the desert.

We, the people, have made mistakes. We have made mistakes in our relationships with those who came before us and the land that holds their histories. We have made mistakes in how we have managed and misunderstood the wild. But after spending a lifetime immersed in our national parks, I believe we are slowly learning what it means to offer our reverence and respect to the closest thing we as American citizens have to sacred lands. Our national parks are places of recognition. When I see a mountain lion's tracks on pink sand in the desert, I am both predator and prey. When I see the elusive Everglade kite hovering above the sawgrass, I am that manifestation of hope and survival. And when I visit the Women's Rights National Historical Park in Seneca Falls, New York, and listen to Sojourner Truth's speech, "Ain't I a Woman," her voice becomes the voice I want to cultivate in the name of courage.

We are at a crossroads. We can continue on the path we have been on, in this nation that privileges profit over people and land; or we can unite as citizens with a common cause—the health and wealth of the Earth that sustains us. If we cannot commit to this kind of fundamental shift in our relationship to people and place, then democracy becomes another myth perpetuated by those in power who care only about themselves.

In my own state of Utah, there are those (including most of our elected officials) who want to see our federal lands returned to the states. At the Western Freedom Festival held in Cedar City, Utah, in 2015, in the proximity of Zion and Bryce National Parks, devotees of the rancher Cliven Bundy, who refused to pay his grazing fees, gathered to protest what they see as an assault on their liberty. From their point of view, any more federal lands "locked up" in the name of wilderness or national parks is a threat to their values as Americans. Why? Because they are sick of the government telling them what to do. Threats of violence are real. Death threats were made. So much so that during the Freedom Festival, employees of all federal land agencies from the Bureau of Land Management to the National Park Service were advised not to wear their uniforms in public so they would not be a target, literally. The windows at the visitor's center at Grand Staircase–Escalante National Monument were replaced with bulletproof glass.

What are we to do with this kind of polarity of vision within the United States of America? How might we begin a different kind of conversation so that our public lands are seen as our public commons, instead of the seedbed of rancor and violence?

The time has come for acts of reverence and restraint on behalf of the Earth. We have arrived at the Hour of Land.

"All the world seems a church and the mountains altars," wrote John Muir. But perhaps the naturalist's most prescient words were these: "When we try to pick out anything by itself, we find it hitched to everything else in the universe."

The world is intertwined. Life is evolving. We, too, are evolving. We revise our ideas over time. What John Muir advocated for in his lifetime—the protection of wild country and our national parks—is still, I would argue, a noble cause, worthy of our admiration and respect. When the environmental historian Donald Worster says that Muir started a new American religion, if I am honest, I am part of his congregation. When I saw Yosemite Valley for the first time, I felt I was standing in Eden. I have followed in his footsteps of environmental activism as an American writer. And when Richard White argued at the Aurora Forum at Stanford University in 2009 that "Muir's vision for the nineteenth century . . . is not going to be a vision for the twenty-first century," I understand his point of view.

"Muir's view that you can protect the mountains while everything else is opened up to development . . . global warming has finished that . . . It's all one world." White goes on to say, "It's not that I'm against wilderness areas, it's not that I'm against national parks, but essentially, we've now instituted a system of change that is going to take over—the entire planet."

What Muir could not see from the vantage point of Mount Ritter in 1872, the same year Yellowstone became America's first national park, was the scale of changes that would be piled onto the Earth by modernity. How could he have imagined that the work of a backcountry ranger now includes picking up five pounds of toilet paper in a two-foot radius on the trail to Half Dome in Yosemite National Park? How could he have comprehended the appetite of an expanding global population and the carbon load now weighing heavy on all of us? We don't need to denounce John Muir's legacy, we need to broaden it.

A decade ago, the writer Rebecca Solnit was part of a rephotographing project in Yosemite National Park with the photographers Mark Klett and Byron Wolfe, where they not only revisited the sites of images taken by famed photographers such as Carleton Watkins and Eadweard Muybridge, but they took the same picture a century or so later. Changes are visible, but most of them out of frame, like parking lots and bulldozers. "Now, wilderness can be seen as a useful fiction, a fiction constructed by John Muir and his heirs and deployed to keep places from being destroyed by resource extraction and wholesale development," Solnit said.

As our thinking about place matures and deepens, becoming more inclusive, as we honor the complexities between culture and wilderness, the irony is this: Muir's call for wilderness in the past is now becoming a clarion call for the preservation of wilderness for our future. The preeminent biologist E. O. Wilson is saying that if we are to survive as a species, half the Earth must be set aside as wilderness. He is not alone in his thinking. Recently, he told me that he wanted to see whether this idea was taking hold, so he Googled three words: "Wilson Half Earth." To his astonishment, 70 million references popped up on his computer screen.

"Something is happening," Wilson said. "A real movement is occurring. Conservation is the global response to the environmental degradation we are witnessing. If we are to find ourselves on the other side of this bottleneck we are in, it must be. The health of the land is the health of the people."

Whether we see wilderness as a "useful fiction" or an ecological necessity, our national parks are akin to oxygen in the twenty-first century—"Oxígeno!" my friend Mercedes Ornelas from Mexico said, when seeing Arches National

Park for the first time. "Espacio abierto en la naturaleza para respirar aire puro."

The poetry of the world is also an open space. When a young poet asked W. S. Merwin what makes a poem, the great poet thought for a moment and then said, "Following what you don't know." Could a national park be seen as a place of poetry? Line by line, step by step, we wander along a path unknown to us, but in the process of discovery, we come to recognize ourselves in each tree, each plant, each bird and face our longing to reconnect with a larger world beyond ourselves. Rather than fear the wilderness ahead, even climate change, we are present inside it. Fear is replaced with engagement. Relationships are forged, resiliency as a species is enhanced.

> *Insects on a bough*
> *Floating downriver*
> *Still singing*
> *—Issa*

These words have been removed from the new version of the *Oxford Junior Dictionary*:

acorn, adder, almond, apricot, ash, ass, bacon, beaver, beech, beetroot, blackberry, blacksmith, bloom, bluebell, boar, bramble, bran, bray, bridle, brook, budgerigar, bullock, buttercup, canary, canter, carnation, catkin, cauliflower, chestnut, clover, conker, county, cowslip, crocus, cheetah, colt, corgi, cygnet, dandelion, diesel, doe, drake, fern, ferret, fungus, gerbil, goldfish, gooseberry, gorse, guinea pig, hamster, hazel, hazelnut, heather, heron, herring, holly, horse chestnut, ivy, kingfisher, lark, lavender, leek, leopard, liquorice, lobster, magpie, manger, marzipan, melon, minnow, mint, mistletoe, monarch, mussel, nectar, nectarine, newt, oats, otter, ox, oyster, pansy, panther, parsnip, pasture, pelican, piglet, plaice, poodle, poppy, porcupine, porpoise, porridge,

*poultry, primrose, prune, radish, raven, rhubarb, sheaf, spaniel, spinach,
starling, stoat, stork, sycamore, terrapin, thrush, tulip, turnip, vine, violet,
walnut, weasel, willow, wren*

These are words that have been added:

allergic, alliteration, analog, apparatus, attachment, bilingual, biodegradable, block graph, blog, boisterous, brainy, broadband, bullet point, bungee jumping, cautionary tale, celebrity, chatroom, childhood, chronological, citizenship, classify, colloquial, committee, common sense, compulsory, conflict, cope, creep, curriculum, cut and paste, database, debate, democratic, donate, drought, dyslexic, emotion, endangered, EU, Euro, export, food chain, idiom, incisor, interdependent, MP3 player, negotiate, square number, tolerant, trapezium, vandalism, voicemail

If we can remove words from a dictionary that are so alive with meaning, and withhold them from our children, removing what is alive in the world becomes easy. The wild is no longer part of our vocabulary. I hear Merwin's words: "Through all of youth I was looking for you without knowing what I was looking for." Nature becomes "a forgotten language."

These are difficult times, transformative times—times of extreme actions especially within our national parks. Extreme drought. Extreme fires. Extreme development with extreme policy shifts needed in the name of global warming. The world is changing dramatically, both ecologically as well as politically. But I believe our greatest transformation as a species will be spiritual. The word "we" must include all species.

The religious scholar Karen Armstrong says compassion is an act, not an emotion. If it were an emotion, it would be discomfort. If we are to understand compassion for Other, we must cultivate the emotions of discomfort and disturbance. By embracing the word "umvelt," honoring the world as it is

experienced by different people, animals, and organisms, our capacity to imagine and empathize will bring us into a more authentic relationship with the Earth. Humility in the face of humanity allows us to see ourselves as "one species among many," not the indomitable center of a human-developed world.

Arvol Looking Horse is the nineteenth-generation keeper of the White Buffalo Calf Pipe bundle and a spiritual leader among the Lakota. He and others are calling for "the Great Healing" to address this separation from the land and each other. "The natural world does not discriminate. We must unite or perish."

When we enter places of grandeur and sites of suffering, and inhabit landscapes of historical import and ecological splendor, we stand on the periphery of awe. How did this happen? Who were the witnesses? And what are we seeing now? The American landscape has a voice, many voices. It becomes us. Our national parks are a burning bush of identities.

This deeper understanding of our individual and shared histories, both human and wild, allows us to touch and be touched by what has occurred in the past and what remains as we contemplate what we can create together by listening to one another with an open heart.

César Chávez said, "After thirty years of organizing poor people, I have become convinced that the two greatest aspirations of humankind are equality and participation." If we can learn to listen to the land, we can learn to listen to each other. This is the beginning of ceremony.

"It is time to weep and sing," wrote W. H. Auden. At a low ebb of hope, I asked my friend Doug Peacock how he staves off despair—this is the man who kept a map of Yellowstone in the back pocket of his fatigues throughout the war and would unfold it at night to keep insanity at bay.

"Insulate yourself with friends and seek out wild places," he said.

Which is exactly what I was doing seeking out my friend on the other side of Yellowstone on the day we learned that the U.S. Fish and Wildlife Service had denied wolverines protection under the Endangered Species Act.

While driving from Jackson Hole to Livingston, I was listening to Vivaldi's *Four Seasons* recomposed by the musician Max Richter. I love this piece of music and I love the story behind it. Richter's favorite piece of music was Vivaldi's *Four Seasons*. He had played it as a musician hundreds of times and had heard it many more times than he had performed it. But the strangest thing started to occur. *The Four Seasons* had become so commercialized, so trivialized, played in elevators and as the sound track for cheap commercials, that he could no longer hear its beauty. It had become lost to him—demoted to musical wallpaper. Max Richter did the unthinkable. He reimagined Vivaldi's masterpiece and recomposed it so it could be heard once again at this moment in time.

"*The Four Seasons* is something we all carry around with us," Richter said. "It's everywhere. In a way, we stop being able to hear it. So this project was about reclaiming this music for me personally. I wanted to fall in love with it all over again," he said. "By getting inside it and rediscovering it for myself—I was able to take a new path through a well-known landscape."

I was listening to the *The Four Seasons Recomposed* as I was en route to Doug. My mind was moving toward reverie with the music. It was exactly what I needed to recompose myself as I was driving through Yellowstone to Montana, inspiring me to reimagine everything, including our national parks. Our institutions and agencies are no longer working for us. It is time to reimagine the wilderness movement as a movement of direct action, time to reimagine our public lands as sanctuaries, refuges, and sacred lands. Time to rethink what is acceptable and what is not. I became lost in the music—and then, as I was driving through the Hayden Valley, the cars in front of me came to a halt. We faced a bison jam: hundreds of bison not only crossing the road but walking alongside us. I was now at a crawl, barely going five miles per hour. I rolled down my window, still listening to *The Four Seasons* with the volume louder than I realized. The bison started moving closer to my car. I started getting nervous, thought about rolling up my window, but then I began noticing the bison turning their heads toward the music, walking even closer to the car. I imagined they were enjoying Vivaldi as I was, and I relaxed as we listened to the music together for close to a mile, all of us, slowly moving down the road.

I was late to Doug's house. He was waiting. I brought him a nice French Bordeaux. We took the bottle and two glasses outside with a view of Paradise Valley. Doug had written a plea on the wolverine's behalf a week before. It was published online in *The Daily Beast*. He had received a note from his editor, Chris Dickey, the son of the poet James L. Dickey.

"I'm sorry," he'd said. "Perhaps this poem from my father will help."

Under a thunderous sky with bolts of lightning adding punctuation, Doug and I read "For the Last Wolverine" out loud to each other, between sips of wine, alternating between stanzas, with tears streaming down our cheeks.

The final lines undid us:

> *Alone, with maybe some dim racial notion*
> *Of being the last, but none of how much*
> *Your unnoticed going will mean:*
> *How much the timid poem needs*
>
> *The mindless explosion of your rage,*
> *The glutton's internal fire   the elk's*
> *Heart in the belly, sprouting wings,*
>
> *The pact of the "blind swallowing*
> *Thing," with himself, to eat*
> *The world, and not to be driven off it*
> *Until it is gone, even if it takes*
>
> *Forever. I take you as you are*
>
> *And make of you what I will,*
> *Skunk-bear, carcajou, bloodthirsty*
>
> *Non-survivor.*
>   Lord, let me die   but not die
> Out.

Doug and I raised our glasses to the mountains, black clouds billowing all around us as a swath of red clouds turned pink.

"To Wolverine!" Doug said.

And then, he turned to me with tears in his eyes. "We lose nothing by loving."

THE GALLERY

Curated with Frish Brandt

 **CARLETON WATKINS (1829-1916)** was a pioneer, an explorer, the man on the moon in a place called Yosemite when he stepped into this landscape with his camera in 1861. Over his lifetime, Watkins made some five thousand photographs, and his work not only brought the majesty of the American West to the masses, but also influenced President Abraham Lincoln's decision to protect the Yosemite Valley through the Yosemite Land Act in 1863.

EDWARD A. RIDDELL (1952-) is a photographer rooted in Jackson, Wyoming. Weather punctuates his pictures: clouds, seasons, shadows. Early on, it was Ed Riddell who brought me to a love of photography. We met as aspiring artists at the Teton Science School in 1974, making  a vow to create a book together, which we did in 2005: *The Range of Memory*, and we reimagined it again in 2015. The frontispiece photograph of the Grand Tetons is an image that hangs in my father's home.

 LEE FRIEDLANDER (1934-): I had the privilege of meeting Mr. Friedlander at the Fraenkel Gallery, where he spoke of a lifelong love of national parks that began when he was a child growing up in the Pacific Northwest. "They taught me how to see," he said. Nowhere is his genius more apparent than in *America by Car* (2010), which includes nearly two hundred images that he took while driving through all fifty states in a rental car. His project is especially poignant regarding our national parks, such as the photograph seen here in Death Valley.

LUKAS FELZMANN (1959–) was born in Switzerland and now teaches photography at Stanford University. His work celebrates the patterns and juxtapositions found within the human landscape and natural world. Each image creates its own narrative. His latest book, *Gull Juju*, is a subtle unfolding of the plastics that now reside on the Farallon Islands off the coast of California. It is a terrible beauty that glimmers in the nests of gulls.

 JAMES BALOG (1952–) is a photographer with a warrior spirit who continues to push the boundaries of art and advocacy. Bolting cameras in place across the Arctic, he has recorded the retreating of glaciers through his Extreme Ice Survey (the focus of the award-winning film *Chasing Ice*), which speaks to both his muscular commitment to climate justice and his brilliance as an artist. When I think of Balog, the word *velocity* comes to mind.

ANSEL ADAMS (1902–1984) set the standard for landscape photography in the modern era, especially when it came to America's national parks. The classic Sierra Club book *This the American Earth*, a collaboration between Ansel Adams and Nancy Newhall, showed me how the power of image and text can align itself with an ethic of place. Ansel Adams was a fierce environmentalist who understood the legacy of love.

 ANONYMOUS: For whom was this picture made, and why? The beauty is that it allows us to think about who saved it and how it found its way to us. Every hand that touched this photograph and passed it on is part of Anonymous. With gratitude to Jonah Samson for this found photograph.

EDITH LEVY (1964–) lives in Toronto, Canada, with her two sons. The horizon holds her attention. As a photographer, she describes her work as "writing with light." A script of light is evident on the dancing water of the Atlantic Ocean. "The sheer size of Acadia National Park makes it possible to carve out a little slice of heaven that you can call your own," she wrote, "even for just a few moments."

SALLY MANN (1951–):   Shadow and light. Sally Mann is a fearless photographer whose strength is rooted in her own home ground. Her focus on family, death and decay, and the haunting battlefields of the Southern landscape have become her signature. We met at the Corcoran Gallery in Washington, D.C., on September 11, 2001. Later, she sent me a photograph of seeds flying from a dry stalk of native grass on her farm in Virginia. It mirrored the falling bodies we all witnessed on that very dark day.

LOIS CONNER (1951–)   has made her life an ongoing pilgrimage to our national parks, part of her remarkable portfolio of place. Her platinum landscape photographs made with her 7"×17"-format banquet camera are shimmering scrolls of panoramic wonder  that hold all the richness and texture of silk tapestries. I met Lois at Emmet Gowin's show *Hidden Likeness*, at the Morgan Library. The shared joy between these two photographers created its own exchange of light.

LIDAR-DERIVED IMAGE OF MARCHING BEARS MOUND GROUP: This image of the Effigy Mounds National Monument was taken by "a remote sensing technology that measures distance by illuminating a target with a laser and analyzing the reflected light." It is of great benefit to archeologists, as it helps map and locate features beneath the forest canopy and vegetation.

JAMES H. EVANS (1954–)   lives in Marathon, Texas. "Outside is the side I'm on," Evans says, and that becomes obvious from his portraits of the  wizened people who live on both sides of the Rio Grande. He not only captures the lines of a face but the strangeness of saguaros, and the eye shine of javalinas at night. Evans became my visual guide in the bareboned landscapes of the Chihuahuan desert of Big Bend National Park.

SEBASTIÃO SALGADO (1944–):   I first met Sebastião and his wife, Léila, at "An Evening of Conscience" at the University of Utah in 2005. It was here that I learned of Salgado's project "Genesis": his desire to photograph the beauty of the Earth's remaining wild places. He spoke of his "soul being sick" from bearing witness to war, particularly in Rwanda, and that the work of restoration was what he needed now. Salgado's images have the power to heal.

EMMET GOWIN (1941-)   is a photographer intrinsically bound to the soul of things. He is one of my spiritual teachers. Luckily for us, he picked up a camera, but whatever he would have chosen to touch would have become a medium of numinosity. When Gowin was given special clearance to photograph the Nevada Test Site and make pictures of the craters in the desert left by the atomic bombs in the 1950s and 1960s—the same bombs responsible for the deaths of my mother and grandmothers—I saw the role of the artist differently. Gowin is a seer in pursuit of both paradox and hard-edged truths.

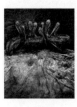

DANIEL BELTRÁ (1964-)   was born in Madrid, Spain, and has traveled the world exposing our human impact on the planet. He has worked as a photographer alongside Greenpeace, as well as with Prince Charles on forest ecology. His passion for conservation burns as bright as his eyes and heart remain open and steady in the face of ecological tragedies. Beltrá's images create both a conversation and a bridge between beauty and despair.

ROBERT ADAMS (1937-):   Is there anyone who feels the sorrow, angst, and beauty of the Earth deeper than Bob Adams? "What pact did we make, Faustian or otherwise, to consume the world?" he writes. When I stood before his exhibit *Turning Back*, which documented the devastation of ancient forests by the logging industry in his home ground of Oregon, I wept. Adams's visual articulation of what changes and what remains dares us to confront our humanity as a species.

MARK KLETT (1952-)   takes his unique perspective as a trained geologist and translates his knowledge of the Earth from the inside out. His transformative "rephotographing" surveys are a documentation of the Western journey, past and present. But it is the way he frames time today with his camera, particularly the desert Southwest, that moves me. In his photographs, Klett maintains a sense of geologic scale as he renders human presence against tentative and enduring landscapes. I admire his wit.

WILL WILSON (1969-)   is a photographer whose formative years were spent inside the Navajo Nation. When I first encountered his work at the Abbe Museum in Maine, the courage and cultural critique of his images made me wonderfully uncomfortable. "Since 2005, I have been creating a series of artworks entitled *Auto Immune Response*, which takes as its subject the quixotic relationship between a postapocalyptic Diné (Navajo) man and the devastatingly beautiful, but toxic environment he inhabits," he states.

 **CHRISTINA SEELY (1976-)** is an artist who draws from the fields of science, architecture, music, and anthropology to find the song lines between darkness and light. Always mysterious, often mischievous, Seely's pictures are searing in both their chill and heat, from the Arctic to the tropics. Climate change is the medium from which she makes art. Darkness is where she has taken refuge. And light is where she emerges as a brilliant messenger of her generation.

RICHARD AVEDON (1923-2004) said, "My photographs don't go below the surface. I have great faith in surfaces. A good one is full of clues." With Avedon, a double helix is created between the artist and his subject. The eyes are held in trust. For months, I tried to track down the portrait of César Chávez and Dolores Huerta standing side by side, but the negative was nowhere to be found. Still, the dignity of both is captured here in the steady gaze of Chávez, who said that Dolores Huerta was the only person he ever feared.

 MARY DANIEL HOBSON (1969-) is a photographer with a fidelity toward natural forms, be they feathers, flowers, or the human body. Through the medium of collage, she expresses a depth and devotion to the integrity of objects: a piece of music, a bottle, a tattoo. Each picture feels akin to ceremony, calling forth a healing grace. "Instead of just describing the surface, which photography does so well," she writes, "I wanted to express something deeper . . . something more emotional."

JONATHAN STUART (1950-) studied with Ansel Adams in the 1970s and was an assistant at the prestigious Ansel Adams Workshops in Yosemite Valley. His work focuses on the modern West in its all its paradox, brutality, tenderness, and grace. An observer with an edge and a very astute mind, Stuart explores the nature of human intimacy with the land. Jon lives in Jackson Hole, Wyoming, where he continues to mentor students of photography.

 LYNN DAVIS (1944-) understands the architectural force of landscape that is sculpted through time by wind, water, and light, be it in Utah's red rock desert, the geometry of Greenland ice, or the façade of a building. The mathematical instinct of her work—clear, clean, and elegant in its visual language—is singular. Portraits of history and the presence of creation are evident in each of her pictures, including the ephemeral force of Old Faithful in Yellowstone National Park.

ANSLEY WEST RIVERS (1982–) lives in Georgia and photographs hidden landscapes: a night sky, a disappearing tree, ghosts rising from water. She fell in love with rivers on her first rafting trip down the Grand Canyon. She took her 4 x 5 camera with a box of film on the river knowing she could lose everything. Instead, she came home with a portfolio of "lunar traces" by following the moon. This descent into deep time changed not only the nature of her work, but the nature of her mind.

SOURCES

The following sources were used to inform the writing of each essay. I also benefited greatly from the natural history associations of each national park that I visited whose books are located within national park visitor centers. They house a wealth of resources, from natural history field guides to books on human history and a literature of place. In this selected bibliography, I have also included recommended reading for each national park represented in *The Hour of Land*.

AMERICA'S NATIONAL PARKS

Burns, Ken. *The National Parks: Our Best Idea*, a film by Ken Burns. 2009. www.pbs.org /nationalparks/about.

Cahn, Robert, and Robert Glenn Ketchum. *American Photographers and the National Parks*. New York: The Viking Press, 1981.

Cronon, William, ed. *Uncommon Ground: Rethinking the Human Place in Nature*. New York: W. W. Norton & Co., 1996.

Duncan, Dayton. *Seed of the Future: Yosemite and the Evolution of the National Park Idea*. San Francisco: Yosemite Conservancy, 2013.

Jacoby, Karl. *Crimes Against Nature: Squatters, Poachers, Thieves, and the Hidden History of American Conservation*. Berkeley: University of California Press, 2001.

Keiter, Robert B. *To Conserve Unimpaired: The Evolution of the National Park Idea*. Washington, D.C.: Island Press, 2013.

"National Parks: A Conversation with William Cronin, James Mills, Richard K. Nelson, and Nevada Barr." *To the Best of Our Knowledge*. National Public Radio, 2015. www.publicbroadcasting .net/wjsu/.artsmain/article/11/1172/1555228/Radio/TTBOOK.National.Parks.

Peacock, Doug. *Grizzly Years: In Search of the American Wilderness.* New York: Henry Holt, 1990.

Soulé, Michael E. *Collected Papers of Michael E. Soulé.* Washington, D.C.: Island Press, 2014.

Spence, Mark David. *Dispossessing the Wilderness: Indian Removal and the Making of the National Parks.* London: Oxford University Press, 2000.

Wuerthner, George. *Yellowstone: A Visitor's Companion.* National Park Visitor's Companion Series. Mechanicsburg, Pa.: Stackpole Books, 1992.

Wuerthner, George, Eileen Crist, and Tom Butler, eds. *Protecting the Wild: Parks and Wilderness, the Foundation for Conservation.* Washington, D.C.: Island Press, 2014.

GRAND TETON NATIONAL PARK

Albright, Joseph, and Marcia Kunstel. "Rockefeller's Last Stand: Historic JY Ranch Returning to Nature." *Jackson Hole* (Summer/Fall 2003).

Craighead, Frank C. *For Everything There Is a Season: The Sequence of Natural Events in the Grand Teton–Yellowstone Area.* Guilford, Conn.: Falcon Books, 2001.

———. *Track of the Grizzly.* San Francisco: Sierra Club Books, 1979.

D. R. Horne & Company. *JY Ranch: Historic American Buildings Survey Documentation.* Laurance S. Rockefeller Preserve, 2010.

Righter, Robert W. *Crucible for Conservation: The Struggle for Grand Teton National Park.* Moose, Wyo.: Grand Teton Association, 1982.

———. *Peaks, Politics & Passion.* Moose, Wyo.: Grand Teton Association, 2014.

Turner, Jack. *Abstract Wild.* Tucson: University of Arizona Press, 1996.

———. *Teewinot—A Year in the Teton Range.* New York: Thomas Dunne Books, 2000.

Williams, Terry Tempest. *A Feather on Phelps Lake*, poetry exhibit inside the Laurance S. Rockefeller Preserve, Grand Teton National Park, 2008.

Winks, Robin W. *Laurance S. Rockefeller: Catalyst for Conservation.* Washington, D.C.: Island Press, 1997.

THEODORE ROOSEVELT NATIONAL PARK

Bakkan Oil Field Fail of the Day. www.facebook.com/Bakken-Oilfield-Fail-of-the-Day-292810960810561.

Box, C. J. *Badlands.* New York: Minotaur Books, 2015.

Brinkley, Douglas. *The Wilderness Warrior: Theodore Roosevelt & the Crusade for America.* New York: Harper Perennial, 2010.

Jenkinson, Clay. *Theodore Roosevelt in the Dakota Badlands: An Historical Guide.* Dickinson, N. Dak.: Dickinson State University, 2006.

Morris, Edmund. *Colonel Roosevelt.* New York: Random House, 2011.

———. *The Rise of Theodore Roosevelt*. New York: Random House, 2001.

———. *Theodore Rex*. New York: Random House, 2002.

Moss, Jesse. *The Overnighters*. Drafthouse Films, 2014. www.theovernighters.com.

Orr, Shannon K., and Rebecca L. Humphreys. "Mission Rivalry: Use and Preservation Conflicts in National Parks Policy." *Public Organization Review* 12, no. 1 (March 2012): 85–98.

Rockin' the Bakkan. www.rockinthebakken.com/Bakken/What-is-the-Bakken.

Roosevelt, Theodore. With an introduction by Stephen E. Ambrose. *Hunting Trips of a Ranchman and The Wilderness Hunter*. New York: Modern Library, 1998.

———. *Wilderness Writings*. Literature of the American Wilderness ed. Layton, Utah: Peregrine Smith Books, 1986.

ACADIA NATIONAL PARK

The Abbe Museum located in Bar Harbor, Maine, is an invaluable resource on Maine's Native American history, culture, art, and archaeology. www.abbemuseum.org.

Curry, Tom, and Carl Little. *Island: Paintings by Tom Curry*. Rockport, Maine: Downeast Books, 2012.

Dawn Land: Abenaki Creation Story. www.youtube.com/watch?v=GgnAR-rwsj0. Based on book by Will Davis (adapter, illustrator) and Joseph Bruchac (author). New York: First Second, 2010.

Dorr, George B. *Acadia National Park: Its Origin and Background*. Burr Printing Company, 1942.

History of Cranberry Isles—a website by the Cranberry Island Historical Society. www .gcihs.org and www.cranberryisles.com/history.html.

Jewett, Sarah Orne. *The Country of Pointed Firs and Other Stories*. Signet Classics ed. New York: Signet, 1960.

Morison, Samuel Eliot. *The Story of Mount Desert Island*. New York: Little Brown & Co., 1960.

Roberts, Ann Rockefeller. *Mr. Rockefeller's Roads: The Untold Story of Acadia's Carriage Roads and Their Creator*. Maine: Down East Books, 1993.

Shetterly, Susan Hand. *Settled in the Wild: Notes on the Edge of Town*. Chapel Hill, N.C.: Algonquin Books, 2010.

GETTYSBURG NATIONAL MILITARY PARK

The Civil War Monitor is a quarterly magazine that portrays the Civil War from many perspectives. I enjoyed the varied articles in each issue written for a popular as well as an informed audience. www.civilwarmonitor.com.

Epstein, Daniel Mark. *Lincoln and Whitman: Parallel Lives in Civil War Washington*. New York: Random House, 2007.

Gates, Henry Louis. "Which Black Man Was Responsible for Burying Bodies at Gettysburg?" www.theroot.com/articles/history/2014/10/battle_of_gettysburg_which_black_man_was_responsible_for_burying_the_bodies.html.

Johnston, Jenny. "Badge of Honor." *Civil War Monitor*, Special Issue: Gettysburg at 150, vol. 3, no. 2 (Summer 2013). I benefited greatly from this article.

McKone, William. *Vermont's Irish Rebel: Captain John Lonergan*. Jacksonville, Vt.: Brewster River Press, 2010.

McPherson, James M. *Battle Cry of Freedom: The Civil War Era*. Oxford History of the United States ed. Oxford: Oxford University Press, 2003.

———. *Hallowed Ground: A Walk in Gettysburg*. Crown Journeys ed. New York: Crown Publishing Group, 2003.

Pitcaithley, Dwight T. "A Cosmic Threat": The National Park Service Addresses the Causes of the Civil War, *Slavery and Public History: The Tough Stuff of American Memory*. Edited by James Oliver Horton and Lois E. Horton. Chapel Hill: University of North Carolina Press, 2009.

Shaara, Michael. *Killer Angels*. New York: Ballantine, 1987.

Smithsonian Institution. *The Civil War: A Visual History*. New York: Dorling Kindersley, 2011.

Winks, Robin. "Sites of Shame: Disgraceful Episodes from Our Past Should Be Included in the Park System to Present a Complete Picture of Our History." *National Parks* (March–April 1994), 22–23.

EFFIGY MOUNDS NATIONAL MONUMENT

Birmingham, Robert A., and Leslie E. Eisenberg. *Indian Mounds of Wisconsin*. Madison: University of Wisconsin Press, 2000.

Effigy Mounds National Monument Scandal. www.desmoinesregister.com/story/news/2015/05/04/effigy-mounds-firing-scapegoat/26877455.

Lenzendorf, Dennis. *Effigy Mounds: A Guide to Effigy Mounds National Monument*. Fort Washington, Pa.: Eastern National, 2015.

Mallam, R. Clark. "Ideology from the Earth: Effigy Mounds in the Midwest." *Archaeology* 35, no. 4 (July/August 1982): 60–62, 64. www.jstor.org/stable/41727426. Accessed July 27, 2015. 19:24 UTC.

Milner, George R. *The Moundbuilders: Ancient Peoples of Eastern North America*. London: Thames & Hudson, 2004.

Mississippi River Facts. National Park Service. www.nps.gov/miss/riverfacts.htm.

Wilson, Jennifer. "The Park That Wasn't." *Iowa Outdoors* 72, no. 1 (January/February 2013): 38–44.

BIG BEND NATIONAL PARK

Bowden, Charles. "Big Bend." *Mountain Gazette* (Boulder, Colo.), April 3, 2012.

Bowden, Charles, Erin Almeranti, and Mary Martha Miles. *The Charles Bowden Reader.* Austin: University of Texas Press, 2010.

Evans, Bill. *Crazy from the Heat.* Austin: University of Texas Press, 2011.

Langford, J. O., with Fred Gipson. *Big Bend: A Homesteader's Story.* Austin: University of Texas Press, 1981.

Nelson, Barney, ed. *God's Country or Devil's Playground: The Best Nature Writing from the Big Bend of Texas.* Austin: University of Texas Press, 2002.

Roorbach, Bill. *Big Bend—Stories.* Berkeley, Calif.: Counterpoint, 2002.

Wauer, Roland H., and Carl M. Fleming. *Naturalist's Big Bend: An Introduction to the Trees and Shrubs, Wildflowers, Cacti, Mammals, Birds, Reptiles and Amphibians, Fish, and Insects.* Louise Lindsey Merrick Natural Environment Series ed. College Station: Texas A&M University Press, 2001.

GATES OF THE ARCTIC NATIONAL PARK

Adams, John Luther, and Alex Ross. *The Place Where You Go to Listen: In Search of an Ecology of Music.* Middletown, Conn.: Wesleyan University Press, 2009.

Banerjee, Subhankar. *Arctic Voices: Resistance at the Tipping Point.* New York: Seven Stories Press, 2013.

Lopez, Barry. *Arctic Dreams.* New York: Charles Scribner's Sons, 1986.

Miller, Debbie. *On Arctic Ground.* Seattle: Mountaineers Books, 1986.

Murie, Adolph. *A Naturalist in Alaska.* Tucson: University of Arizona Press, 1961. Reprint, 1990.

Murie, Margaret E. With a new foreword by Terry Tempest Williams. *Two in the Far North.* Portland, Ore.: Alaska Northwest Publishing, 1962. Reprint, 2003.

Nelson, Richard K. *Make Prayers to the Raven: A Koyukon View of the Native Forest.* Chicago: University of Chicago Press, 1986.

Pielou, E. C. *A Naturalist's Guide to the Arctic.* Chicago: University of Chicago Press, 1995.

GULF ISLANDS NATIONAL SEASHORE

BP Settlement of $18.7 Billion in Deepwater Horizon Oil Spill Claims. www.wsj.com/articles/bp-agrees-to-pay-18-7-billion-to-settle-deepwater-horizon-oil-spill-claims-1435842739; www.nytimes.com/2015/10/06/business/bp-settlement-in-gulf-oil-spill-is-raised-to-20-8-billion.html; www.nola.com/business/index.ssf/2015/09/bp_oil_spill_claims_56_billion.html.

Oreskes, Naomi, and Erik M. Conway. *The Collapse of Western Civilization: A View from the Future.* New York: Columbia University Press, 2014.

Pendleton, Elizabeth A. *Coastal Vulnerability Assessment of the Gulf Islands National Seashore to Sea-Level Rise*. Washington, D.C.: Department of the Interior, USGS, 2013.

Safina, Carl. *A Sea in Flames: The Deepwater Horizon Oil Blowout*. New York: Broadway Books, 2011.

Stephenson, Wen. *What We Are Now Fighting For Is Each Other: Dispatches from the Front Lines of Climate Justice*. Boston: Beacon Press, 2015.

U.S. Environmental Protection Agency. *The Gulf Islands National Seashore, Florida & Mississippi*. Washington, D.C.: BiblioGov, 2013.

CANYONLANDS NATIONAL PARK

Abbey, Edward. *Desert Solitaire*. New York: Touchstone, 1968. Reprint, 1990.

Childs, Craig. *The Secret Knowledge of Water: Discovering the Essence of the American Desert*. New York: Back Bay Books, 2001.

deBuys, William. *The Great Aridness: Climate Change and the Future of the American Southwest*. Oxford: Oxford University Press, 2013.

Diné Bikéyah and the Bears Ears National Monument Proposal. www.utahdinebikeyah.org; www.bearsearscoalition.org.

Frost, Kent. *My Canyonlands: I Had the Freedom of It*. London: Abelard-Schuman, 1971. Reprint, 1990.

Quintano, Jen Jackson. *Blow Sand in His Soul: Bates Wilson, the Heart of Canyonlands*. Moab, Utah: Friends of Arches and Canyonlands, 2014.

Udall, Stewart. *The Forgotten Founders: Rethinking the History of the Old West*. Washington, D.C.: Island Press, 2012.

Wilkinson, Charles F. *Fire on the Plateau: Conflict and Endurance on the Colorado Plateau*. Washington, D.C.: Island Press, 2004.

Williams, David B., and Gloria Brown. *A Naturalist's Guide to Canyon Country*. Guilford, Conn.: Falcon Guides, 2000.

Williams, Terry Tempest. "What Love Looks Like: A Conversation with Tim DeChristopher." *Orion* magazine, January/February 2012.

ALCATRAZ ISLAND, GOLDEN GATE NATIONAL RECREATION AREA

Fortunate Eagle, Adam, with Tim Findley. Foreword by Vine Deloria. *Heart of the Rock: The Indian Invasion of Alcatraz*. Norman: University of Oklahoma Press, 2002.

Johnson, Troy R. *The Occupation of Alcatraz Island: Indian Self-Determination and the Rise of Indian Activism*. Chicago: University of Illinois Press, 1996.

Johnson, Troy R., and Joane Nagel Duane, eds. *American Indian Activism: Alcatraz to the Longest Walk*. Champaign: University of Illinois Press, 1997.

Klayman, Alison. *Ai Weiwei: Never Sorry.* MPI Home Video, 2012. DVD.

Spalding, David. *@Large Ai Weiwei on Alcatraz.* San Francisco: Chronicle Books, 2015.

Thompson, Erwin N. *The Rock: A History of Alcatraz Island, 1847–1972.* Edited by Kurtis Toppert, National Park Service. Damascus, Md.: Penny Hill Press, 2000.

Weiwei, Ai. *Weiwei-isms.* Edited by Larry Warsh. Princeton, N.J.: Princeton University Press, 2012.

GLACIER NATIONAL PARK

These newspaper articles were helpful regarding the "Summer of Fire 2003": www .missoulian.com/lifestyles/territory/remembering-glacier-national-park-s-summer-of -fire/article_5d073ba0-06a7-11e3-b445-0019bb2963f4.html; www.canyoncollective .com/threads/nps-valor-awards.6444/; www.glacierparkfoundation.org/InsideTrail/IT _2004Win.pdf.

Ashby, Christopher S. *Blackfeet Agreement of 1895 and Glacier National Park: A Case History.* Missoula: University of Montana Press, 1985. See also this video of Blackfeet elders speaking about their relationship to Glacier National Park, full of insight: www.bing.com /videos/search?q=blackfeet+and+glacier+national+park&FORM=HDRSC3#view =detail&mid=A2E899EF6E5B16BA6DF4A2E899EF6E5B16BA6DF4.

Chadwick, Douglas H. *A Beast the Color of Winter: The Mountain Goat Observed.* San Francisco: Sierra Club Books, 1983.

Kittredge, William, and Annick Smith. *The Last Best Place: A Montana Anthology.* Helena: Montana Historical Society Press, 1988.

Locke, Harvey. *Protecting the Ecological Integrity of Waterton Lakes and Glacier National Parks: Flathead Valley and Crowsnest Pass (Highway #3), British Columbia* (spiral-bound). Ottawa: Canadian Parks and Wilderness Society, 2001.

Smoak, Gregory Ellis. *Ghost Dances and Identity: Prophetic Religion and American Indian Ethnogenesis in the Nineteenth Century.* Berkeley: University of California Press, 2008.

Thompson, Sally. *People Before the Park: The Kootnai and Blackfeet Before Glacier National Park.* Helena: Montana Historical Society, 2015.

CÉSAR E. CHÁVEZ NATIONAL MONUMENT

Armstrong, Karen. "On Compassion," plenary remarks at the Parliament of World Religions. Salt Lake City, Utah. October 17, 2015.

Chávez, César. *An Organizer's Tale: Speeches* (Penguin Classics). Edited and with an introduction by Ilan Stavans. New York: Penguin Books, 2008.

Cohen, Michael P. *The Pathless Way: John Muir and the American Wilderness.* Madison: University of Wisconsin Press, 1996.

SOURCES

Klett, Mark, Rebecca Solnit, and Bryan Wolfe. *Yosemite in Time: Ice Ages, Tree Clocks, Ghost Rivers*. San Antonio, Tex.: Trinity University Press, 2008.

MacFarlane, Robert. *Landmarks*. United Kingdom: Hamish Hamilton Ltd. (an imprint of Penguin Books), 2015.

Matthiessen, Peter. *Sal Si Puedes (Escape If You Can): Cesar Chavez and the New American Revolution*. Berkeley: University of California Press, 1969.

McLeod, Christopher, and Robert Wild. *Sacred Natural Sites*. Best Practice Protected Area Guidelines Series, no. 16. Paris: UNESCO, 2008.

Merwin, W. S. *Migration: New and Selected Poems*. Port Townsend, Wash.: Copper Canyon Press, 2007.

Oxford Junior Dictionary replacement of natural words: www.theguardian.com/books/2015 /jan/13/oxford-junior-dictionary-replacement-natural-words; www.telegraph.co.uk/travel /artsandculture/travelbooks/11503501/Robert-Macfarlane-interview-Natures-lost -language.html.

Peacock, Doug. *Walking It Off: A Veteran's Chronicle of War and Wilderness*. Spokane, Wash: Eastern Spokane University Press, 2005.

Peterman, Audrey. *Our True Nature: Finding a Zest for Life in the National Park System*. Plantation, Fla.: Earthwise Productions, Inc., 2012.

Presidential Proclamation—Establishment of César E. Chávez National Monument, October 8, 2012. www.whitehouse.gov/the-press-office/2012/10/08/presidential-proclamation -establishment-cesar-e-chavez-national-monument.

Rasmussen, Larry L. *Earth Honoring Faith*. Oxford, UK: Oxford University Press, 2013.

Richter, Max. *Vivaldi's Four Seasons, Recomposed*. Filmed live at (Le) Poisson Rouge, New York City, December 20, 2012. www.youtube.com/watch?v=g3fOVDTg9pU.

Wilson, Edward O. *A Window on Eternity: A Biologist's Walk Through Gorongoza National Park*. New York: Simon & Schuster, 2014.

Wolf, Andrea. *The Invention of Nature: Alexander von Humboldt's New World*. New York: Alfred A. Knopf, 2015.

Worster, Donald. *A Passion for Nature: The Life of John Muir*. Oxford: Oxford University Press, 2011.

Worster, Donald, and Richard White, with Jon Christensen. "A Passion for Nature: Exploring the Life of John Muir." Aurora Forum at Stanford University. May 7, 2009. http:// auroraforum.stanford.edu/files/transcripts/Aurora_Forum_Transcript_John%20Muir _05.07.09.pdf.

AMERICA'S NATIONAL PARKS

ALASKA (8)

NATIONAL PARK	YEAR ESTABLISHED
DENALI	1917
GATES OF THE ARCTIC	1980
GLACIER BAY	1980
KATMAI	1980
KENAI FJORDS	1980
KOBUK VALLEY	1980
LAKE CLARK	1980
WRANGELL–ST. ELIAS	1980

AMERICAN SAMOA

AMERICAN SAMOA	1988

ARIZONA (3)

GRAND CANYON	1919
PETRIFIED FOREST	1962
SAGUARO	1994

ARKANSAS

HOT SPRINGS   1921

CALIFORNIA (9)

CHANNEL ISLANDS   1980
DEATH VALLEY   1994
JOSHUA TREE   1994
KINGS CANYON   1940
LASSEN VOLCANIC   1916
PINNACLES   2013
REDWOOD   1968
SEQUOIA   1890
YOSEMITE   1890

COLORADO (4)

BLACK CANYON OF THE GUNNISON   1999
GREAT SAND DUNES   2004
MESA VERDE   1906
ROCKY MOUNTAIN   1915

FLORIDA (3)

BISCAYNE   1980
DRY TORTUGAS   1992
EVERGLADES   1947

HAWAII (2)

HALEAKALĀ   1961
HAWAI'I VOLCANOES   1916

IDAHO

YELLOWSTONE   1872

KENTUCKY

MAMMOTH CAVE   1941

MAINE

ACADIA   1916

MICHIGAN

ISLE ROYALE   1940

MINNESOTA

VOYAGEURS   1975

MONTANA (2)

GLACIER   1910
YELLOWSTONE   1872

NEVADA

GREAT BASIN   1986

NEW MEXICO

CARLSBAD CAVERNS   1930

NORTH CAROLINA

GREAT SMOKY MOUNTAINS   1934

NORTH DAKOTA

THEODORE ROOSEVELT   1978

OHIO

CUYAHOGA VALLEY   2000

OREGON

CRATER LAKE　1902

SOUTH CAROLINA

CONGAREE　2003

SOUTH DAKOTA (2)

BADLANDS　1978
WIND CAVE　1903

TENNESSEE

GREAT SMOKY MOUNTAINS　1934

TEXAS (2)

BIG BEND　1944
GUADALUPE MOUNTAINS　1972

U.S. VIRGIN ISLANDS

VIRGIN ISLANDS　1956

UTAH (5)

ARCHES　1971
BRYCE CANYON　1928
CAPITOL REEF　1971
CANYONLANDS　1964
ZION　1919

VIRGINIA

SHENANDOAH　1935

WASHINGTON (3)

MOUNT RAINIER	1899
NORTH CASCADES	1968
OLYMPIC	1938

WYOMING (2)

GRAND TETON	1929
YELLOWSTONE	1872

ACKNOWLEDGMENTS

"Seize your space," writes Margaret Atwood. The men and women of the National Park Service do this every day. My first acknowledgment is to them, past and present: the naturalists, the backcountry rangers, the trail and maintenance crews, those in the offices and those on the ground, the historians, the archaeologists, the law enforcement rangers, and each superintendent who presides over each particular unit. Jon Jarvis, the eighteenth director of the National Park Service, whom I admire greatly, says, "Climate change is the biggest threat we have ever faced in terms of integrity of the National Park System." This kind of visionary leadership, with an eye toward the future in the midst of the immediate challenges of overcrowding and underfunding, is where I place my faith and gratitude.

My second bow goes to the 200,000 volunteers nationwide who are giving their time and hearts to our national parks. They are largely seniors, veterans, and young people. Without them, our national parks could not function.

In writing *The Hour of Land*, each park I visited comes with its own set of acknowledgments:

Grand Teton National Park: Steven C. Rockefeller, Larry Rockefeller, Douglas Horne, John Carney, Nancy Carney, and the late Clay James, who executed Mr. Rockefeller's vision on the ground; Superintendent David Vela and Leslie Mattson of the Grand Teton National Park Foundation for their Pura Vida program, which mentors local Latina students; Ranger J. J. King for his stunning portrayal of Stephen T. Mather; Larry Ann Castle-Fericks for her warmth and guidance at the Laurance S. Rockefeller Preserve; Bill Resor for his encyclopedic knowledge, which helped me tremendously with historical facts and essential timelines; Bob Righter, who remains singular for his essential writings; Marcia and Joe Albright for their excellent article on the LSR Preserve; Bob Schuster, his integrity; Jack Turner, his embodied knowledge; Jim Kleine, watchful gatekeeper. We acknowledge the Collection Center for Creative Photography, University of Arizona © 2015 The Ansel Adams Publishing Rights Trust, for use of the photograph by Ansel Adams, with a bow to Jeanne Adams, who along with Ansel Adams was a guest of Mr. Rockefeller at the JY Ranch. And this blessed community: Edward Riddell; the Carlman women, Lee, Susan, and Maryellen; Joan and Ted Major; Joanne Dornan; Malinda and Yvon Chouinard; Tom Mangelson; Charlie Craighead; Madi Quissek; Kathleen Harrington; K'Lea Andreas; Christian Beckwith; Giovannina Anthony, her power; Story Clark Resor, her wisdom. Annette and Ian Cumming, their love.

Theodore Roosevelt National Park: Superintendent Valerie Naylor is a heroic figure for her leadership on behalf of the Dakota Badlands. Her passion for the National Park Service earned her the Stephen T. Mather Conservation Award from the National Park Conservation Association. My respect for her is immense. Lillian Crook, for introducing me to this landscape; Clay Jenkinson, for his words in describing it. Douglas Brinkley brought Theodore Roosevelt to life. And I want to acknowledge the wisdom and spiritual strength of my brother Hank Tempest. He is a workingman who faces the wind every day with courage, kindness, and an uncommon intelligence.

Acadia National Park: Mariah Hughs and Nick Sichterman, bedrock; Ann Backer, perspective; Bill Backer, creativity; Tim Elliott, sustenance; Susan Longacre, spirit; Susan and Ray MacDonald, roots; Tom Curry and Kim Ridley, anchors; Rob Shetterly, conscience; Susan Hand Shetterly for her phrase "the Settled Wild"; Lynne Tempest and Steve Earl, family; Anne and John Milliken for bringing us to Mount Desert Island as godparents to Annabelle; Phoebe Milliken, faith; Roger Milliken, restoration; Jim Singerling for his hospitality; Phil Whitney, gratitude for his work at the Cranberry Island Historical Society; Justin Bunker and David Bunker, kin, and a day well spent on Cranberry Island; Roxanne Quimby for her active vision of land protection; Lucas St. Clair for his soul work on the ground and his belief in a new national park with a view of Mt. Katahdin; the visionaries of RESTORE, Jym St. Pierre, Jamie Sayen, George Wuerthner, Brock Evans, John Davis, and Michael Kellett (among them), who drew the first map; and Beth and Gary Lawless for poetry.

Gettysburg National Military Park: Cornerstone Farm Horseback Tours and the amazing Andie Custer Donohue as our guide, who brought Picketts Charge to life; William McKone for his story; Louis Gakumba for his companionship and insights on war; *saltfront* literary magazine for publishing them; Naomi Natale and Susan McDonald for their vision of One Million Bones; Ellen Friedman, Jennifer Sokolove, and Rebecca DiDomenico of the Compton Foundation for supporting the One Million Bones Project; Rick Bass for his storytelling, abiding friendship, and love.

Effigy Mounds National Monument: Chief Ranger Bob Palmer for his generosity of spirit. He introduced us not only to the land but to the context of Effigy Mounds through time.

Larry Roelandt for a beautiful walk up the Fire Point Trail with his grandson, Reese; Albert LeBeau for his integrity and candor regarding indigenous imperatives within cultural archaeology, specifically surrounding Effigy Mounds, and for his artistry in turning a satellite image into art; Todd Kahn, Frontier Motel.

Big Bend National Park: Bill Summers, the National Park Service volunteer and distinguished vet from Desert Storm, for his commitment to homeland security in protecting wilderness; Dale Vice for his hospitality and depth of knowledge at the Chisos Mountain Lodge and the gift of the Roosevelt Stone Cabins; the extraordinary volunteers behind the desk at each visitor center who answered endless questions, from the color of lichen to insects; the late Charles Bowden for his spirit that remains in this bone-dry country; the Lannan Foundation, which gave me the time and space to write in west Texas—I am grateful to Patrick Lannan, Martha Jessup, and Douglas Humble; Jane Mead for her poetic pragmatism; Jean Valentine for her joy; Will Mackin for his stories; Lawrence Fodor for the color vermilion boxed as a koan; Brandon Shinoda and Dot Devota for their poems that became compass points; Alan Vana, his faith; and Elena Radford for her holy water that entered the Rio Grande.

Gates of the Arctic National Park: Our dear friends from Arctic Treks, Carol Kasza and Jim Campbell with their son, Kyle, not only shared this wild country with us but showed us how one listens. Richard Nelson's "Make Prayers to the Ravens" accompanied me north once again, as did John Luther Adams's music. My dear brother Dan Tempest camped inside my heart and remains there as a soulmate. Jennifer Sahn helped craft this piece for the fiftieth anniversary of the Wilderness Act, which appeared in *Orion Magazine*, September 2014; Cindy Shogan of the Alaska Wilderness League is my sister; Debbie Miller, Mike Matz, and Lenny Kolm remain warriors. The images of Subhankar Banerjee and Florian Schultz are testaments of beauty; and my devotion to Sonya and Tom Campion, true Arctic champions, only increases as they continue to show us how a passion for all things Arctic is changing the political landscape. The Alaskan natives from G'witchen elder Sarah James to Inupiak Robert Thompson to the next generation of leaders like Princess Daazhraii Lucaq are calling for both ecological integrity and environmental justice. Bless them.

Gulf Islands National Seashore: My love and respect belongs to Becky Duet for her sisterhood, the courage of her voice, and her spiritual stamina in the wake of the BP oil spill. Avery Resor was my trustworthy companion; I am grateful for her empathy and strength. Bill Weaver's watchful eye kept us awake to subtleties; Tom Hutchings, our pilot, gave us not only an aerial perspective but a political one. Without his greatness of spirit, our view would have been greatly diminished. And Jerry Cope, whose eyes on the ground made all the difference. I am deeply grateful for all the people in the Gulf who allowed me to interview them and tell their stories, Margaret Curole among them. Another bow, to Jennifer Sahn and Chip Blake at *Orion Magazine* for their editorial support.

Canyonlands National Park: This is home and there are many debts: Andy Nettell of Back of Beyond Books for his generosity of spirit; Bruce Hucko, Chris Noble, Jeff Foott,

ACKNOWLEDGMENTS

Judith Zimmerman, and Resford Rouzer for their stunning images of home ground; Bill Hedden, Eleanor Bliss, Chloe and Sarah Hedden, family; Laura Kamala, a healing grace; Christy Williams Dunton, voice; OB and Mary O'Brien, vigilance; Dave Erley, leadership; Anna Brady who created the table of gratitude; Gavin Noyes, and Jonah Yellowman of Diné Bikéyah; Scott Groene, Matt Gross, Liz Thomas, savvy; Matt Rothschild, editor extraordinaire; Trent Alvey, art; Glen Lathrop, scribe; Clarke Abbey, witness; Miso Tunks, joy; Jen Jackson Quintano, future; Peter Lawson and Anne Wilson, roots; Kate Cannon, commitment; Eleanor Inskip, muse; Karla Van der Zanden, water; Cindy Hardgrave, and Walt Dabney, the long view; Monette Tangren Clark, trust.

Alcatraz Island, Golden Gate National Recreation Area: Tim DeChristopher for his courage, fearlessness, and joy in the face of cultural complacency; Dylan Schneider for her leadership of the heart; Avery and Felicia Resor, scouts; Ai Weiwei, artistic defiance.

Glacier National Park: The Tempest Clan who survived the fire: John, Jan Sloan, Steve, Ann, Callie, Andrew, Sara, Diane, Dan, and Thalo Porter; Christopher Burke of the National Park Service; and the man in yellow who flew in to calm our nerves and as quickly disappeared when the smoke subsided.

César E. Chávez National Monument: Dolores Huerta for her indomitable spirit and inspiration; Lori de Leon at the Dolores Huerta Foundation for her stories surrounding the United Farm Workers and help in locating the Avedon portrait; Erin Harris from the Richard Avedon Foundation; Peter Matthiessen, his knife-blade perceptions; Mercedes Ornales, her translation.

These individuals shaped my ideas about culture and landscape: Oren Lyons, Arvol Looking Horse, Mary Evelyn Tucker, John Grim, Gus Speth, Katrina Gore, Louie Psyhoyis, Mickey Houlihan, Charles Wilkinson, Dennis Sizemore, Michael Soule, Kieran Suckling, David Johns, Eileen Crist, Harvey Locke, Tim Egan, Todd Wilkinson, Jean Shinoda Bolen, Dr. Linda Lancaster, Susan Griffin, Rebecca Solnit, Bill McKibben, Lisa Consiglio, Colum McCann, Greg Kahlil, Rob Spillman, Ron Rash, Tyler Cabot, Sheri Parks, Cindy and Luis Urrea, Lauret Savoy, Andy Friedland, Terry Osborne, Ann Kapusciniski, Carol Folt, David Pert, Ross Virginia, Morgan Curtis, Leehi Yona, Kim Wind, Jeff Sharlett, Steve Tatum, Robert Newman, Melody and John Taft, Mark Bergstrom, Jeff McCarthy, Michael Lerner, Eric Karpeles, Philippe Jaroussky, Jenepher Stowell, Teresa Cohn, Barry Lopez, Wendell Berry, Gary Snyder, Geralyn White Dreyfous, Robert Redford, E. O. Wilson, Greg Carr, and Kris and Doug Tompkins.

A special bow to Michael Kellet for his vigilance on our national parks and providing daily reports on current events.

Paula and William Merwin continue to inspire me through their partnership of love and land.

Betsy Burton of The King's English Bookshop helped ground-truth this book. Jan Sloan has been part of the conversation from the beginning as a calm and nurturing presence. I benefited greatly from Greg Smoak's sharp and corrective eye on chapters regarding Indian history and his expertise on Gettysburg. Alisha Anderson provided background information on each national park early in the process and was a trustworthy sounding board. Alexandra Fuller provided a spirited critique of the manuscript that served as an outline for later drafts—shared cups of tea, critical to sanity.

Two women held me through this project: Linda Asher read every draft of every chapter followed by detailed notations, and helped me work out ideas in rigorous conversation before they found their way on the page. And Lyn Dalebout was the midwife to *The Hour of Land* with her astute understanding of national parks and all things wild.

Doug Peacock has always walked point for me and commands my heart and deepest respect for the force of his word and the size of his heart for America's wilderness. He is a bear of a man and a radiant friend.

Frish Brandt has been my co-conspirator throughout *The Hour of Land*. One of the great joys of this book has been working with her and the photographers who shaped not only this book but the text as well. Emily Lambert has been a steady inspiration; Rebecca Brown secured permissions with grace; and I am so grateful to these photographers who have been fellow travelers in this ambitious project: Jeanne Adams and the Ansel Adams Center for Creative Photography; Robert Adams for his trust; the Richard Avedon Foundation; James Balog; Daniel Beltrá; Lois Conner; Lynn Davis; James Evans; Lukas Felzmann; Lee Friedlander; Emmet Gowin; Mary Daniel Hobson; Mark Klett; Edith Levy; Sally Mann; Edward Riddell; Ansley West Rivers; Sebastião Salgado; Jonah Samson; Christina Seely; Jon Stuart; and Will Wilson. Photographs by Robert Adams and Lee Friedlander are courtesy of the Fraenkel Gallery, San Francisco.

Sarah Crichton, my editor, challenged me to tell the stories straight. Because of her, I found new writing muscles. She is tough and tender at once, even as she supported my own vision that, at times, was contrary to hers. The most one can ask of an editor is honesty. She gave me this gift. My respect resides in the relationship we have forged.

The entire team at Farrar, Straus and Giroux has been a remarkable collaboration, beginning with Marsha Sasmor, who has been the center point of *The Hour of Land*, from editorial work to managing each photograph with care. All things flowed through her. I want to thank Abby Kagan for her beautiful design; Rodrigo Corral for guidance; Alex Merto for his innovative cover; Debra Helfand, Amy Vreeland, Sarita Varma, and especially Bobby Wicks, for their front-line work and enthusiasm; and the sharp-edged, magnetic vision of Jeff Seroy.

Steven Barclay is the godfather of this book. Without him, I never would have written it. The subject was so close, I couldn't even see it. He did, and I trusted him. *The Hour of Land* is dedicated to him with love.

Gail Hochman, my agent, in her wisdom held the space left empty by my beloved Carl Brandt, who passed away on August 13, 2013. His hand is forever on my shoulder.

ACKNOWLEDGMENTS

My father, John Tempest, is my hero. He tells the truth. His influence infiltrates every page. From the moment we could walk, we walked behind him on the trail. It is still that way. I am so grateful for his long and spirited life.

And lastly, my love belongs to Brooke, who explored these parks with me, joyously. For more than forty years, we have been in partnership without a map, only a lifelong search for Beauty. He is the strongest person I know and the most wild.

PERMISSIONS ACKNOWLEDGMENTS

Grateful acknowledgment is made for permission to reprint excerpts from the following material:

The author would like to thank the Laurance S. Rockefeller Preserve for the use of the poem "A Feather at Phelps Lake," by Terry Tempest Williams, that appears on the walls in the visitor center.

Selected lines from "WE" by Jorie Graham are used with special permission of the poet.

Excerpt from "Variation on a Theme," from W. S. Merwin's *The Moon Before Morning*, is used by permission of the poet and Copper Canyon Press (Port Townsend, Wash: 2014).

The letter written to Edward Abbey appeared in slightly different form in *Postcards from Ed: Dispatches and Salvos from an American Iconoclast*, edited by David Peterson (Minneapolis, Minn: Milkweed Editions, 2006).

The letter written to John Wesley Powell appeared in slightly different form in *The Progressive*, December 2013/January 2014.

Excerpt from James L. Dickey's poem "For the Last Wolverine" reprinted by permission of his children: Christopher, Bronwen, and Kevin Dickey.

Terry Tempest Williams is the author of fifteen books, including *Refuge: An Unnatural History of Family and Place*, now considered an environmental classic, and *When Women Were Birds*. She has received a John Simon Guggenheim fellowship and a Lannan Literary Fellowship in creative nonfiction. Williams appeared in the *National Parks* PBS series produced by Ken Burns and written by Dayton Duncan. The recipient of the John Muir Award by the Sierra Club and the Robin W. Winks Award from the National Parks Conservation Association, Williams lives in Castle Valley, Utah, with her husband, Brooke Williams.